BALTIC FACADES

In the same series

BALTIC FACADES

Estonia, Latvia and Lithuania since 1945

ALDIS PURS

REAKTION BOOKS

Published by Reaktion Books Ltd
33 Great Sutton Street
London EC1V ODX
www.reaktionbooks.co.uk

First published 2012
Transferred to digital printing 2014

Printed and bound by Chicago University Press

British Library Cataloguing in Publication Data
Purs, Aldis.

Baltic facades : Estonia, Latvia and Lithuania since 1945. – (Contemporary worlds)
1. Estonia – History – 1940–1991.
2. Estonia – History – 1991–
3. Latvia – History – 1940–1991.
4. Latvia – History – 1991–
5. Lithuania – History – 1945–1991.
6. Lithuania – History – 1991–
7. Estonia – Social conditions. 8. Latvia – Social conditions.
9. Lithuania – Social conditions – 1945–1991.
10. Lithuania – Social conditions – 1991–
I. Title II. Series
947.9-dc23

ISBN 978 1 86189 896 8

Contents

Preface

This book is intended as a thought-provoking, detailed introduction to Estonia, Latvia and Lithuania for those that were once pejoratively called 'the chattering classes', and is not aimed specifically at the professional historians, political scientists, economists and Baltic specialists in their midst. This book is meant primarily for the bankers, architects, librarians, lawyers, doctors, teachers, clerks, accountants, brand managers and those of a thousand more trades and professions who are interested in the world beyond their block, city, region or state; for those that approach the world with a healthy intellectual curiosity, but are unable or unwilling to commit a great deal of time, energy and resources to exhaustive, in-depth studies. This book is meant for the curious traveller, for example, who is considering or planning a trip to the region and wants to know more than is in a tourist pamphlet; and for the concerned citizen who hears about political and economic events in contemporary Estonia, Latvia and Lithuania, and yearns for more context than newspapers or, more likely, television segments provide.

Since the book is not intended for academic specialists, I have foregone traditional academic footnoting and referencing. I have opted for endnotes as cues to suggested reading instead of providing laundry lists of such sources at the end of chapters. The books and articles cited may not even agree with the points that I make. Instead they are meant as a starting point for examining any given topic in more detail. For example, I mention Lithuanians and their national and social identity in the later nineteenth and early twentieth century only briefly. I suggest, however, that if the reader finds this an area of particular interest they turn to Tomas Balkelis's *The Making of Modern Lithuania*. This source, of course, is not the only one to address the topic, but it is a good place to begin, and from it an eager reader can find other sources. Further, I have only referenced sources in the English language. This is unfair to the bulk of academic work on Estonia, Latvia and Lithuania, which is primarily in Estonian, Latvian and Lithuanian as well as in German, Russian and a smattering of other languages. Nevertheless, the English source base is impressive, and it seems convincing to me that most of the readers for whom this book is intended will remain within it.

Even still, this book may fail the reader for whom it is intended, and if that is the case, the blame lies solely with me. I have tried to weave a kind of narrative that holds up to however the reader will experience Estonia, Latvia and Lithuania. If months later the reader notices a news piece on the fervour of Latvian hockey fans, they may understand the hysteria from some of the context provided in this book. Ultimately, I hope that this book provides its readers with a sense of Estonia, Latvia and Lithuania.

Introduction

'Who the f*** are the Balts to us?'[1]

To imagine the slightly portly, perennially bow-tied Toomas Hendrik Ilves, graduate of Columbia University and the University of Pennsylvania, being upset about being labelled a 'Balt' underscores how fundamentally flawed and incomplete Baltic identity is. Ilves's life story has crisscrossed continents, professions and citizenships. Born in Sweden to Estonian refugees of the Soviet occupation of their homeland, he spent his formative years in the United States, where he excelled academically and received degrees in psychology from two of the most esteemed universities in the USA. He worked as a journalist for Radio Free Europe in the 1980s, using the position to vault himself into Estonia's politics prior to independence. After renouncing his US citizenship in favour of his Estonian (by virtue of his parents' pre-Second World War status), he moved through the ranks of the Ministry of Foreign Affairs, serving as ambassador to his former home, the USA, going into parliament, and later becoming Minister of Foreign Affairs from December 1996 until September 1998. In 2003 Ilves became a member of the European Parliament and by the autumn of 2006 was elected president of the Republic of Estonia by Estonia's parliament, the Riigikogu. Ilves's pedigree as a leading scion of the Estonian émigré community, and as a steadfast opponent to the Soviet occupation of Estonia (and its repercussions), would suggest that he, together with like-minded Latvians and Lithuanians, would nourish a Baltic common cause. Instead his attacks on the core of the Baltic idea, developed while he was Minister of Foreign Affairs, have become the most celebrated and withering critiques of the entire concept.

Ilves's rejection of the Baltic label was most thoroughly developed in a speech to the Swedish Institute for International Affairs on 14 December 1999. In many respects Ilves's speech was a modern incarnation of Jonathan Swift's *A Modest*

Proposal. In a satirical and whimsical yet biting speech Ilves chided West European academics, diplomats and businessmen for knowing very little (and much of that incorrectly) about Estonia, for their attachment to the 'clichés and stereotypes' that lump all post-Communist countries together, and for their fondness for the Baltic concept. Speaking less than two weeks before Christmas, Ilves suggested, somewhat playfully, a new conceptual identity for Estonia, that of a 'Yule-land', which lumped it together with Finland, Sweden, Norway, Denmark, Iceland and the British Isles. Ilves began with a similar vocabulary for the winter solstice among these nations and drew on other similarities between them, including the character traits of their populations, such as being 'rational, logical, unencumbered by emotional arguments . . . businesslike, stubborn and hard-working', the fact that these countries are international pace-setters in Internet and mobile phone penetration, and his impression that the people of these states are inherently against corruption. The 'Yule-land' idea was short-lived and many failed to register Ilves's attempts at humour within the speech, but his short, yet thorough, deconstruction of the Baltic concept touched on a growing sentiment shared with Lithuania. His suggestion that Estonia could be classified as a Nordic country set off a long-lasting debate whose fundamental starting point reinforced Ilves's claim. Academics and government officials disagreed on whether Estonia could or should be included as a Nordic state, but they limited their discussion to Estonia, essentially affirming that Estonia was different from Latvia and Lithuania; countries which, by implication, had little or no claim to a Nordic title.

Ilves was not alone in searching for a new identifying concept for Estonians and he stated his reasons for dismissing the Baltic label clearly:

I think it is time to do away with poorly fitting, externally imposed categories. It is time that we recognize that we are dealing with three very different countries in the Baltic area, with completely different affinities. There is no Baltic identity with a common culture, language group, religious tradition.[2]

Ilves concluded that the Baltic idea was mostly foreign to Estonians. He declared:

Unfortunately most if not all people outside Estonia talk about something called 'The Baltics'. This is an interesting concept, since what the three Baltic states have in common almost completely derives from shared unhappy experiences imposed upon us from outside: occupations, deportations, annexation, Sovietization, collectivization, Russification. What these countries do not share is a common identity.[3]

Lithuania's president, Algirdas Brazauskas, had already declared Lithuania's identity to be more Central European than Baltic. Echoing Brazauskas, Lithuanian diplomats suggested occasionally that Lithuania could belong to the Visegrad Group, a loose alliance consisting of the Czech Republic, Hungary, Poland and Slovakia formed to encourage European integration. It would seem that Latvia's politicians stand alone in not criticizing the Baltic concept, but Latvia's political scientists, notably Daunis Auers and Dzintra Bungs, have drawn similar conclusions to the politicians of Lithuania and Estonia. Auers has summarized that 'historically the Baltic states usually have been more separated than united', while Bungs has dissected the Baltic idea and found it to be an essentially Latvian one.[4] Recently Latvian politicians have joined their Estonian and Lithuanian counterparts in drawing more attention to the differences between the Baltic states than to their similarities.

The Baltic states, as a singular concept, is a construct, and one that after 50 years of frequent usage is under attack. European historians eager to move away from Cold War typologies have more generally re-examined geographic constructs since the late 1980s, and in many cases, including in the larger Baltic Sea region, have offered new conceptual frameworks. Historians such as David Kirby, Marko Lehti, Jörg Hackmann and Alan Palmer have offered regional models that to some degree encompass all the countries with coastlines on the Baltic Sea. Recent academic work on 'Nordosteuropa' or northeast Europe suggests a concept that is larger and more inclusive than the Baltic alone. Contemporary German scholars such as Klaus Zernack, Ralph Tuchtenhagen and Stefan Troebst are the leading champions of this re-conceptualization of the region that includes more than just the sea and its coast. Although each of these approaches is encouraging and may ultimately gain general acceptance, they still stumble amid the many historical incongruities in the multitude of experiences that the states that border the Baltic Sea have had. Even a recent reassertion of common policy goals by the diplomats of the traditional Baltic states, Estonia, Latvia and Lithuania, underlines the artificial nature of the term 'Baltic states'. 'Baltic' has become the preserve of contested academic discourse or an alignment potentially to be used or abandoned within the shifting constellations of European Union politics. There is little tangible Baltic identity on the ground in Estonia, Latvia or Lithuania; the number of people that would exclusively identify themselves as Baltic is infinitesimally small.

Nevertheless, throughout the twentieth (and into the twenty-first) century, the larger international stage has looked at and acted upon the three states collectively and thus the Baltic states concept continues to have meaning. As Ilves remarked in his Yule-land speech, the Baltic states suffer as a 'cliché, untrue, but repeated precisely because it is a received idea'. In other words, as small states Estonia, Latvia and Lithuania are forced to live with the Baltic concept because others insist upon using it. For some the term 'Baltic states' is a kind of shorthand simplification that reduces three states into one larger whole. Either devoting specific attention to nation-states that are individually smaller than are dozens of cities is too taxing for these people, or they prefer aggregates and generalizations over nuance and detail. Still, despite all of the shortcomings of the Baltic concept, it can still produce insightful observations.

The Baltic idea is essentially a Latvian one, although not in its historical roots. As small countries, Estonia, Latvia and Lithuania look naturally for a larger cohesive body to which they belong. Estonia can argue that it is a Nordic country or a Yule-land, Lithuania can claim to be a part of Central Europe, but Latvia has little else to turn to. Furthermore Latvia is the glue that holds Estonia and Lithuania together. Latvia can claim a similar socio-economic development to that of Estonia or a linguistic and cultural closeness with Lithuania. Estonia and Lithuania, on the other hand, are almost entirely bound by 'unhappy experiences' and little else. Therefore the Baltic concept begins in Latvia and ripples out to include Estonia and Lithuania. Often these ripples are weak and imbalanced or they are thematically confined: one ripple is the academic study of Soviet occupation, one ripple is joint military exercises, and another is a common front in Brussels. As a result the Baltic concept is weak precisely because it holds little value outside of these thematic myopias. Historians, economists and tourists all speak of the Baltic states, but few others do. There is however, a broad, sweeping gestalt-like approach that more successfully unites the experience – past and contemporary – of Estonia, Latvia and Lithuania. As with other Baltic ideas, this one likely originates in Latvia and its ripple effect is not always uniform, but the core idea revolves around how Balts identify and place themselves within their nation-state, region and continent.

The Body Politic of the Baltic states

Quite a while ago, a fashionable academic trend was to relate a nation-state's development to that of an individual. Some states were young, while others were the 'sick men of Europe'. At times the metaphor was used reassuringly to describe the development of foreign relations, as with British opinion that the American colonists' revolution was the act of an impetuous, headstrong teenager that with time returned to the fold, like a prodigal son, to develop a special relationship with the former fatherland. Thankfully the trend passed from most serious discussions, although the press is still fond of referring to the young age of a state to explain its unsatisfactory behaviour. The reason the metaphor was abandoned was simple: those states that described themselves as in their primes wielded the old/senile and young/immature labels with the same condescension and paternalism generally reserved for parents. Such crude abuse rightfully doomed the 'state as living organism' metaphor, but with many caveats the metaphor can still provide a kernel for useful commentary. Rather than describing the development, ageing and passing of an individual, it can be revived to explore the maladies plaguing a state, which have a descriptive, analytical similarity to the maladies and syndromes that shape people's lives. The metaphor need not be confined to medical terms; my wife, for example, is fond of perceptively describing the US as emblematic of the cardinal sin of gluttony. The Baltic body politic can be defined, using this metaphor, as suffering from body dysmorphic disorder or – in layman's terms – a preoccupation with perceived defects in its physical features.

This preoccupation – how the Baltic states see themselves and how they imagine others see them – is the unifying trope of this study. This obsession is not unique to the Baltic states and probably ties in to a more general, universal, postmodern search for identity. This obsession was the starting point of Toomas Hendrik Ilves's aforementioned speech on 'Estonia as a Nordic Country'. Almost at the outset, Ilves declared that he would focus 'on how Estonia is viewed, where it resides subjectively in the perceptions of the West'. He concluded that 'aside from foreign diplomats stationed in Estonia', Western perceptions betray a 'lack of understanding, that often can be perceived in Estonia as arrogance and haughtiness, if not downright prejudice'. The Baltic states' struggles with the rest of the world's 'lack of understanding' of them or, worse, its complete lack of knowledge of them, pulses through all of the upcoming chapters. In the more obvious cases – in their historical experience, in art and architecture or in sport and spectacle – the Baltic states see their accomplishments as battles won in a larger public relations war. Conversely their defeats and failures become more ominous. Even in issues such as how the Baltic states imagine their relationship with physical geography, the spectre of how the larger world understands the same geography looms large. The Baltic states, like many small countries, have an overwhelming desire to be

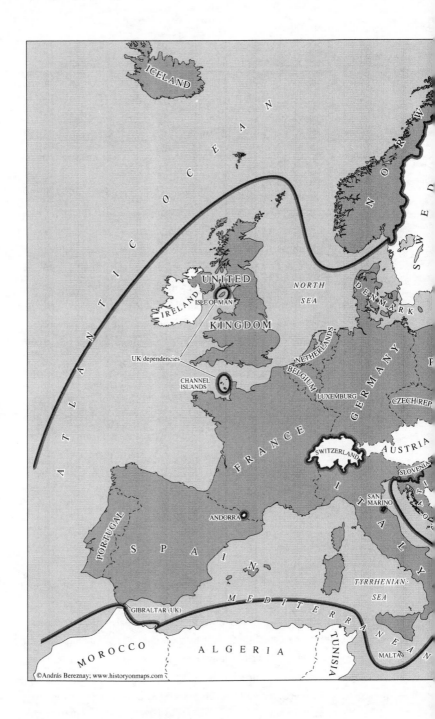

ICELAND

ATLANTIC OCEAN

NORWAY

SWEDEN

UNITED KINGDOM

IRELAND

ISLE OF MAN

NORTH SEA

DENMARK

UK dependencies

CHANNEL ISLANDS

NETHERLANDS

BELGIUM

LUXEMBURG

GERMANY

CZECH REP.

FRANCE

SWITZERLAND

AUSTRIA

SLOVENIA

SAN MARINO

ITALY

PORTUGAL

SPAIN

ANDORRA

TYRRHENIAN SEA

GIBRALTAR (UK)

MEDITERRANEAN

MOROCCO

ALGERIA

TUNISIA

MALTA

©András Bereznay; www.historyonmaps.com

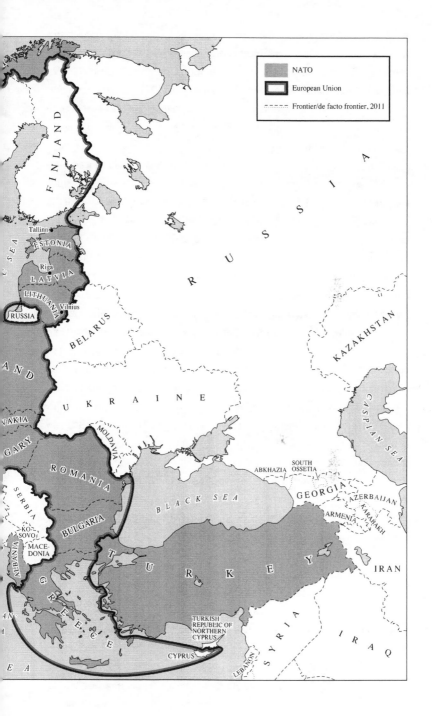

recognized and accepted – in the Baltic case, by the European fold. Yet each step towards being a part of a larger identity generates an almost equal and opposite reaction in Baltic declarations of uniqueness and exceptionalism. History, sport, landscape or folk traditions can set the Baltic states apart. The two related currents, the desire to be recognized as a part of something larger and the equal need to preserve and celebrate Baltic uniqueness, act as the warp and weft of the larger tapestry of Baltic identity.

My approach to the Baltic states has clear benefits. Instead of being an encyclopaedic description of events or an account heavy in political history, this study will offer a feel for the Baltic states, a sense of place. This sense will be new in detail, but familiar as well, because the struggle over identity in a world recently made flat is ubiquitous across Europe. This account is ideal for the reader looking for an introduction to the Baltic states that is engaging, slightly unorthodox and iconoclastic and ultimately comments as much on how we are all similar as it does on how the Baltic states are different. This account, therefore, is far from ideal for the reader looking for certainty and precision in discussing specific people, events or dates. It will offer little to Baltic specialists. The task of condensing three states into one description is almost impossible; moving quickly through many topics will be far too reckless for the specialist that has devoted a career to a painstaking study of a phenomenon that I mention in a cursory note. Fortunately the ranks of Baltic specialists have swelled in the last twenty years and they have been equally prolific. Readers unsatisfied with this account or who have had their curiosity whetted can now turn to a vibrant academic debate in almost any discipline focusing either on the individual states or all three.

I am indebted to a great many of these Baltic specialists. Their work (collectively and individually) is invaluable; it is challenging long-held assumptions about the Baltic states and moving away from the simplistic, partisan works of the Cold War era. More specifically the new scholarship on the Baltic states has opened academic debate far beyond questions of the Second World War, Soviet occupation and national movements. Inquiry into the Baltic states has become as variegated, complex and rich as the academic study of most parts of the world, with many of the same research methodologies and questions.

David Kirby was an early proponent of examining the long history of the entire Baltic Sea region in his comprehensive two-volume history of Northern Europe. His second volume, *The Baltic World, 1772–1993: Europe's Northern Periphery in an Age of Change*, tackled an increasingly difficult challenge to this approach, finding regional trends in an era defined by nation-states.[5] Mostly his study rewards the reader with a sense of the transition from agricultural societies to modern states that affected the entire Baltic region. The ongoing dilemma, however, is how to discuss the horror and despair that the twentieth century visited on the eastern side of the Baltic Sea while the northwestern side developed advanced, progressive social welfare states. The brutalities of world wars and foreign occupations compare poorly, even with states such as Denmark and Norway that experienced considerable suffering in the Second World War. Alan Palmer's *The Baltic: A History of the Region and its People* is even more ambitious, covering most of recorded history between its covers.[6] As with Kirby, the challenge remains: how to create a regional history without writing a history of the regional imperial powers' attempts at hegemony? For Estonians, Latvians and Lithuanians each of these sources is an exciting, yet incomplete, breakthrough. Including these states as instrumental players in regional history is groundbreaking for English-language sources that traditionally give short shrift to these small nations. Still, focus on the larger powers continues to dominate the written word, as it has the geopolitical world. The challenge remains that Estonia, Latvia and Lithuania want to be included in the history of the region and of Europe on their own merits while simultaneously underlining their exceptionalism and the travesties visited upon them by their neighbours. The difficult balancing act is to include these states meaningfully in a regional history, document their tortured twentieth century and showcase their individuality.

Surprisingly in the discipline of history there have been very few integrated accounts of Estonia, Latvia and Lithuania. Instead, most titles that claim to present such a history almost immediately split their subject-matter into its three component parts. One notable exception is Romuald Misiunas and Rein Taagepera's *The Baltic States: Years of Dependence, 1940–1980*, which successfully and purposefully brings the events in each republic together into one narrative.[7] Unfortunately their account is of a fairly brief period, including their expanded and updated edition, which runs to 1990. Misiunas and Taagepera's account drew inspiration from a similarly successful study by Georg von Rauch on the interwar era, *The Baltic States. The Years of Independence: Estonia, Latvia, Lithuania, 1917–1940*.[8] These excellent sources, however, suffer from two shortcomings, neither of which is the fault of the authors. The first stems from the authors' severely limited access to source material in Estonia, Latvia and Lithuania. They all wrote at the height of the Cold War and thus did not have free and unfettered access to archival collections or published work inside the Soviet Union. The second shortcoming was the almost universal assumption of the day, later pilloried by Toomas Hendrik Ilves, that

Soviet rule was forging a common identity among Estonians, Latvians and Lithuanians. Misiunas and Taagepera assumed that 'the Baltic peoples have come to identify themselves as a unit' (p. xi), whereas fewer than twenty years later, Ilves would declare that Baltic identity proved ephemeral after 'the shared unhappy events' of Soviet occupation had passed.

Other historians, notably John Hiden, have successfully penned Baltic histories that cover Estonia, Latvia and Lithuania as their subject-matter, but focus on a more specific theme. Hiden, for example, has written prolifically on Estonia, Latvia and Lithuania in interwar international relations (either with a single state, Germany, or more generally). He has also written a masterful study of Dr Paul Schiemann, arguably one of the most profound Baltic German politicians and thinkers of the interwar period.[9] Still, even from Hiden, there is no concise history of the Baltic states. Instead he and many other historians have produced thoughtful, well-researched and convincingly argued edited collections with titles that suggest Baltic comprehensiveness. These volumes are compendia of collected essays on specific subjects or individual nation-states. At times this trend reaches its logical extension when three separate studies are folded together into one large source, as with *The Baltic States*, written by David Smith, Artis Pabriks and Aldis Purs, and Thomas Lane.[10] The four authors wrote solid and for a short while definitive surveys of Estonia, Latvia and Lithuania respectively, and their works were later republished as a single volume. It was well suited to the reader interested in the experiences of each state individually, but did not offer an integrated analysis of the three states. This approach is little different from separate histories of Estonia, Latvia and Lithuania. Of these, Andrejs Plakans's *The Latvians: A Short History* and Toivo Raun's *Estonia and the Estonians* stand out as thorough, well constructed surveys of their respective states and nations.[11] Most recently, Andres Kasekamp's *A History of the Baltic States* and Andrejs Plakans's *Concise History of the Baltic States* provide masterful, comparative overviews of the three states from earliest inhabitation to the present.[12] Much of what this account does not do is done well in these essential books.

If, for historians, the challenge of a single integrated survey of the Baltic states is particularly difficult, such an analysis may be slightly more manageable in political science and economics. These analyses include successful new conceptual approaches to a Baltic Sea regional conglomeration and studies of ongoing political developments within the recently expanded European Union. Marko Lehti's work on the emergence of a Baltic group within the EU is particularly well focused and also addresses a larger European development: the growing power of regions.

Jörg Hackmann, who melds history with the contemporary debates about the meaning of historical events, places recent developments in Estonia, Latvia and Lithuania in the context of similar events around the Baltic Sea.[13] Lehti and Hackmann both underscore the continuing importance of historical memory for the Baltic region and by extension for Europe as a whole. Dovile Budryte's *Taming Nationalism? Political Community Building in the Post-Soviet Baltic States* also focuses on alternate memories of the repressive aspects of Soviet rule with judicious balance and tact.[14]

Still, even the most successful analyses of political scientists and economists suffer a short shelf life, particularly in the Baltic states. If, for example, the political scientist Juris Dreifelds wrote about a *Latvia in Transition*, which included many open questions about the shape and nature of post-Soviet economic transformations, Marja Nissinen wrote of *Latvia's Transition to a Market Economy* as a fait accompli just three years later.[15] Even Nissinen's skilful analysis of the political economy of market reforms was rendered somewhat obsolete by Latvia's entry to the EU and its rapid economic growth from 2002 to 2008. Yet again, accounts from these years, with optimistic forecasts of 'Baltic tigers', are equally dumbfounded by Latvia's economic meltdown in the recession of 2008 to 2010 (for Latvia, a depression). And again, near contemporary accounts predicting a lasting moribund status, near bankruptcy and economic and political rudderless-ness are, to paraphrase Mark Twain on reports of his death, somewhat premature, considering the beginnings of economic recovery in late 2010 and 2011.

Why is it so difficult to produce a lasting, integrated survey of Estonia, Latvia and Lithuania? The answer lies in problems with the subject-matter and with the dearth of qualified and willing writers. On the first count, the historical survey has barely materialized because of the lack of a single, common chain of events for all the lands of the present-day states of Estonia, Latvia and Lithuania. The exception is in the twentieth century, where the common chain is shared unhappy experiences. The majority of the histories of Estonia, Latvia and Lithuania under Nazi or Soviet occupation also focus almost exclusively on a history of victimhood, of what was done to these states and nations. Such accounts, over time, become sacrosanct litanies that limit historical study more than they encourage it. Integrated surveys in political science and economics, although initially far more successful, are victims of being produced in interesting times. Each of the momentous events of the last twenty years towers over the horizon, but for only a moment before being replaced by the next momentous event. To successive scholars, the movements for independence were replaced by independence achieved, followed by struggles to join the EU and NATO, followed by admission to these bodies, followed by tremendous economic growth, followed by catastrophic economic collapse. Accounts that stick too closely to contemporary events are perpetually in danger of falling into the 'newest is best' curse, particularly those that follow too closely the political fortunes of cabinets and politicians.

If the challenge of a survey of Estonia, Latvia and Lithuania is daunting, the wise and prudent have not undertaken it. Throughout most of the Cold War there was simply no unrestricted access to archival or published material. Histories relied on limited archival and library holdings housed outside the USSR and problematic émigré sources. Discussions of life in Soviet Estonia, Latvia and Lithuania relied on equally incomplete sources, or struggled with the biases and distortions of official Soviet publications and/or rumours and hearsay from dissidents. More recently the source quandary has reversed itself: where once there were few, now there are almost too many. Equally daunting in the struggle is the language problem. Latvian and Lithuanian are related, but Estonian, a Finno-Ugric language, is not. The number of people that are fluent in all three languages is very small; trained academics among them are even fewer. Add to these three languages and their major dialects the importance (historically or currently) of sources in German, Russian, Yiddish, Hebrew, Polish, Latin, Finnish and English, and the pool of qualified authors shrinks away almost completely. I am woefully deficient on most of these accounts and cannot produce a comprehensive and integrated account of Estonia, Latvia and Lithuania; nor would I try. Instead my novel approach embraces my Latvia-centric background and training and takes advantage of the considerable time I have spent in Estonia, Latvia and Lithuania and the sum of my academic training and career to develop, not a comprehensive account, but a common thematic motif that runs through the developments in these three nations. As with all things Baltic (including the idea itself), this motif begins in Latvia and ripples outward. This theme also overcomes the quick obsolescence of many sources – it is less time-sensitive and hopefully illuminates future developments as well as past ones. Therefore *Baltic Facades* is about Latvians', Estonians' and Lithuanians' obsessions with their identities, about how they see themselves and about how others see them. Currently their identity crises are fixed and fixated upon being recognized as equal members of Europe. Still, each step towards Europe produces a reaction that declares Estonian, Latvian and Lithuanian uniqueness. This theme acts as a keystone for the discussions of twentieth-century history, politics, economics, art, architecture, geography, memory, sport and spectacle. This thematic approach, however, is not complete or flawless: there exist dozens of other potential constructs of the Baltic. Some are more traditional, others more unorthodox; many of each would take issue with much of this study. Still, this salvo awaits its replies.

CHAPTER 1

Historical Background

If the Baltic idea is contested in the twentieth and twenty-first centuries, a long history of the Baltic states built around such a Baltic concept is, to paraphrase Benedict Anderson, an 'imagined history'. The disparate historical developments across the eastern Baltic littoral are the primary reasons why individuals such as Ilves have discredited the Baltic concept: there has simply been no common language, religion or identity whatsoever in the region over the many millennia of human history. Equally difficult and conceptually problematic is the validity of writing the history of Estonia, Latvia and Lithuania back into antiquity. All three states are modern creations with histories of less than a hundred years. The history of the region before these states is a history of dozens of political entities that rarely, if ever, had political borders that matched those of modern-day Estonia, Latvia or Lithuania. Still, the political legacies and populations inherited by the modern Baltic states fundamentally shaped and influenced their twentieth-century development.

The earliest permanent human settlement near the eastern shores of the Baltic Sea came with the retreat of the glacial coverage of the last great glacial period. The physical conditions of the time and the composition of the first human artefacts (primarily wood, furs, bones and other material generally not suited to long-term preservation) complicate any attempts at dating the earliest human arrivals with any degree of exactness. The ever more sophisticated technological approaches and tools available to today's archaeologists have slowly pushed this first arrival further back into time. Early hunters and temporary settlers conceivably moved into the region as soon as the ice thinned, let alone retreated, roughly 11,000 years ago (9000 BC). The oldest verified archaeological sites, however, are considerably younger (from 7000 to 6000 BC). Although very little is known of these earliest settlers, conventional wisdom labels them as early Finno-Ugric people. Finno-Ugric people are primarily united by linguistics, sharing a root language that is not Indo-European. Modern-day Hungarian, Finnish and Estonian are the largest surviving Finno-Ugric languages, but they are joined by more than a dozen other languages spread across Scandinavia, central Russia and Siberia. Understanding how and when Finno-Ugric peoples populated the places in which they now live relies primarily on historic linguistic reconstructions, few of which are universally accepted and scientifically verified. Still, in the case of early Finno-Ugric people on the eastern shores of the Baltic Sea, consensus has it that they pre-dated a proto-Baltic migration into the region by several thousand years. As such the distant ancestors of Estonians, Finns, Livs and Sami were likely well settled in the current lands of Latvia and Estonia by 6000 to 4000 BC. To present-day archaeologists these people and their settlements do not possess our modern national identities, nor are they seen as early, proto-Estonians. Rather their culture is defined by the style of their most common archaeological relics, pottery decorated with a comb-like pattern; thus they are called the Comb Ceramic Culture or the Pit-Comb Ware Culture.

These early Finno-Ugric people began to share the territory of the Eastern coast of the Baltic Sea with early Indo-Europeans, also known as proto-Baltic peoples – or, in current archaeological terms, the Corded Ware Culture – in the fourth and third millennia BC. This group of people either moved into the region in one of the great migrations of Indo-European peoples into Europe or they preferred their ceramics decorated with the imprints of string, cord and rope. How these two cultures cohabitated is largely unknown. We do know that Finno-Ugric people pushed further north into modern-day Estonia and Finland, while proto-Baltic people settled more into modern-day Latvia and Lithuania. We do not know if this population displacement was forced, negotiated or organic. Potentially the differences between these communities and peoples were marginal, while similar patterns of agriculture, husbandry, hunting and fishing unified all inhabitants in the difficult struggle to survive in Neolithic northern Europe.

The labelling of these early inhabitants as proto-Balts, ancestors of Estonians or as Comb Ceramic peoples hints at the greater underlying problem behind our knowledge of the prehistoric Baltic region. Ultimately we know very little about the long beginnings of human habitation along the Baltic Sea. What we do know comes from occasional shards of pottery, grave sites and a quasi-forensic linguistics that uses remnants of oral traditions to recast ancient belief systems. We do not know what language these people spoke, how they identified themselves or any specifics of their history. These issues are by and large not the concerns of archaeological researchers, who track the material relics of cultures and try to recreate how people lived. Obsessions about language, identity and history are modern concerns. Modern nationalists look to archaeological evidence to support implicitly their political goals concerning national sovereignty and legitimacy. If Estonians, Latvians or Lithuanians can lay claim to living on the territory for more than 3,000 years, the reasoning goes, they must have greater political legitimacy as 'founding nations' of the modern nation states than more recent migrants of a few hundred years or a few decades. Ultimately, however, there is no way to substantiate claims of a common ancestry with the early settlers of the Baltic Sea region and no correlation between modern national demands and the lives of these early inhabitants. Their lives were overwhelmingly shaped and determined by the exceedingly harsh natural environment in which they lived: short growing seasons and long, dark, cold winters. Society was based largely on subsistence and survival and the prevalence of ceremonial weapons in some grave sites (the Corded Ware Culture is occasionally referred to as the Battle Axe Culture for this reason) suggests that this struggle was often violent – either in defence or in aggression to seize resources.

Archaeology tells us that, with time, the accumulation of resources moved people beyond simple indentations on pottery to greater adornments, most notably the use of local amber, and the beginnings of long-distance trade. This amber trade generated the first written acknowledgement of the people of the eastern shores of the Baltic Sea in texts by ancient Greeks and Romans and in Scandinavian sagas. The Greek and Roman texts can hardly be considered first-hand accounts of the region and amount to little more than a few lines describing the origins of amber and other hearsay. The archaeological record, however, becomes more complex and begins to give us more information about the peoples of the region. Baltic amber was known in the Mediterranean world and metals not cast locally began to appear at Baltic sites, with the Roman historian Tacitus alluding to amber and peoples likely to be Estonians by AD 98. Although no direct contact was likely, the early inhabitants of present-day Estonia, Latvia and Lithuania occasionally partook in trade with neighbours, setting off a cascade of trade that ultimately took their local goods to far destinations. Simultaneously and through similar trade, these same inhabitants of the Eastern Baltic region received products created far away. The costs of such long-distance trade suggest that early societies in the Baltic were becoming more differentiated; some more privileged individuals could command greater resources and partake in such trade. Although there is little evidence of state formation at this early date, societies were probably organized along clan networks with defined chiefs and religious shamans.[1] This elite would most likely have benefited from the very occasional trade connections, although in material standards the distance between them and their compatriots was probably quite small. As before, life was defined by subsistence and survival, with trade playing a small part in societies that continued to be dominated by seasonal (slash and burn) agriculture, foraging, hunting and fishing. Life continued to be punctuated with aggressive and defensive violence, perhaps even more so than before, since early trade could often appear to be more like pillaging than negotiated exchange.

As the expanse of the written word receded with the collapse of the Roman Empire, the peoples of the eastern Baltic Sea also receded from the historical record for almost 1,000 years. By AD 900–1000, when European records again mention the Baltic, its society initially seems similar on the surface, but growing differentiation, technological change and increasing contact with other parts of Europe had begun to transform the region. Traditional national Estonian, Latvian and Lithuanian histories describe the uninvited and unwelcome arrival of German merchants (followed by knights and priests) near the beginning of the thirteenth century. This narrative, however, is severely flawed and is intended as the opening salvo of the '700 years of German oppression' myth in Latvian and Estonian nationalist historiography.[2] Instead, by 1100, Baltic societies were moving toward primitive states with established ruling classes and religious hierarchies that were increasingly involved in long-distance trade. Baltic peoples were aware of the growing might and influence of Kievan Rus' and some paid tribute and/or entertained emissaries and orthodox priests. The first arrival of Christianity to the eastern Baltic region came from the southeast, with a decidedly Slavic flavour. Still, there was no wholesale or prominent conversion to orthodoxy before the Mongol destruction of Kievan Rus' in the early thirteenth century (1237–40). With the sudden absence of encroaching Russian and Orthodox influence from the East, German Catholic advances from the West found more fertile ground.

By the twelfth century Western, Central and Scandinavian Europe had clearly emerged from the greater isolationist trends of the Middle Ages and begun a process of state consolidation and expansion. Expansion into Europe's northeast seemed inevitable, although the region was not entirely unknown. A more pronounced and permanent mercantile and religious presence pushed into the region from the 1100s on. The local inhabitants, who had already differentiated into linguistic groups that would serve as the linguistic ancestors of modern Estonians, Latvians and Lithuanians, also curried the favour of these new Germanic and

Danish merchants. The German founding of Riga in 1201 is usually cited as the opening salvo of the northern crusades into the last bastion of paganism in Europe. The arrival of German knights and priests is often presented as the beginning of German hegemony over Latvia and Estonia and the impetus to more centralized state formation in Lithuania. More probably the twelfth and thirteenth century were complicated times of shifting alliances that saw the eventual triumph of a Catholic, German military-religious order (the Livonian Order) in modern-day Latvia and southern Estonia, Danish rule in northern Estonia and its islands, and a firm rebuttal in Lithuania. The century-long battle for conversion in modern-day Estonia and Latvia suggests that the campaign of Christianization and conquest included considerable doses of local political rivalries between indigenous political groupings. More often than not, German or Danish crusaders exploited animosity and rivalry between local clan leaders to gradually extend Catholic influence into the eastern Baltic region. The Livonian Order's defeat by the forces of the Russian prince Alexander Nevsky in 1242, on the frozen ice of Lake Peipus, stopped further eastward incursions into Slavic lands. Several hundred years later, nationalists would bemoan the lack of unity among Baltic peoples against the crusaders, but that lack of unity itself suggests that initially crusaders were not seen as an overwhelmingly clear, common enemy. Still, the national historical narratives of Estonians, Latvians and Lithuanians draw considerable attention to the occasional battles that display some building of alliances between Baltic groups against crusaders, or that produced temporary military defeats for the crusading orders. These temporary alliances and short-lived victories did little to slow the establishment of German and Danish Christian hegemony over modern-day Estonia and Latvia, which was unquestioned and complete by the end of the thirteenth century.

The Lithuanian case was remarkably different, and is a strike against a common Baltic experience regarding the arrival of German crusaders in the twelfth and thirteenth centuries. Lithuanian society was probably in greater contact with the nearby growing political state power of Poles and Kievan Rus'. Geographically Lithuanian lands included the heavily forested lands that dominated to the north, but also more open land leading into the great Eurasian steppe. The steppe, long a veritable highway for marauding, nomadic armies, also encouraged greater contact and trade among peoples. As a result, in Lithuania the arrival of crusaders spurred concrete state formation and consolidation, which resulted in a Lithuanian kingdom that successfully rebuffed German advances. Much of this early work was accomplished by the Lithuanian leader Mindaugas, whose struggle to unite Lithuanians by force or persuasion ultimately led to his coronation as king of Lithuania in 1253.[3] Many resented either the dominance of a king or the dominance of Mindaugas, and he was assassinated in 1263. Despite the formal dissolution of his kingdom and a return to multiple Lithuanian duchies, a Grand Duke acted very much like a king in coordinating military campaigns against the German Christian orders. Some of these Grand Dukes expanded Lithuanian power considerably over the next 150 years.

The Grand Dukes Gediminas (*reg* 1316–41) and Algirdas (*reg* 1345–77) particularly pressed Lithuanian expansion to the east and to the south. These lands, traditionally ruled by Russian princes aligned with Kiev, had become a political vacuum after the Mongol destruction and subjugation of Russian lands. As Mongol expansion ceased, Lithuanian authority nibbled away at its furthest reaches, particularly appealing to those eager to escape paying Mongol tributes. As a result, Slavic patterns of governance and record-keeping entered the Lithuanian court and impressed the Lithuanian nobility. By the time of Algirdas's rule Lithuanians were probably a minority among the Grand Duke's subjects. The Grand Duchy's orientation would become even more confused when Algirdas's successor, Jogaila, married the queen of Poland in 1386. This marriage necessitated the baptism of the Lithuanians in 1387, marking an end to the final pagan state in Europe. Jogaila's marriage formally introduced Polish and Catholic influence to the Lithuanian court and its nobility.

The Grand Duchy of Lithuania would reach its zenith in terms of geopolitical power and influence under the Grand Duke Vytautas (*reg* 1392–1430). Vytautas continued the past practice of expansion into modern-day Belarus, Russia and Ukraine, and at his territorial peak extended Lithuania's rule to the Black Sea. Vytautas was equally successful in warding off the still expansionist German knightly orders. In 1410 he was one of the crucial military leaders of a Polish and Lithuanian army that virtually annihilated the Teutonic Order, the vehicle for German expansion into northeast Europe, at the Battle of Grunwald/Tannenberg. In a telling commentary on how divisive this history can be, Poles and Slavs refer to the battle as Grunwald, Germans as Tannenberg, and Lithuanians as the Battle of Žalgiris. Although the battle was an unqualified military success, and ended any further medieval German expansion into the lands of modern-day Lithuania, the Grand Duchy's ties to Poland grew ever stronger. By the sixteenth century the political elite of the Grand Duchy of Lithuania was thoroughly Polish in culture.[4]

The radical turns of events on the shores of the eastern Baltic in this time period (1150–1410) stand out in greater detail than earlier history because written records also began in this era. Historians can confidently name individuals, tribes

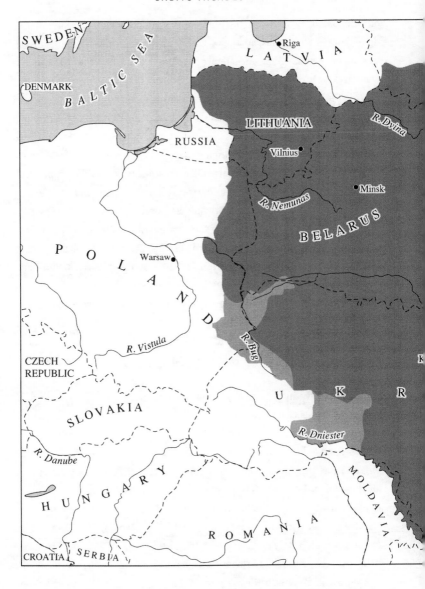

and battles. They can also comb early record-keeping and multiple sources to produce more nuanced and informed descriptions of the societies of the day. Still, the overwhelming majority of these written records are the records of the 'victors': the chronicles of how crusading knights and priests brought Christianity to Europe's last pagans or the more tedious and less inflated records of feudal relationships and obligations. All historical documents are subjective (influenced

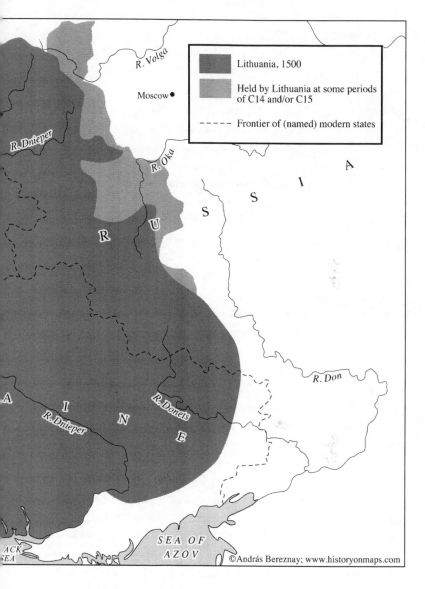

Map legend:

- **Lithuania, 1500**
- **Held by Lithuania at some periods of C14 and/or C15**
- – – – – **Frontier of (named) modern states**

©András Bereznay; www.historyonmaps.com

by the conditions and whims of the author), but these are spectacularly so. The Book of Chronicles, for example, sang praises to the victories of God and his followers more than it sought to carefully record events. More troubling is the lack of documents from the 'losing side' to use as a corrective to the vainglory and cultural superiority of the German documents. In this way, those that fought and lost against the crusading Germans became a 'people without history'.[5] But, even with troublesome and biased sources, we are slowly able to piece together the societal framework of Europe's last pagans.

The experiences of modern-day Estonia, Latvia and Lithuania with the forceful intrusion of German and Danish Christianity from the twelfth to the early fifteenth century were fundamentally different in their end results (subjugation in Estonia and Latvia, state formation and successful defence and expansion in Lithuania), but there are also core similarities. Throughout the region, prior to the thirteenth century, clear state formation was still in its infancy. Clan and tribe chieftains united geographical territories and built hilltop fortresses to assert their authority and control trade. Pagan belief systems included individuals who acted as intermediaries with divine forces, but they did not create an entrenched, religious caste. The distance in material possessions, power and authority between members of society was likely not enormous. Prior to German arrival, local chiefs were in increasing contact with states and societies across Scandinavia and the Russian lands. These contacts brought material and cultural gain, but also spurred ever greater state formation, which led to bitter, contested rivalries between claimants to a potential unified crown. The Mindaugas case is the most clear and successful (if short-lived), but initial alliances forged with the Germans and Danes in Estonia and Latvia suggest a similar process at work. In Latvia and Estonia, German and Danish technological superiority (steel swords, stone castles and access to a powerful hinterland for resupply and reinforcements), with time, overwhelmed local attempts at state building and created the Livonian Order, a collection of medieval power and authority vested in a patchwork of bishops, priests and knights. In Lithuania union with Poland reinforced earlier successes against the Germans, but ultimately came at a similar price, with the acceptance of Christianity, and the ruling elite's wholesale conversion and replacement with a 'foreign' culture.

From the nineteenth century on, the way in which modern Estonians, Latvians and Lithuanians have recreated and reimagined these centuries is also remarkably similar. Latvian and Estonian nationalists particularly struggled against the local power of Baltic Germans, the scions of the German invasion. They, unlike the Lithuanians, were handicapped by having had one of the 'national awakenings' in Eastern and Central Europe but not being able to claim a great medieval kingdom (and thereby garner legitimacy). The remedy to both ills was to vilify German conquest. Estonian and Latvian nationalists portrayed the actions and plans of German knights and priests as duplicitous and inhumane, with one ultimate goal: to conquer and rule the lands of the eastern Baltic littoral. Local chiefs, warriors and would-be kings were resurrected from passing references in the old medieval chronicles and presented as brave leaders fighting against German invasion. Disunity was characterized as the gravest flaw in Estonian and Latvian defences. Once German power was established, '700 years' of oppressive rule over the Estonians and Latvians began.

Lithuanians, on the other hand, have a glorious medieval history complete with stunning military victories and a state which at its zenith nearly stretched from the Baltic Sea to the Black Sea. The early assassination of Mindaugas, the merger with the kingdom of Poland and the gradual fall of Lithuanian influence within the dynastic union are blamed on treacherous division and discord. Lithuania's 'fall and subjugation' to 'foreign influence' brought Lithuanians to the same starting point as the Estonians and Latvians; at least, to nineteenth-century Lithuanian nationalists struggling against Polish and Russian hegemony.

The historical memory forged by nationalists in the nineteenth century has persisted through the twentieth and into the twenty-first century. Even though many of its details are not fabrications, the narrative is too simplistic and reads the conflict of the nineteenth and twentieth centuries back into the historical record. Discord and disunity can equally be explained as the real and perceived differences between the tribes and clans of the eastern Baltic. Clearly some leaders and groups preferred German or Danish and Christian rule and worked for its ultimate triumph. Likewise the oppressive character of rule under Germanic feudal lords and priests is contested. Nevertheless mass rebellions, most notably the 1343 St George's Day Uprising in Danish-ruled Estonia, showcased the potential for widespread social unrest. The rebellion, although short-lived, led the Danish crown to sell its possessions to the Livonian Order, thus bringing most of Estonia and Latvia into Livonia. Serfdom, the great social and economic injustice fresh in the minds of Estonian, Latvian and Lithuanian nationalists in the nineteenth century, was not initially introduced following the German conquest. German knights and priests in Estonia and Latvia monopolized the distribution of justice and they exacted dues from their subjects, but these demands may have been tempered by material benefits such as the expansion of trade and the growth of urban centres. Almost inevitably, much of the middle ranks of society was made up of locals that adapted well to the newly introduced culture. Furthermore the early modern centralizing king likely exacted more from his subjects to finance his ambitions, whereas the eastern Baltic was a supremely decentralized region. The travails of war and the exactions of great, centralizing kings between the sixteenth and the eighteenth century likely scarred and oppressed the peoples of Estonia, Latvia and Lithuania more than did the arrival of German and Danish Christians in the twelfth to the fourteenth century.

The medieval social order in the Eastern Baltic began to break down soon after Martin Luther challenged Catholicism in Western Europe in 1517. Baltic German lords and the urban populations of the Livonian lands quickly adopted Protestantism out of religious conviction and socio-political calculation. In Lithuanian lands, where Polish rule and custom had asserted itself, the Counter Reformation remained more powerful. As a result the still dominant religious divide among the Baltic states emerged: Estonia and Latvia share a Lutheran historical and religious experience, while Lithuania is firmly Catholic. The Reformation also set into motion the chain of events that would lead to a written Estonian and Latvian language (and the Counter Reformation was equally responsible for written Lithuanian). The Reformation also more immediately ushered in competition between expansionist national monarchies that all coveted the lands on the shores of the Eastern Baltic. The kings of Sweden, Poland and Russia had all exerted growing influence on the Livonian state for some time, but in 1558 Tsar Ivan IV opened a military campaign, the Livonian Wars, designed to destroy and annex the territory.[6] Muscovy saw this campaign as an extension of its gradual 'reclamation' of the Grand Duchy of Lithuania's Slavic territories. Ivan's initial offensive proved successful in Narva and Dorpat (today known as Tartu); the existing Livonian armies were unable to halt his advance. In desperation some Baltic German elites turned to Sweden and/or Denmark, which purchased the island of Saaremaa/Ösel, while other Baltic Germans looked to Poland for aid. The Livonian War quickly became a contest of three regional powers vying for regional supremacy. Ultimately the Treaty of Altmark, signed in 1629, brought an end to more than 70 years of protracted, yet intermittent, war. Muscovy was repulsed and the spoils of war were divided between Sweden and Poland. Sweden extended its rule into modern-day Estonia, northern Latvia and the city of Riga, while Poland reaffirmed its rule over Lithuania and acquired southeastern Latvia, also known as Latgale (Inflanty to Poles). Central and western Latvia became the semi-autonomous Duchy of Courland, a vassal state to the king of Poland that enjoyed a brief period of overseas colonial enterprises during the reign of Duke Jakob.

The seventeenth century witnessed economic and demographic recovery after the almost cataclysmic, long Livonian Wars. Famine and plague had repeatedly struck the region during the wars and depopulation across the region was considerable. But peace also brought new rulers eager to reap rewards from their new conquests. The frequent assertion that 'Swedish rule' in the Baltic lands was a comparable golden age are likely misleading and reflect more on later unhappy experiences with other rulers or with the changing opinion of Sweden itself.[7] In the seventeenth century the Swedish king may have been eager to break the control of local German nobles, but less out of concern for the peasantry than desire to fill his coffers. As Swedish fortunes continued to wax those of the Polish crown waned, in part due to ongoing struggles with the power of the Polish aristocracy. Muscovy, after a century of turmoil following the death of Ivan IV, first the Time of Troubles and then the Great Schism in the Russian Orthodox Church, refocused on the eastern Baltic, particularly when the energetic and ambitious Peter I took the throne in 1696. Peter, eager for access to the sea and great, imperial power, revisited the Livonian War. Allied with Denmark and Saxony, Peter's engagement in the Great Northern War began in 1700.

In the Great Northern War Peter I defeated the occasionally brilliant but tempestuous Swedish king Charles XII and humbled Polish ambitions.[8] More than in the case of the Livonian War, the Russian Empire was a determined and modernizing adversary that ultimately captured Swedish-held territory in Estonia and Latvia, including the city of Riga. As before, local power changed little as the Baltic German nobility accepted tsarist rule in exchange for special domestic privileges and rights. In other words, the local aristocracy adapted to a new, distant, national monarch, but continued to rule over local populations. This local rule had developed into classic and near total serfdom for most of the rural population of Estland and Livland (the north of Estonia and the south of Estonia/northeast of Latvia respectively). Although many of Poland's possessions in present-day Latvia and Lithuania remained, her power was broken. Through the eighteenth century Russia was able to more forcefully intervene in the dynastic successions of the Duchy of Courland and in Polish affairs more generally. By the reign of Catherine II, Russia, Prussia and the Habsburg Empire had consumed a weak and decentralized Poland in a series of three partitions. Lithuania, which had long played a reduced and junior role in Polish affairs, became a part of imperial Russia in the course of these partitions. Similarly the Duchy of Courland expired with the Polish state and became a part of imperial Russia. A sliver of Lithuanian lands became part of the kingdom of Prussia. The Baltic German nobility from the Duchy of Courland fared considerably well through the eighteenth century in Russian politics, even greatly influencing Tsarist policies and succession.

By 1800, for the first time in its history, most of the lands of modern-day Estonia, Latvia and Lithuania shared a common ruler, the Russian tsar. Still, the region was not ruled uniformly, nor did the different areas share the same characteristics of socio-economic development. In most of modern-day Estonia and Latvia Peter I conferred special status upon the Baltic German nobility in return for loyalty. As all these lands became Russian possessions, they became administratively referred to as the Baltic Provinces of Estland, Livland and Courland. The German nobility maintained considerable local rights and preserved an aristocratic assembly (the diet). In the more rebellious eastern Latvia, Lithuania and Poland, administrative rule followed the harsher patterns of rule in Polish-occupied lands. The local nobility and the Catholic Church were suspected of Polish loyalties, and the peasantry was seen as an explosive social element. The lands were administratively ruled in a pattern similar to Great Russian provinces.

Much about the eighteenth century on the eastern shores of the Baltic Sea is contradictory. The century can rightly be described as the apogee of the Baltic German nobility. The nobility successfully parlayed their stalwart loyalty for special privileges, including the nearly universal extension of serfdom to the great majority of peasants on their lands. Serfdom reached its most extreme level, with almost unchecked power and authority in the hands of lords. Baltic German nobles aggressively courted the Russian court throughout the century and helped orchestrate the expansion of imperial Russian might through the entire region. They played central roles in the palace coups and machinations that defined much of imperial Russian politics. To the peasantry, the Russian tsar and administration were distant and vague, most noticed when individual young men were chosen for 25 years of service in the imperial army – they received a funerary celebration when departing due to the very slim chance of their return. The enserfed peasants were almost entirely Estonians and Latvians, although their ethnic identity was still very vague. Through the century, however, they would begin to share most of the hallmarks of a common identity with their fellow serfs: they spoke a similar language; they suffered under the same social order; they attended the same confession and used a common Bible in their language. The beginnings of modern nationalism in Estonia and Latvia would not stir until the middle of the nineteenth century, but many of its foundations were set in the eighteenth.

Still, society continued to transform and modernize. Urban centres continued to slowly grow and develop, increasingly as termini for European–Russian trade. These cities were becoming ethnic mosaics, although they were still dominated by centuries of German hegemony. City burghers and guilds were almost entirely German, but this was more a linguistic, cultural stratum than a firmly ethnic, discriminatory system. Latvian and Estonian peasants that had escaped the countryside co-mingled with Germans and often assimilated over the course of a few generations to produce a nebulous social world of blurred ethnicity and social station. Added to this mix were Russian administrators and merchants, Jewish communities and a smattering of others, all inhabiting the most paradoxical of places, a city in imperial Russia. If the Baltic countryside of the eighteenth century created many of the foundations from which Estonian and Latvian nationalism would grow in the nineteenth century, then the urban centres took shape as the crucibles of many of the developments of the nineteenth century: massive demographic growth, industrialization and radicalism.

In Lithuanian lands the gradual decay and then the rapid and complete loss of statehood defined the eighteenth century. To complicate matters, however, the lost state was Polish. The Lithuanian component of the once great Polish-Lithuanian state had dissolved well before. By the end of the eighteenth century that which was Lithuanian was almost entirely the peasantry. The most important urban centre, Vilnius, was a centre of Polish and Jewish culture, not Lithuanian. If nineteenth-century Estonian and Latvian nationalists could not reference a great medieval state of their own, Lithuanians could, but they could not show its physical continuity. There was no longer a Lithuanian nobility nor a Lithuanian elite, and modern Lithuanian national identity rested entirely on the rural, Catholic identity of serfs and peasants. Although the end of the eighteenth century would suggest a common starting point for a joint Baltic history, with one ruler (the Russian tsar) and predominantly enserfed peasant nations, the similarities end there. Considerable commonalities exist for Estonians and Latvians, but less so with Lithuanians. This trend would intensify during the nineteenth century, primarily because of the revolutionary transformations of urban places in Estonia and Latvia as well as the different administrative conditions of the Baltic Provinces and Lithuanian lands and even more so given the small numbers of Lithuanians living in Prussian territories.

The period from 1796 to 1914 in the Baltic region has been referred to as a long century of reforms.[9] The chronology is particularly appropriate for Estonian and Latvian lands, whereas in those of Lithuania most of the reforms were compressed into a time frame from 1861 to 1914, with important breaks and disruptions even in this half-century.[10] Nevertheless the entire region went through such radical transformations that the society and peoples at its beginning seem entirely foreign by the eve of the First World War. The fundamental social fabric of the region, specifically serfdom, but more generally a landed gentry ruling over a peasantry burdened with restrictions and obligations, ceased to exist. In its place land, labour and agricultural production gradually developed as separate commodities. The old nobility fought (often successfully) to retain power, wealth and influence, while smallholders and landless agricultural labourers emerged in a volatile, contested countryside. As the population expanded rapidly, many fled the poverty and misery of the countryside altogether for the promise of work in the nascent industrialization of the region's urban centres. Others abandoned their homelands entirely and migrated to Siberia for the promise of greater access to land. Still others, notably the region's Jews, who were reacting to periodic outbreaks of pogroms and intimidation in tsarist Russia, fled westward, often as far as the United States and Canada, in the great European migrations of the late nineteenth century. National identity developed to explain and place people's identity in this maelstrom of events while radicals and revolutionaries imagined sweeping political programmes that would cure society of poverty and inequality.

The century of reforms began hesitantly, but significantly, with the occasionally liberal-minded Russian tsar Alexander I. Alexander toyed with the idea of reforming serfdom, but was sidetracked by the European-wide convulsions set off by the French Revolution and the Napoleonic Wars (Napoleonic armies marched extensively through Lithuanian lands and a sliver of Latvian land during their ill-fated invasion of Russia). Afterwards, his governing policy became more conservative, but he oversaw the emancipation of the serfs in the Baltic Provinces of Estland, Livland and Courland. The Baltic German nobility of the Baltic Provinces successfully used their position and influence to take over the drafting of the legislation, and the end results reflected their priorities. Essentially the nobility emancipated their serfs without giving them land or civil rights. The material condition of serfs seemed to drop precipitously, but over the next several decades crucial rights were extended to the destitute peasantry. To alleviate overcrowding in the countryside, peasants more easily acquired the right to move to towns and cities. Likewise they won the right to purchase land and own it as private property. Both of these reforms acted as valves that released some pressure from the countryside, but neither was a long-term solution. Most peasants that remained in the countryside did not purchase land, but worked as agricultural labourers or sharecroppers for their former lords or for a small but growing minority of Estonian and Latvian smallholders. The peasants that migrated to urban centres primarily exchanged rural for urban poverty; the dream of rapid advance and riches in towns and cities, for most but not all, was illusory. Still, these radical societal changes enabled the great societal transformations of the second half of the nineteenth century: the emergence of nationalism and socialism.

The Estonian and Latvian 'national awakenings' began in the middle of the nineteenth century, building on the academic work of educated Baltic Germans influenced by Johann Gottfried von Herder (1744–1803). Herder's celebration of the *Volk* and his use of folk songs and customs inspired other German educated thinkers, particularly in East and Central Europe, to examine local peasant languages and cultures. In the Baltic Provinces the first Estonian- and Latvian-language newspapers and journals were a direct result of this trend; written by Baltic Germans, primarily for other Baltic Germans, but in 'peasant tongues'. Through the first half of the nineteenth century this activity was primarily a parlour game, an opportunity to demonstrate erudition, not to advocate for the actual peasant peoples. German remained the cultural, administrative and mercantile lingua franca of the Baltic Provinces. By the middle of the century, however, the old pathways of assimilation, open to the best and most successful sons of Estonian and Latvian peasants, were less appealing. An early generation of nationalist intellectuals demonstratively refused to assimilate and declared themselves Estonians or Latvians. Initially this was a difficult assertion for Baltic Germans to understand; their view of German-ness was one of station and education, not blood. By moving as far as the university level entirely in German, these individuals, to Baltic Germans, were Germans. Latvian-ness and Estonian-ness were specific to being peasants, hence the many references to peasant nations and peasant tongues. The first generation of Estonian and Latvian nationalists primarily sought to raise their respective languages and nations up from their current peasant condition. If proper European nations had national epics, literature, arts and a vocabulary capable of expressing the new, modernizing, scientific world, Estonian and Latvian would need these stepping stones as well; epics and novels were written, plays, music and theatre presented, and new words invented. Much of this activity would have been another parlour game if not for the social transformations of the countryside and urban centres. Estonian and Latvian peasants and city dwellers became a growing and eager market for the cultural production of the first generation of nationalists. This trend was accelerated by the breakdown of old methods of urban assimilation and acculturation that stressed a German milieu, but could not handle the exponential influx of migrants in the second half of the nineteenth century.

As the Baltic German elite began to see the potential threat in these national awakenings, and started to move to block, restrain or heavily censor their cultural output, the early nationalist intellectuals began to move from a cultural programme to one that also included political demands. These, however, were difficult to voice in imperial Russia, where the tsar was an absolute ruler. Furthermore the tsars of the nineteenth century moved fitfully to centralize and modernize their domains. In the Baltic Provinces this included an initiative to standardize administrative practice with the rest of the Empire. Over the next decades, in legal political space,

Estonian and Latvian nationalists and Baltic German noblemen attempted to out-manoeuvre each other and gain favour in tsarist circles. The Baltic German nobility highlighted its similar aristocratic worldview and centuries of loyal service to the Russians, while Estonians and Latvians depicted themselves as closer and more in line with the Slavic world, unlike the alien Baltic Germans, who conceivably could align themselves with national compatriots in Prussia or – later – a unified Germany. Early Estonian and Latvian intellectuals hinted that they could displace the Baltic Germans as the local elite and more thoroughly serve the imperial court. They initially (and logically) supported a late nineteenth-century Russification plan as a step toward weakening the hegemony of the German language. Both arguments fell in and out of favour and neither camp was thoroughly routed or dismissed, but overall Baltic German hegemony remained strongly in place at the turn of the twentieth century.

By 1900, Socialism, which reflected the massive transformations of society in the Baltic Provinces, emerged as a new threat to the existing political order. Socialist thought captured the imaginations of a second generation of Estonian and Latvian nationalists upset with the gross inequities and injustices of landless peasants and urban workers. They were equally annoyed with the slow, gradualist reform approach of the previous generation of activists. As opposed to working within the imperial framework to displace the Baltic German elite, the Socialists believed change required the overthrow of tsarist rule. They did not hope for an indigenization of local rule, but a radical change in the nature of rule itself. Hounded by tsarist secret police, beset by interminable infighting between radical groups and factions, and seen as a foreign and irreligious element by most peasants and workers, the radical parties made few inroads prior to 1905. Still, the Socialists' concerns for equality and justice had much wider currency. Approaching 1905, the Baltic Provinces of Estland, Livland and Courland were a cauldron of change and had been so for several generations. The socio-economic fabric of an almost medieval, peasant society was drastically overturned by rapid urbanization, indus-trialization and modernization in the last two decades of the nineteenth century. National identity and class identity (often the two were seen as the same) were, broadly speaking, two approaches to explaining societal changes while simultane-ously offering a programme for reform or revolution.

In the Lithuanian lands and in the Latvian-inhabited areas just to the south and east of the Baltic Provinces, these changes were much slower to develop. These lands' incorporation into imperial Russia did not include any special privileges for the existing elites. They were simply incorporated into existing Russian administrative provinces. As such, the end of serfdom came with the great Russian emancipation of 1861. Furthermore the close involvement of Lithuanians and Catholics in the frequent but unsuccessful Polish rebellions (most notably in 1830 and 1863) lumped these lands together with Polish ones for harsh, tsarist repression. As a result, the nearly century-long string of developments in modern-day Estonia and Latvia prior to the explosion of 1905 were compressed to fewer than 40 years in Lithuania. If, for example, Estonian and Latvian activism began with cultural activity in the 1850s followed by a more radical young generation in the 1890s, Lithuanian and Latgalian activism was just beginning before political events overran them. As a result of the later emancipation and development of national identity (and nascent radical identity), Lithuanian lands had less of the Baltic Provinces' cauldron of socio-economic industrialization, modernization and urbanization. As a result, the cauldron did not boil over as it did in Estland, Livland and Courland.

The Revolution of 1905 in imperial Russia began after a disastrous war with Japan, a mounting campaign for more public involvement in affairs and increasing radicalization among industrial workers.[11] The tinder for the revolution came when tsarist troops fired upon a peaceful procession in St Petersburg that planned to present a petition to Tsar Nicholas II; the day immediately became known as Bloody Sunday. In the Baltic Provinces a similar, but angrier, procession marking the Petersburg massacre produced similar results in Riga when police fired into the crowd, killing dozens. Anger over the lethal response merged with more general discontent across society to produce a short-lived, general movement demanding substantive reform. In many ways this was similar to the Revolution's development throughout Russia: Tsarist authorities were initially unable to use repressive means to end protests, but protestors were unable to move beyond general demands to overthrowing the existing order. By the end of 1905, particularly after the October Manifesto guaranteed an elected, consultative body (a pre-parliament), the Revolution lost unity and momentum. Gradually the army and the police restored order throughout Russia. In Estland, Livland and Courland, however, the Revolution was more intense and more widespread, moving out of industrial, urban centres into the countryside.[12] Armed peasant bands attacked and burned manors, looted government stores and created short-lived local governments. Noticeable revolutionary activity lasted throughout 1906. Eventually tsarist order was restored, often leading to a period of counter-revolution, in which previously besieged manor lords directed punitive expeditions as much for revenge as for pacification.

The simplest reason for the greater intensity of violence and radicalism in the Baltic Provinces is that national and social identity did not compete with each other, but joined forces. In other words, Estonian and Latvian peasants and workers acted against Baltic German lords and factory owners out of national and social outrage. They understood little difference between the slogans 'Down with the bosses!' and 'Down with the Germans!' Although this apparent merger of enemies played its part, equally important was the longer period of time over which modernization had transformed the socio-economic foundations of the Baltic Provinces without offering any political release valves for discontent. This may also explain the lesser amount of radicalism and violence (relative to the Baltic Provinces, not to Russia itself) in Lithuanian lands and Latgale through 1905.

Radical Estonian and Latvian socialists, moving quickly into illegal, Marxist Social Democratic Workers' Parties, monopolized the political legacy and mantle of the failed Revolution. They could claim many of the martyrs of the Revolution and even more of the radicals deported to Siberia or fled to the West. Likewise their political language dominated the discourse during and after the Revolution. As a result, the Revolution of 1905 is remembered in Estonia and Latvia as a Red event, a memory cultivated by Bolshevik and Soviet propagandists as a pre-cursor to a 'natural and legitimate Soviet Baltic'. Nationalists, on the other hand, have struggled awkwardly to force the Revolution of 1905 into a nationalist narrative as an early national uprising against German and Russian rule. This argument is shaky at best, but its lack of precision or authenticity does not mean that the 'Red Revolution' is entirely accurate either. Instead the Revolution of 1905 was a massive outpouring of frantic political and social work where no such opportunity had existed before. Few peasants and workers understood the intricacies of party platforms (if they existed). They did not know politicians and activists in any great detail. Rumour and chaos defined the year; progressives became reactionaries and radicals became moderates in quick succession. The revolution's outpouring of action should be understood as a statement for change. There was near universal support for a democratically elected legislative and executive body; in other words, the idea that the people should decide and influence government policy through elected leaders. Overwhelmingly the issues of policy that most needed to be addressed were landlessness in the countryside, poor conditions and wages for workers, and the injustice of preferential treatment and rights for some accorded by their station or ancestry. Little of this was accomplished in 1905 or in its after-math as the Duma, the elected consultative body the Tsar acquiesced to, lacked real power. The complexity of Estonian, Latvian and – to a lesser degree – Latgalian and Lithuanian society, on the eve of the First World War, muddles the simple narratives of socialists and nationalists alike about the relationship of Estonians, Latvians and Lithuanians with imperial Russia.

The complex and contradictory nature of Baltic society on the eve of the First World War is alternately understood as a revolution in waiting or as the beginning of reform. The partisan nature of the writing of the history of Estonia, Latvia and Lithuania through much of the twentieth century puts the events of the First World War and its aftermath back into the era preceding the war. Soviet historians who understood the Bolshevik Revolution of 1917 as inevitable found its roots before the war. Liberal, conservative and nationalist historians, however, who understood the rise of the Bolsheviks as a coup in the midst of extenuating circumstances, saw more promise in the haphazard steps towards reform of the imperial system. Neither is completely accurate; the complexity of Estonian, Latvian and Lithuanian society on the eve of the First World War contained elements of discontent and revolution as well as agents of organic change and reform. Estonian, Latvian and Lithuanian elites clearly emerged to challenge for greater influence locally and in the Empire. Politically, elected members in the Dumas and in municipal and parish councils joined with educated specialists in government ministries (and officers in the armed forces as well) to showcase Estonian, Latvian and Lithuanian efforts to work within the existing imperial system for more power. In a few towns Baltic German political dominance stumbled as Estonian and Latvian council members formed a majority in the Valka municipal council and Estonian and Russian members formed a majority in Tallinn. Economically, Estonian, Latvian and Lithuanian merchants and industrialists were among the phenomenally wealthy and successful, but more significantly created an emerging middle class of small business and property owners (joined by increasing farm ownership in the countryside). Culturally many of the crowning achievements of the modern Estonian, Latvian and Lithuanian arts were produced and openly celebrated within a larger tsarist milieu. If these politicians, merchants and artists wanted radical change, they wanted it to recognize their contributions.

To many radicals and revolutionaries, however, the failures of the Revolution of 1905 were lessons for a future, successful revolution. To these revolutionaries, mass politics were remembered as diffuse and amorphous. They also questioned the viability of a common cause with class enemies, assuming that the collapse of the Revolution was largely due to the bourgeoisie betrayal following the October Manifesto. Not surprisingly many gravitated toward the Bolshevik vision of the Social Democratic party that stressed the role of a secretive, professional revolutionary vanguard. To those radicals and revolutionaries of 1905 who were driven underground or in exile, preparations were not made for reform and organic work within the tsarist system, but for scuttling the entire old regime if given the chance.

In the endless debate between national and social identities, however, there existed a running debate that split both camps. This debate revolved around the Latvian, Estonian and Lithuanian place within Russia, near to Germany and in a larger Europe. Katrina Schwartz has elegantly summarized this discourse as a debate between an identity rooted in expansion and the future and an insular, backward-looking identity.[13] This divide applies as much to the first 'national awakeners' as to politicians and intellectuals today. In short, nationalists (or socialists, for that manner) that placed Baltic identity in an expanding context, which included most of the national awakeners and the Marxist socialists, saw progress through a greater engagement with the larger world. Nationalists such as the Latvian Krišjānis Valdemārs famously and pointedly pushed Latvians to move into the merchant marine as a symbol of a new worldview. A key component of this perspective was proving Estonian, Latvian and Lithuanian value and place in Europe. Others, however, clung to the powerful and simple symbol of the land and the person working it as the cornerstone of Baltic identity. In Latvia this idea became encapsulated in the idea 'of each person's little corner of land' as the be-all and end-all of political action and development. To these intellectuals Latvia's identity was tarnished by contact with the European world and was more pure in its distant past. Finding a place in Europe was not needed, but reclaiming the past was.

Although the outward- and forward-looking perspective dominated among most of the emerging elites of the late nineteenth and early twentieth century, how far this sentiment was shared by the peasants and workers of the Baltic was unclear. It is likely that any single, simple description would be inaccurate: intellectuals, peasants, workers and merchants all vacillated between the two dialectical ideas, struggling to use them to find meaning in the rapidly changing world around them.

The actual demographic and socio-economic changes to Baltic society by the eve of the First World War further discredit the simple narratives of nationalists or socialists. Urban centres, most specifically Riga, were imperial cities. Riga was a multicultural centre with multiple, vibrant Baltic German, Latvian, Russian and Jewish communities, as was Vilnius in its own way.[14] The hackneyed description of Baltic German lords and Estonian or Latvian peasants or workers hardly applied to cities with major Russian and Jewish populations as well as variegated German and Latvian ones. Cities enjoyed the amenities of a modern urban environment, from public transportation, sanitation and electricity to expanding health care and education, and they were a part of a sophisticated network of trade, communication and finance (with the telegraph, railways, ports, banks and foreign investments). Yet overcrowding and abysmal slums coexisted with prosperity.

The greatest obstacle in tsarist Baltic society remained the inability to act meaningfully in political decision-making. This absence placed a ceiling above the upwardly mobile Estonian and Latvian elites that would never be entirely removed during tsarist rule. The lack of ability to change things through the system always reinforced the argument of revolutionaries. The tenuous balance of these many forces after the Revolution of 1905 collapsed completely under the weight of the First World War, which exposed all tsarist society's weaknesses and stripped its accomplishments of all their splendour. The War ultimately led to the collapse of imperial Russia, Germany, Austria-Hungary and the Ottoman Empire. Finland, Estonia, Latvia, Lithuania and Poland emerged from the former Russian Empire, with Polish lands also coming from German and Austrian-Hungarian lands. Further across Central Europe, the collapse of empires led to the emergence of Czecho-slovakia and Yugoslavia. Romania experienced a considerable redrawing of its borders and Austria, Hungary, the Weimar Republic, the Republic of Turkey and ultimately the Soviet Union began their existences in the territorial rump of old Empires. Several other states, most notably Ukraine, Belarus, Armenia, Georgia and Azerbaijan, suffered through a short period of independence before succumbing to Soviet aggression.

When war broke out in Europe in 1914, almost all observers and governments imagined it would be quick and decisive. As the war became a marathon battle of attrition that approached total war (a war that mobilized all of society for its effort), imperial Russia – of all the major combatants – was least prepared for the demands of modern warfare. Russia's advantage in numbers became meaningless when facing more advanced German armies, greater German industrial might and its more comprehensive transportation and resupply networks. Russia's initial offensive into Prussia became an abject rout after the Germans' unequivocal victory at the Battle of the Masurian Lakes. German forces advanced into imperial Russian territory and occupied most of modern-day Lithuania and half of Latvia from the summer of 1915. Hundreds of thousands of civilian refugees fled – some by compulsion, some by choice – eastward into the interior of Russia.[15] Although academic debate continues about the First World War and its causal relationship with the end of tsardom and the advent of Soviet Russia, along the eastern shores of the Baltic Sea the First World War led to the independence of Estonia, Latvia and Lithuania, not to mention Finland and Poland. Estonia, Latvia and Lithuania all saw unprecedented societal disruption, which resulted in focused movements for outright sovereignty and political independence that had not previously existed. The road to this independence, even if only four years in the making (from the outset of war to independence), was impossibly tortured, complex and unique in each Baltic state.

Prior to the First World War there were no systematic movements for an independent Estonia, Latvia or Lithuania. Individuals may have dreamed of the idea, but no major political movement advocated for independence. The most radical demand was for autonomy (poorly defined) within a democratic Russia. This was largely a result of a realistic assessment of the international situation in Europe at the dawn of the twentieth century. Small nations and states were anomalies, and the concept that expansionist imperial states would suddenly break apart into their ethnic components seemed more of a Balkan possibility than a Baltic one. But the trauma of the First World War rent imperial Russia asunder, and although the experiences of war were drastically different across the Baltic region, the end results were uniform: a concerted political and military drive for a fully independent nation-state. The totality of German victories in 1915 translated into the bulk of Lithuanian lands experiencing German occupation and rule for the majority of the First World War. Vejas Liulevicius has skilfully examined how this experience of occupation shaped future Nazi attitudes and policies in his *War Lands on the Eastern Front*, but it also forced Lithuanians to consider their place within a post-war Europe.[16] As the war tortuously approached its endgame, a renewed Polish entity seemed more and more likely (though the degree of its autonomy and independence was still hotly debated). To Lithuanian nationalists, the emergence of a new Polish state reopened the debate about the Lithuanian glorious past subsumed into a Polish union. If Poland re-emerged, whither Lithuanian national ambitions? Lithuanian statehood, potentially subservient to German oversight, became a counter to a renewed Polish influence as well as to the contagion of atheist, Soviet Russia. The question of how that state would emerge, and what its borders – and its relations with Germany and Poland – would be, remained unanswered. Unlike Estonia or Latvia, the question of Russia was much less central apart from the categorical rejection of the Soviet alternative to the great majority of inhabitants.

For the Latvian lands the First World War categorically meant displacement.[17] Industry, which had modernized and transformed Riga, was evacuated to the Russian interior. Neither Riga nor Latvia would recapture an industrial character until the city was once again (and forcibly) incorporated into a Soviet political entity. More traumatically, the great majority of the population of Courland fled into the Russian interior after a combination of scorched earth tactics by retreating Russian troops, rumours of expected German atrocities and outright evacuation orders from the Tsarist military command. These refugees and the organizations that emerged to organize their aid and relief moved beyond demands for autonomy within a reorganized Russia.[18] As the Baltic German nobility flirted with unification with imperial Germany, Latvian nationalists struggled to find viable alternatives. After the Bolshevik seizure of power, many concluded that Latvians no longer had common ground with either a German- or a Russian-dominated state. The only alternative was a Latvian nation-state that was slowly and fitfully embraced by its elite and inhabitants alike.

Only in Estonia did the standard nationalist narrative fit closely with events on the ground. Although thousands of Latvian refugees fled into Estonian lands, far fewer Estonians fled further east. German occupation did not come until well into 1917. By this late date the Baltic German nobility in Estonia seemed a clear, reactionary force and Soviet Russia an unpalatable revolutionary option. War, revolution and occupation provided the opportunity for a hitherto unrealized dream: independence. Aided and abetted by nationalist Finns, Estonian nationalists quickly rallied public support for an independent state and moved to win its borders militarily and achieve their recognition diplomatically. In Latvian and Lithuanian land independence remained elusive as significant domestic and international obstacles remained. In all three states the contest between Germany and Soviet Russia surrounding the harsh terms of the Treaty of Brest-Litovsk complicated the declarations and winning of independence. In Lithuania activists declared independence on 16 February 1918, with German approval. The state initially seemed destined to be a client of imperial Germany. In Estonia, however, nationalist forces loyal to an existing legislative body, the Maapäev, defeated local Bolsheviks on the eve of a German offensive and declared independence on 24 February 1918 as German troops entered Tallinn. Within a few weeks the German authorities had crushed the Estonian provisional government and arrested many of its members. This action spurred the UK and France to recognize (de facto) Estonian independence as a spur in the side of imperial Germany's eastern front. In Latvian lands a declaration of independence did not come until 18 November 1918, after the collapse of the German war effort. Latvia's complications, as well as those of Estonia and Lithuania, included a defeated German army eager to withdraw from the east, leaving a military vacuum into which Bolshevik forces were eager to move to recoup earlier territorial losses. Through November and December 1918 Bolshevik forces moved swiftly across the territory before finally meeting determined resistance west of Tartu in Estonia and near the banks of the Venta river in western Latvia. Estonian forces with Finnish volunteers quickly pushed the Bolsheviks out of Estonian territory by February 1919.

In all three states victory came not just with the defeat of Bolshevik enemies, but also with the defeat of remaining German forces, freebooters and White forces involved in the Russian Civil War. The military forces involved in all three states were a dizzying kaleidoscope of uniforms that include the three national armies, ethnic and Russian Bolshevik forces, partisans, German forces, freebooters, White Russian and Polish armies, Finnish volunteers, British and French gunboats and more.[19] At the beginning of 1920 each state signed a peace treaty with Soviet Russia, establishing de jure recognition. Allied powers extended this same recognition soon after, with the USA notably recognizing the three states' independence considerably later. The wars that led to independence left unresolved border disputes. Ironically, demarcating the border between the three Baltic states and Soviet Russia (the major combatants of the wars) proved simple and straightforward. Latvia's borders with Estonia and Lithuania, who had been allied during the wars, proved more difficult and ultimately required international adjudication. Lithuania's border with Poland remained unresolved. As war ended with Soviet Russia, Polish troops unilaterally occupied Vilnius, the expected capital of the state. This occupation would last until the Second World War and throw relations with Poland into permanent crisis throughout the interwar years. Furthermore the loss of Vilnius would feed irredentism and discontent in Lithuania domestically as well.

Following the wars for independence, the newly independent Baltic states shared many challenges, from economic reconstruction to state formation. All three states embarked on radical agrarian reform to ameliorate rural landlessness. In Estonia and Latvia this primarily meant dispossessing the Baltic German nobility of their lands (with little or no compensation) and distributing this land to the rural landless. As a result many, but not all, Baltic Germans were bitterly opposed to these new states. War and revolution effectively destroyed the industrial enterprises of Estonia and Latvia; all three states became overwhelmingly agricultural societies. The city of Riga felt this transformation most drastically, going from an industrial and mercantile imperial hub to a largely administrative capital. It was considerably reduced in population as well. Still, all three states experienced a period of robust and frenzied economic and social development, as school systems were expanded and modernized, transport and communications systems developed, and cultural output soared.

All three states, however, struggled to adapt to a parliamentary system of government. In each republic social democrats polled strongly but largely stayed in parliamentary opposition. Liberal electoral laws saw parliaments with many parties and fragile coalition governments cobbled together from frequently competing interests. Patriarchal figures closely tied to the wars for independence (either as first Minister Presidents or as victorious generals) towered over the seeming political chaos and instability. These characters were not universally loved and were often painted as corrupt, petty despots. Still, they commanded enough power and patronage to be the most likely figures to take power in any coup orchestrated from above. In 1926, largely due to the constant political instability surrounding the Vilnius question and the unease nationalists felt about the left-wing government in power, Antanas Smetona emerged as president of Lithuania with near dictatorial powers. He remained president until 1940. In Estonia and Latvia authoritarian coups did not succeed until 1934, after the Great Depression handicapped consensus-building, when Konstantin Päts in Estonia and Kārlis Ulmanis in Latvia seized power.

A balance sheet of the interwar republics and of their authoritarian regimes is difficult to produce. Estonian and Latvian nationalists quickly enshrined national narratives that linked an independence lost in the thirteenth century to one regained in the twentieth. Lithuanian nationalists referenced the Grand Duchy of Lithuania at its height as its pedigree, but remained obsessed with its incomplete restoration for as long as Vilnius remained under Polish authority. In all three states the authoritarian leaders wrapped their regimes in ethnic nationalism, using the power of the state to weaken the position of Germans, Jews, Russians, Poles and others. Measured against the democratic, progressive spirit of the founding of the states and of their initial constitutions, this homogenizing ethnic impulse was a travesty. Compared to the brutal and murderous path to the same ends employed by authoritarian regimes across Central and Eastern Europe and Eurasia, the Baltic cases seem more benign. Still, as authoritarianism and extremism became more of the norm for much of Europe, the fascist aesthetic captivated the regimes of all three states. As more and more research delves into the inner workings of each of these regimes, the desire to use the power of the state to transform society into a totalitarian state devoted to the dictates of its leader emerges. That these regimes, however, were unable or unwilling to turn many of these desires into sustained practice is equally telling.

If the domestic record of Estonia, Latvia and Lithuania is mixed, their foreign policies failed, albeit not of their own accord. The fundamental objective of a state's foreign policy is to ensure its survival and the Baltic states could not achieve this most basic need. All three were fortunate in exploiting an unprecedented international crisis to achieve statehood. The two great regional powers, Germany and Russia, were both weak and isolated. Allied powers, the UK and France, were mildly supportive of Baltic independence. Soon after the Baltic states enjoyed general recognition, they moved into more difficult waters: how to protect and guarantee independence? An early initiative to create a union or alliance from Finland to Poland quickly collapsed. As France and the UK's interest and ability to guarantee Baltic sovereignty waned, the states were left with few options. As Hitler's Germany and Stalin's Russia emerged from a prolonged period of weakness, the Baltic states' survival was in doubt. Without other allies, the Baltic states realistically could curry favour with Soviet Russia or with Nazi Germany and thereby become the de facto client of one or the other. Or they could do nothing and hope for the best. Ultimately Estonia and Latvia hoped to use what little negotiating space they had with each of their neighbours, but eventually retreated into neutrality. Lithuania's foreign policy – like almost everything else – was complicated by the Vilnius question. Lithuania's fundamental foreign policy objectives were to survive and to regain Vilnius. As such, their foreign policy was more aggressive in its goals than Estonia's or Latvia's, but failed equally. None of the three states successfully preserved their independence through the Second World War, although it is almost inconceivable how this could have been accomplished.

CHAPTER 2

Potemkin Republics

In 1787 Empress Catherine II visited the recently acquired Crimean peninsula and either did or did not see elaborate facades along the banks of the Dnieper river. Historians still argue about the apocryphal 'Potemkin villages' that her supposed paramour General Grigori Aleksandrovich Potemkin allegedly constructed for her viewing pleasure. Whatever the provenance of the original theatre-like sets, the term 'Potemkin village' entered the general political lexicon to denote an elaborate, false construct designed to conceal an unpleasant or unwanted situation. The history of Estonia, Latvia and Lithuania from 1940 until 1991 is largely the history of three Potemkin Baltic Republics. For most of this period they were Potemkin Baltic Soviet Socialist Republics and the chasm between the facade and conditions on the ground was at its deepest. During this era the facade consisted of multiple overlapping and intertwined deceptions that were internal, international, domestic and societal. After 1991, however, the metaphor did not completely disappear and there is still something to the idea of Baltic Potemkin republics within the European Union.

The Second World War Descends upon Estonia, Latvia and Lithuania

Although geopolitical events such as the Munich Crisis (when the Allied Powers agreed to the dismemberment of Czechoslovakia without consulting the Czechoslovaks) foreshadowed the inevitability of the Second World War consuming the Baltic Republics, its beginning was the infamous Nazi–Soviet Non-Aggression Pact of 23 August 1939, more frequently referred to as the Molotov–Ribbentrop Pact. The pact gave the green light to Nazi Germany's invasion of Poland, but also doomed other Eastern European states, most notably Estonia, Latvia and Lithuania, all of which relied on Nazi–Soviet rivalry as a perilous safeguard of their independence.

Estonia, Latvia and Lithuania had no military safeguards for their independence other than their own armed forces (which were mostly small and outdated). In the early 1920s a few optimistic statesmen entertained the idea of a grand alliance of Poland, Finland, Estonia, Latvia and Lithuania, but it collapsed over two insurmountable obstacles: Finnish tepidity and, more importantly, Poland's occupation of Lithuania's cherished Vilnius.[1] Through the 1920s an occasional intrepid minister of foreign affairs would broach some novel security arrangement for the Baltic states with multiple great parties guaranteeing (and thus ensuring) their independence. These schemes were largely ignored and by the 1930s Baltic security was perilous. Estonia made some inroads into military cooperation with Finland and signed a treaty of cooperation with Latvia, but neither produced a significant defensive bloc for securing independence. The overall frailty of Baltic independence was harshly exposed when Hitler forced Lithuania to cede Klaipeda (Memel) in March 1939: this aggressive manoeuvre led to few international consequences for Hitler. By the summer of 1939 the likelihood of war between Germany and Poland increased significantly and the capitals of Europe were abuzz with efforts to stave off war or cement alliances in the event of its outbreak. Long the pariah, the Communist leadership in Moscow became a coveted ally for the UK, France and Nazi Germany alike. If the Soviet Union would fight against Nazi Germany, Hitler would be faced with a multiple front situation comparable to that of the First World War. If the Soviet Union sided with Germany, Poland's defence would be virtually hopeless. To Estonia, Latvia and Lithuania, their last remnants of maneuverability in foreign policy would be lost with a negotiated understanding between Hitler's Germany and Stalin's Russia. As news broke of a Soviet–German rapprochement, diplomats from Estonia, Latvia and Lithuania scurried to understand its consequences, and to verify the rumoured secret protocols that addressed the Baltic states.

The Non-Aggression Pact did indeed contain secret protocols that divided much of Eastern Europe into spheres of influence where each state would have a free hand.[2] Initially Estonia and Latvia were earmarked for Soviet Russia, while Lithuania fell into the German sphere. In late September Nazi Germany bartered Lithuania to the Soviet Union for gold and steel. In early October a further round of negotiations ceded the troubled city of Vilnius to Soviet influence. The existence of the secret protocols, discussed in diplomatic circles in 1939 and publicized in the West at the Nuremberg Trials that followed the Second World War, was categorically denied by the Soviet Union until 1991. More recently revisionist historians in contemporary Russia have sought to minimize the impact of the Pact and its protocols, downplaying their role in the outbreak of the Second World War. Their reinterpretations, however, struggle to explain the rapid chain of events that followed in Poland and the Baltic Republics. Nazi Germany invaded Poland a week later, followed by a Soviet invasion of eastern Poland on 17 September.

If panic descended on the Estonian, Latvian and Lithuanian ministries of foreign affairs, the regime-controlled media in each state put on a brave face. Regime newspapers that had conspicuously reported little about Soviet or Nazi terror inside their own countries insisted that the regimes' policy of neutrality had saved the states from the flames of war. The same policy forced the Baltic states to intern Polish troops that fled from Soviet and German forces into their countries. More difficult to explain were the Mutual Assistance Pacts that Moscow forced on the Baltic states in early October 1939. In belligerent and belittling late-night meetings at the Kremlin, Molotov and Stalin cajoled the Baltic ambassadors to accept Soviet troops into their states or face dire consequences. Baltic cooperation in the face of this threat amounted to little more than frenzied communications with each other about the terms of the pacts. The appearance of Soviet bases in the territories of Estonia, Latvia and Lithuania compromised their territorial integrity and the large numbers of stationed troops made the states virtually defenceless to further Soviet demands. To add to the funerary feeling in Estonia and Latvia, the majority of Baltic Germans 'voluntarily repatriated' to Germany in the autumn and winter of 1939 and in the spring of 1940. These Baltic Germans had centuries-long roots in the community and very little connection to the Reich. Still, German, Estonian,and Latvian pressure, coupled with the realization of likely Soviet advances, convinced most of them to leave. As before, regime newspapers trumpeted these latest developments as successes. In Latvia the loss of the Baltic German community and the state's inability to protect its citizens was described as a victory in making Latvia a more ethnically Latvian ideal. This was a bitter foreshadowing of the general indifference to the plight that Latvia's Jews would suffer under Nazi occupation in less than two years. In Lithuania, on the other hand, Soviet forces ceded control of Vilnius (taken from Poland on 19 September 1939) to Lithuania. The Lithuanian army marched triumphantly through the city at the end of October, having accomplished the long-held dream of unification quite accidentally.[3]

Soviet pressure on the Baltic Republics abated after the bases were established on their territory. Soviet attention was likely focussed on a similar plan of action with Finland. Finland refused to acquiesce and waged the Winter War with the

USSR until the early spring of 1940 before finally suing for peace. Soon thereafter, just as Nazi tanks invaded France, the USSR issued an ultimatum to Estonia, Latvia and Lithuania. It cited manufactured border incidents and the 'hostile' nature of the Estonian–Latvian alliance from the early 1930s as evidence of the three states' betrayal of the Mutual Assistance Pacts of 1939. With Soviet troops massed on the borders of each state, Moscow demanded the entry of troops and the dismissal of acting governments, which were to be replaced by ones amenable to (and picked by) Soviet emissaries. In Estonia and Latvia Konstantin Päts and Kārlis Ulmanis acquiesced, but in Lithuania President Smetona fled the country before his replacements finally agreed to Soviet demands. In each state a new puppet government prepared for incorporation into the USSR.

This year of Soviet occupation is almost entirely remembered in Estonia, Latvia and Lithuania backwards; or, rather, the events of the end of the year of occupation are remembered as the salient features of the entire year. These events include the first mass deportations of Estonian, Latvian and Lithuanian citizens to the USSR, which occurred from 13 to 14 June 1941. Although remembering this single monumental tragedy is understandable, it does not convey the sense of confusion and uncertainty, rather than abject dread and terror, that defined the start of Soviet occupation. At first the puppet cabinets seemed to be assemblies of progressive journalists, scientists and cultural figures rather than leftist, let alone Communist, politicians. This was a smokescreen: some of these figures had secretly been Communist Party activists for years while others had no power whatsoever. Still, for bewildered populations desperately anxious to avoid war, the compositions of these cabinets promised a glimmer of hope. Furthermore the promise of parliamentary elections (abrogated in all three states) suggested that some degree of public participation in government and rule was possible. The continuing presence of Konstantin Päts and Kārlis Ulmanis as the state presidents of Estonia and Latvia respectively further hinted at compromise and continuity. As Ulmanis had implored over the radio as Soviet troops occupied his state: 'Stay in your places, I will stay in mine.' Almost everyone did, and held their breaths.

The nature of Soviet occupation began to show itself with the supposed elections to people's parliaments in July 1940. Although the elections were publicized as free, electoral commissions, closely staffed and monitored by Soviet personnel, refused to allow the formation or registration of rival political parties. In all three states broad coalitions of political parties and well-known cultural figures tried to offer a nationalist, yet progressive, alternative to the Soviet-supported workers' list of candidates. In all three states security agents harassed the alternative parties' organizational work and arrested many activists and proposed candidates.[4] With the exception of a few isolated individuals, most notably in Estonia, the electorate went to the polls in July 1940 to find only one electoral list for which they could vote. Further voting 'irregularities' included an extreme disregard for the legal procedure of elections as defined in each state's constitution, voting by Soviet armed forces and others not eligible to vote, the lack of secret ballots, and implied and direct threats throughout the process. Not surprisingly the puppet cabinets declared nearly unanimous victories for the Soviet-supported lists and almost immediately began to stress that these newly elected people's parliaments would push for incorporation into the USSR. At the beginning of August 1940 delegates from Estonia, Latvia and Lithuania travelled to Moscow and formally requested the incorporation of their states into the USSR. Stalin graciously acquiesced. The three Baltic Republics became the Estonian, Latvian and Lithuanian Soviet Socialist Republics. Foreign embassies shuddered throughout the Baltic while diplomatic personnel of the former 'bourgeois' republics were ordered to return. Not surprisingly, few did. Some states refused to recognize the legality of this process and continued to insist that the Baltic Republics had been forcefully occupied and annexed. During the heat of the Second World War, however, this policy of non-recognition could provide nothing more to the Baltic states or their inhabitants. The elections clearly demonstrated that Soviet occupation would lead to Soviet political rule without any space for compromise, consensus-building or opposition. The political elites of Estonia, Latvia and Lithuania clearly understood that after the sham elections and the manufactured incorporation into the USSR, all three states would begin a crash course of Sovietization – the transformation of their independent states to adhere to Soviet political, economic, social and cultural norms.

Still, in August 1940, even in January 1941, few would have predicted the mass deportations that were to come by June. Soviet rule was seen as heavy-handed and clumsy and the stressful conditions of a world at war were blamed for Soviet excess. Many hoped that conditions would soften with time. Furthermore the Soviet state took active steps to build support among sectors of Estonian, Latvian and Lithuanian society even while they continued to identify, isolate and remove anti-Soviet elements. Workers received wage increases, the landless received land in a new round of agrarian reform, social democrats and leftists were welcomed into administration (but not decision-making), and minority groups were extended some cultural rights. By far the most impressive play for public support remained the transfer of Vilnius to Lithuania in 1939, prior to Soviet occupation. By the autumn of 1940, however, Lithuanian nationalists' attempts to Lithuanianize the city in the winter of 1939 and spring of 1940 were rapidly replaced by efforts to Sovietize the city in the remainder of 1940 and in the first half of 1941.

The limited attempts at building public support failed miserably under the dual pressures of Soviet economic transformation and deepening political control. Workers may have received more money, but the introduction of the Soviet ruble at ridiculously inflated rates wiped out earlier savings. Most wealth was national-ized, prices soared and serious shortages of consumer goods became commonplace. Complaints and opposition to this new economic course were interpreted as anti-Soviet behaviour and often led to political arrests. Rather than building support, Soviet policies pushed Estonians, Latvians and Lithuanians into opposition to Soviet rule. By the winter of 1940 Estonians, Latvians and Lithuanians understood that the arrival of Soviet troops in June 1940 had led to the simple, outright and complete occupation of their states. Independence had been lost. Still, few imagined that mass deportations were the next planned step, in part because the newspapers of the authoritarian regimes of the 1930s downplayed the existence of Soviet terror in the USSR.

The mass deportations of June 1941 shocked and befuddled the inhabitants of Estonia, Latvia and Lithuania; nothing like them had happened before. On the night of 13–14 June 1940 tens of thousands of people were detained, transported to railheads and deported. Ultimately the deported were sorted and separated. For the most part, adult males went on to the Gulag as enemies of the state; only a very few returned. Their wives and families were sent into administrative exile in the far expanses of Siberia. If political terror had targeted individual politicians and activists until this date, the June deportation targeted the political elite of the old states as a whole, lumping them together as suspect social classes. In the country-side this could often be summarized as the parish elder, the militia commander and the wealthiest inhabitant from before Soviet occupation; or, in other words, the political figurehead, the law and order figurehead and the economic repre-sentative of the old regime. These individuals were not arrested alone, however, as the bulk of those arrested and deported were the rest of their families: women, children and the elderly.

From 1991 historians in Estonia, Latvia and Lithuania have dissected these first mass deportations at great length.[5] We have ascertained the number deported and their individual fates. We know who drew up the lists of those to be deported, who went out to homes and farmsteads to arrest families, and what happened to much of the property of those arrested. We even know with relative certainty how the broad outlines of the operation were discussed and agreed upon in Moscow in early

1941. If we are beginning to have a degree of certainty about these deportations, the inhabitants of Estonia, Latvia and Lithuania had none the week following the deportations themselves. Rumours abounded about who had been deported and why, and if more deportations were imminent, but confusion and secrecy still surrounded the particulars. The surviving members of the elites of the old republics realized that the Soviet state considered them class enemies and intended to eliminate them. Into this atmosphere of confusion, rumour, shock, despair and anger marched the invading armies of Hitler's Germany. Hitler's propagandists, ably aided by Estonian, Latvian and Lithuanian collaborators, would reshape the first mass deportation as the signature piece of Soviet occupation, the defining moment of what Nazi propagandists would refer to in Latvia as the 'horrible year'. They were particularly adept at linking this carnage and all of Soviet rule to the local Jewish communities, particularly those of Latvia and Lithuania. But German occupation would be similarly horrible and more murderous.

On the eve of 22 June 1941 the entire territory of Estonia, Latvia and Lithuania was occupied by Soviet troops and all three republics were well into the process of Sovietization. The Nazi–Soviet Non-Aggression Pact had cleared the way for Soviet occupation, but within hours invading German armies had rendered it meaningless. German troops advanced quickly through Lithuania and western and central Latvia.[6] Soviet forces were completely surprised and showed little ability or inclination to counterattack. Most Soviet forces and Communist Party officials fled haphazardly. In several places, including Riga, Latvia and most notably at Červene, Lithuania, retreating Soviet forces massacred political prisoners in custody before fleeing; thousands were executed. In most places across Lithuania and Latvia the German army advanced at a rapid pace across the territory, only occasionally leaving Soviet pockets for later attention (such as in Liepaja). This later attention lasted for hours and days, not longer. By the middle of July, in less than a month, German armed forces had swept across Lithuania and Latvia and established occupation authorities. In Estonia German forces arrived as quickly, by early July 1941, but their attention was focused on capturing Leningrad. Much of Estonia remained in Soviet hands until German troops stalled on the outskirts of Leningrad. With the invasion thrust slowed, German troops fanned back into Estonia, capturing Tallinn at the end of August and not securing the Estonian islands until October. As a result Estonia suffered the most in these first months of the German invasion as Soviet troops destroyed much of worth in the summer of 1941 and Estonian partisans waged guerilla war in return.[7] In Lithuania and Latvia the question of an interregnum between Soviet and German rule is more difficult, and more loaded.

The volatility of the idea of an interregnum in Latvia and Lithuania revolves around local initiation of and participation in the murder of Latvia's and Lithuania's Jews.[8] Each state had a large, vibrant, historical Jewish community and the city of Vilnius was a centre of Jewish culture, learning and tradition in Eastern Europe. Although Latvia and Lithuania produced many hardships for these communities, the amount and degree of anti-Semitism did not approach the murderous excesses of much of Eastern Europe. Latvia and Lithuania were measured sanctuaries, hence the greater surprise and tragedy of the Holocaust in the Baltic Republics. Although there were some Bolsheviks from a Jewish background, Jewish communities were primarily conservative, religious and mercantile, and thus suffered extensively under Soviet occupation. Still, Jews were linked with Soviet rule in popular perception and this idea was relentlessly exploited by Nazi propaganda during the occupation. Within the first six months of Nazi occupation the great majority of Latvia's Jewish population had been murdered in the Holocaust, often with local, Latvian participation. After most of Latvia's Jews were murdered, Latvian concentration and internment camps became terminal points in the Nazi's pan-European Holocaust project. Jews were transported from Hungary and further abroad, and were often guarded and occasionally murdered by Latvians under German command. Latvian military detachments in German armies participated in actions targeting Jewish communities in Belarus and Ukraine and served as guards at notorious camps in Poland. In Lithuania there may have been even greater local participation in the killing of Lithuania's and Vilnius' Jews, but there were many fewer Lithuanian troops under German command involved in further atrocities. In Estonia, where the Jewish community before the war was less than a thousand, local participation was even less pronounced, largely because German troops were able to exterminate almost all Estonian Jews themselves in short order. A Nazi officer tasked with implementing the Holocaust in the occupied Baltic Republics, Franz Walter Stahlecker, even proudly reported that by December 1941 Estonia was 'Free of Jews' (*Judenfrei*), but this was almost entirely due to executions carried out by the Nazi Einsatzgruppe A. Still, Estonia also became a terminal point in other Nazi Holocaust sites with local, Estonian participation.[9]

In Latvia and Lithuania the degree of local participation and complicity in the murder of local Jews demands greater attention and focus. Both states witnessed particularly brutal episodes in the larger European Holocaust context and in both cases some of the most disturbing events are preserved on film and in photographs (executions carried out by German soldiers outside of Liepaja and a brutal beating death in Kaunas are two of the most notorious examples). Some Lithuanians and

Latvians quickly volunteered to assist the Germans in the arrest, detainment and eventual murder of Jews who were their compatriots. In Lithuania ad hoc militias, roughly reconstituted from police and local militia forces from before Soviet occupation, were largely responsible for local participation in the Holocaust. In Latvia Viktors Arājs formed a Latvian auxiliary police unit (better known as the Arājs Kommando or Sonderkommando Arājs) under German command within days of the German arrival in Riga. This unit, with a core of 300 to 500 men, but which mushroomed to 1,500, travelled across Latvia to small regional towns and villages, executing Jews detained by local police and authorities. They were also central actors in the burning of Riga's largest synagogue on 4 July 1941 and in the forced march and execution of many of the inmates of the Riga ghetto. The Arājs Kommando alone may be accountable for at least 26,000 murders. If we include the number of police assigned to general guard duty, those that ransacked and stole from Jewish homes and apartments and those that exploited Jews from the ghettos as slave labour, the number of Latvians and Lithuanians that were actively complicit in the Holocaust increases considerably. They dwarf the very few that actively tried to hide, protect or save Jews from death. The honorary title 'Righteous Among the Nations' recognizes a little over 100 Latvians and nearly 800 Lithuanians for their good deeds in saving Jews from the Holocaust.[10] Similarly Japan's lone righteous gentile, Chiune Sugihara, was Japan's Consul-General in Kaunas prior to Soviet occupation, but after the Nazi and Soviet invasion of Poland. Sugihara disobeyed his superiors and issued visas to Lithuanian Jews for travel to Japan. His actions likely saved from 3,000 to 5,000 Lithuanian Jews.

The great majority of Estonians, Latvians, Lithuanians and Consul-Generals were not as brave and selfless as the righteous gentiles, just as the great majority were not active participants in the Holocaust. The roles, responsibilities and guilt of the majority are far more difficult to appraise. Clearly the grand and local operational decision-making at all levels of the Holocaust was in German hands. Latvian and Lithuanian collaborators (Estonian as well) followed orders; they did not create or issue them. Likewise, as sovereign, political actors, Estonia, Latvia and Lithuania were occupied and unable to exercise the wills of their people. Still, none of the three states has entirely come to terms with the murder, with local participation, of one of their component, historic communities. The memory of the Holocaust and its remembrance are strong indicators of the important work that has been undertaken, but much more remains to be done. The governments of Estonia, Latvia and Lithuania have all taken important symbolic steps to demonstrate to the international community – particularly the international Jewish community – their commitment to Holocaust education and remembrance. The reconstruction of Riga's sole surviving synagogue and the attendance of much of Latvia's political elite at its unveiling on 26 August 2009 is the most recent example of these actions. Among the more general public, however, much is not known about the Holocaust and the recent rise of xenophobia, intolerance and extremism has included anti-Semitic currents. Furthermore most Latvians and Lithuanians find it difficult to discuss the Holocaust and Latvian and Lithuanian participation without raising tenuous links to Soviet occupation and the persecution of Latvians and Lithuanians.

Beyond the Holocaust, the German occupation of Estonia, Latvia and Lithuania was similar to Soviet occupation in its overall themes: both regimes moved forcibly to eradicate the vestiges of the independent states; both pillaged the states economically and created an administration designed to serve the interests of the occupier and not the populace. The Reichsmark, for example, was introduced at exchange rates as appallingly bad as those given on the introduction of the ruble. Agricultural and industrial production were entirely retooled and redirected to the German war effort. Tens of thousands of Estonians, Latvians and Lithuanians were enticed or coerced into travelling to Germany as a labour force. Opposition to these changes or to any part of Nazi administration led to arrest, imprisonment and often death, as did belonging to any one of the many other categories of people marked for extermination, such as Roma (gypsies), homosexuals and Jehovah's Witnesses.

The Nazi administration attempted to co-opt local elites to staff the local levels of administration. This succeeded most in Latvia and least in Lithuania, where resistance to Nazi plans was organized quickly. As war with the Soviet Union turned decisively against the Germans (particularly after the Battle of Stalingrad), greater German efforts were aimed at mobilizing Estonian, Latvian and Lithuanian resources including troops. In Lithuania this mobilization failed in the face of active Lithuanian resistance and hence there were no ethnic Lithuanian divisions in the German army. In Estonia and Latvia these calls to arms were slightly better received and with mobilization orders, the Nazis were able to draft one Estonian division and two Latvian divisions into the ranks of the Waffen-ss. The divisions had Estonian and Latvian officers and were initially used in defence of Estonia's and Latvia's territory.

There were multiple causes for collaboration with the Nazis, as with the Soviets. Some individuals were clearly motivated by base emotions such as greed (the plundering of Jewish property) and revenge (belief in Nazi propaganda that equated Soviet crimes against humanity with the local Jewish population). Many were simple careerists with weak moral compasses. Others believed that service in the Nazi cause would lead to better conditions for Estonia, Latvia and, to a lesser degree, Lithuania after the war. This flawed line of thinking diverged into two streams. Some believed that loyal and exemplary service would beget national rewards at a later date. Others believed that a presence within the administration and armed forces would be central to the rise of independent states at the end of the Second World War. These misguided idealists wished to see a return to conditions at the end of the First World War, with exhausted enemies (Soviet Union and Nazi Germany) and the rebirth of the independent states. In some cases these individuals had contacts with – and shared similar post-war hopes with –resistance movements in Estonia, Latvia and Lithuania.

Estonians' and Latvians' resistance to Nazi rule was primarily passive, and nationalist activists were slow to organize concerted, collective action against German rule. In both states national resistance councils formed around a united front of pre-war politicians and cultural figures.[11] These organizations made tenuous contacts with Allied diplomatic representatives in Sweden and with each other. The Councils drew their political legitimacy from their interwar standing and declared their intent to renew the independent republics of Estonia, Latvia and Lithuania. Armed resistance was virtually non-existent, although a renegade unit of military deserters, irregulars and others moved close to such action in the west of Latvia in 1944. The Nazis executed most of the officers in this, the Kurelis Affair, before the unit's organizational ability could prove too dangerous.[12] Far greater and more accomplished resistance to Nazi rule came from Red Partisans operating under Soviet high command and from partisans, particularly Jewish partisans, fighting German occupation in Lithuania. Jewish partisans were especially active and organized in the forests surrounding Kaunas. Resistance to Nazi rule for most, however, was tied to the steady counter-offensive of Soviet forces. By the summer of 1944 Soviet troops were pressing back into Latvia, Estonia and Lithuania and a nearly impossible mental calculus weighed on the minds of most Estonians, Latvians and Lithuanians: is either occupation a lesser of two evils, does a principled stand against all occupation have any real chance of success, is flight the best option or is a personal policy of neutrality and non-involvement best? To most, the return of a triumphal Soviet army was the most feared outcome; Soviet occupation policies had embarked on a physical assault on class enemies (very loosely defined), and advance rumours of retribution against all who had collaborated or not actively resisted German rule circulated widely. Many of these emphasized the degree of violence and brutality that had become commonplace from 1940 on. In

Daugavpils, for example, the common refrain in Soviet-inspired rumours was that the Latvians had helped kill the Jews, and now it would be their turn.[13] The entire region had descended to such a degree that collective guilt and punishment were commonplace.

Perhaps not surprisingly a massive wave of refugees fled from the Soviet advance. Some feared Soviet retribution for their role in the German occupation, but most feared that they would be seen as class enemies and ultimately be deported. Most of these refugees became displaced persons in occupied Germany at the end of the war and, after several years of this status, emigrated to the USA, Canada, Australia, the United Kingdom and elsewhere.[14] These people organized tirelessly to promote the cause of Baltic independence in their new host countries, but internally became classic examples of émigré communities in their conservatism and insularity. Ultimately they played very little role in the affairs of Estonia, Latvia or Lithuania until the mid-1980s, despite the KGB's obsession with them.[15]

The great majority of Estonians, Latvians and Lithuanians remained when the Soviet army and the governments of the Socialist republics returned through the course of late 1944 and the first half of 1945. Soviet retribution was swift and final against the highest-ranking officials of the German occupation. In Riga several of the most notorious war criminals, including Friedrich Jeckeln, were hanged at a public execution in February 1946. Thousands of others were tried and sentenced to hard labour and entered the Soviet Gulag system. Many of the soldiers that were captured at armistice were interned in filtration camps for months while their service history and political beliefs were checked, but they were then released. Ultimately, however, the stain of service in the German army often led to future arrest and persecution.

The return of Soviet power in Estonia, Latvia and Lithuania was the return of Soviet occupation. In many ways Soviet occupation began where it had left off in 1941 with the Nazi invasion of the USSR. The Soviet Socialist Baltic Republics continued on a path toward full Sovietization of all aspects of society so as to standardize their administration, economy and culture with the norms of the USSR at large. The war and Nazi occupation, however, added an entirely new layer to the return of Soviet occupation. Extensive collaboration with Nazi administration, the sporadic but numerous cases of war crimes, conscription into the German army or into German labour and the mass flight westward reinforced the view of Soviet security personnel that all Estonians, Latvians and Lithuanians were suspect. In 1940 and 1941 Soviet police operated under the assumption that all three republics had many class enemies and that such enemies of the Soviet state needed to be liquidated. Returning to these same lands after three and half years of enemy occupation, these same security personnel were further convinced of even more class enemies that needed to be exposed and punished. They went about this work with homicidal intent. Soviet planners were simultaneously faced with the stupendously large task of reconstruction across the entire USSR. The war killed tens of millions, millions more were displaced and even more were to some degree disabled; the material destruction was as great a hurdle. To planners and civil administrators the post-war USSR, and particularly the Baltic Republics, needed the restoration of Soviet power and order, but also reconstruction on a massive scale. The seeming caprice of Josef Stalin loomed over each of these impulses as Soviet officials tried desperately to crush almost universal dissent and opposition and build Soviet society. As a result Soviet policies in the immediate post-war period often worked at odds with each other. In the displaced persons camps of occupied Germany, for example, Soviet personnel tried to convince and cajole Estonian, Latvian and Lithuanian refugees to return to their homelands. The Soviet need for labour, particularly skilled labour (in many professions almost the entire living work force had fled westward), was desperately acute. At the same time, to security personnel, these refugees, having fled Soviet power, were by definition hostile: class enemies. Generally the demands of Soviet security organs trumped all others, but their heavy hand crippled all attempts at managed recovery and reconstruction. In a vicious Catch-22, Soviet repressive practices alienated the bulk of the population of the Baltic Republics, which then more openly resisted Soviet rule or worked poorly and inefficiently, reinforcing suspicions of sabotage and resistance and leading to even more repression.

The partisan wars in Estonia, Latvia and most significantly in Lithuania are the most obvious cases of open resistance to Soviet occupation in the immediate aftermath of the Second World War.[16] There were waves of partisan activity in each republic and they share similarities as well as having unique aspects. The earliest partisan warfare included a considerable amount of activity by soldiers from the German army who refused to surrender and had taken to the forests to continue to fight. Using such disruptive and diversionary forces was a Nazi tactic in retreat and thus Soviet propagandists tarred most early partisans as disgruntled Nazi sympathizers. Most, however, became partisans following Soviet repressive actions or in fear of impending ones. Through 1945 most of these partisans waged a fairly active campaign against symbols of Soviet power and targeted Communist Party personnel. They believed that the grand alliance between the United Kingdom, the USA and the Soviet Union would rapidly collapse and lead into a new pan-European war between these former allies. Partisan tactics revolved around weakening Soviet power and preparing for future warfare against the USSR allied with the UK and the USA. Western intelligence forces exploited these hopes to use partisans for information gathering, but contacts were generally weak and quickly uncovered by Soviet forces. As the partisans' initial hopes faded, their opposition became more defensive and retributive. Partisan warfare was most extensive in Lithuania, and had the greatest amount of international contacts, particularly with partisans in Poland and Ukraine, but its ultimate fate was similar. Year after year, aid from the West did not arrive and the ongoing Sovietization of society continued at a rapid pace.

The Soviet response to partisan activity changed over time. Initially the Soviet regime preferred the use of military detachments with heavy auxiliary local forces, known as destroyer battalions.[17] These troops and irregulars would target perceived partisans (in Soviet language, they were almost always referred to as bandits) and partisan supporters, and periodically 'comb the forests' in mass actions that systematically swept through forests suspected of housing partisan forces. These combing actions were notoriously ineffective. Occasional amnesties tried to coax partisans out of the forests, but the frequent arrests of those that surrendered made future amnesties highly mistrusted. Ultimately the Soviets' most successful tactic against the partisan was a policy of deception and subterfuge. Soviet agents infiltrated partisan ranks and passed their locations on to Soviet security personnel. Combined with the widespread use of corpse mutilation and public display, partisan ranks became bitterly distrustful of each other and their effectiveness was paralysed. Still, despite the neutralization of the partisan threat, each new wave of Soviet repression produced new partisan recruits. Partisan war against Soviet occupation did not effectively end until after Stalin's death in 1953. Some partisans remained in the woods and were periodically captured by Soviet personnel, some as late as into the 1980s.

Soviet repression and persecution of partisans, relatives of partisans and suspected supporters of partisans was swift and severe. Tens of thousands were deported in each Baltic republic, but Soviet terror did not end with partisans. Soviet political arrests targeted 'bourgeois nationalists' at universities, schools and institutes. Jehovah's Witnesses were targeted in 1951 in all three republics, and Lithuanian Jews were arrested in the aftermath of the Doctors' Plot in 1953, a fabricated conspiracy of Jewish doctors who supposedly poisoned – and planned to poison – Communist Party leaders. The 'unmasking' of the Doctors' Plot initiated a broadly anti-Semitic purge across the USSR. Germans living in Estonia, Latvia and Lithuania were deported immediately after the war in the only mass deportations to target people because of their ethnic identity. The deportations of 'kulaks', or wealthy peasants, in 1949 in Estonia and Latvia were the largest deportations, even dwarfing the mass deportations of June 1941. In Lithuania a mass deportation in May 1948 targeted partisan sympathizers and kulaks alike (the Soviets saw little differentiation between these two categories) and deported more than 40,000 people.

The 1949 deportations in Estonia and Latvia were the culmination of a campaign to collectivize agriculture according to Soviet norms. After the war the Soviet regime built model collective farms to encourage farmers to voluntarily join such institutions while simultaneously using tax policy and heavy restrictions on the employment of labour to make private smallholding farming non-viable. Peasants continued to resist the collectivization campaign and, as in the Soviet Union at the end of the 1920s, the state unleashed mass terror to complete collectivization. The kulaks were blamed for partisan activity and peasants' fear of joining collective farms. 'Unmasked' as class enemies of the Soviet regime, entire kulak families were detained and sent into administrative exile in Siberia. The definition of kulak would, if not for the horrendous consequences, be comical; anyone who had employed labour, who had multiple livestock and so on, could be labelled a kulak and deported. Nearly 100,000 farmers across Estonia, Latvia and Lithuania were displaced in this manner. The deportations resulted in the almost universal collectivization of agriculture in the Baltic Republics by the end of 1949, by which point the Baltic Republics were almost entirely Sovietized. Private, large-scale business, farming or trade had ceased to exist and the economy was organized according to central planning originating in Moscow. The Communist Party exercised complete political control through its all-powerful security organs, which extended their influence through culture and society at large. Resistance would continue throughout the entire period of Soviet occupation, but after 1953 there was very little armed resistance. Resistance became an intensely personal and private act, or tilting at windmills.

With almost complete control, how did the Soviet Union try to transform the Baltic Republics? The Soviet Union defined itself as a modern, industrial world power, even if its actual industrialization was uneven. The Baltic Republics, in Soviet plans, were integral to post-war reconstruction and to their continuing, aggressive plans for massive state development of heavy industry and armaments. The period from 1945 to 1959 saw massive Soviet investment in tying Estonian, Latvian and Lithuanian transportation, communication, energy and production networks into the larger Soviet system. The Baltic Republics were to be economically integrated into the planned Soviet economy while serving as a particularly industrialized segment of it. The needed investments were huge: material reconstruction after the destruction of the war was substantial and supply systems had to provide the energy- and resource-poor Estonian, Latvian and to a lesser degree Lithuanian factories with fuel and natural resources. Equally pressing was the need for labour, which Estonia, Latvia and Lithuania could not provide after war-era deaths and displacements and ongoing Soviet deportations. Labour migrants from the rest of the Soviet Union, particularly from Russia, Ukraine and Belarus, flooded into Estonian and Latvian industrial centres. This game of ethnic subtraction and addition was seen (and still is seen) by most Estonians and Latvians as a method of social control and designed Russification. The pattern of removing ethnic Estonians and Latvians and the influx of primarily Slavic workers is understood as an orchestrated campaign to fundamentally alter the ethnic composition of the Baltic Republics and to push their very ethnic survival into doubt. The bulk of Soviet occupation is understood as a corollary to this fundamental goal. The validity of this argument, however, is doubtful and unclear. Although Soviet officials in Moscow clearly imagined the dominance of Russia and the Russian language as a lingua franca in the Soviet Union, there is little to support the idea that full assimilation was the immediate goal (particularly in light of the great expenditures for national cultures across the USSR).[18] Security officials may have seen benefits to Slavic immigration into the Soviet Baltic Republics, and may have favoured Slavic populations in terms of benefits and opportunities, but they did not determine population movement solely as a tool of social control. In addition recent research suggests that Estonian, Latvian and Lithuanian officials influenced and created policy more than was previously accepted. Although All-Union policy directives originating in Moscow overrode all others in importance or authority and set the general parameters for any activity, local, political intra-party battles also influenced the face of the Soviet Baltic Republics.

The face of Soviet Estonia, Soviet Latvia and Soviet Lithuania was the republic-level Communist Party and its leadership, long considered little more than stooges and henchmen to Moscow directives. The single most remarkable example of the power that a local (republic) Communist Party general secretary could wield was Lithuania's Antanas Sniečkus. Sniečkus was a devoted Bolshevik from as far back as 1920 (when he was seventeen years old) and served the Soviet Union in its first year of occupation, from June 1940 to June 1941. He helped orchestrate the terror surrounding the staged parliamentary elections of July 1940 and became the First Secretary of Lithuania's Communist Party on 15 August 1940. Sniečkus implemented much of the Sovietization of Lithuania, authorizing the deportations of June 1941 (including the deportation of his brother), the post-war deportations and the collectivization of agriculture. Still, he successfully defended other Lithuanian Communists from All-Union persecution and was able to limit immigration into the Lithuanian Soviet Socialist Republic. Most remarkably, appointed as a trusted Stalinist at the height of Stalin's power, Sniečkus continued in his post through the 'reformist' Khrushchev years, and then into the Brezhnev era. The only force capable of removing him from his post, despite the vicissitudes of Kremlin politics, was his natural death in 1974.

The Stalinist-era Communist Party First Secretaries in Estonia and Latvia, Nikolai Karotamm and Jānis Kalnbērziņš respectively, were not as colourful, long-lasting or independent as Sniečkus, but they and their ethnic associates played a more central role in initiating and directing the Sovietization of their republics than was initially believed. They were not simple puppets directed by Moscow, but often initiated or directed policy decisions. Karotamm, for example, played a central role in organizing the deportations of 1949, while Kalnbērziņš often played a mediating role between differing radical factions within Latvia's Communist Party. It is likely that these First Secretaries and those that followed them used their positions, with their insider's knowledge of Moscow's policy and goals. They were the undisputed interlocutors of the Kremlin's desire until challenged and deposed. The most savvy First Secretaries carried out the direct directives of the Kremlin with zeal while carving out niches of independence and initiative where Kremlin guidance or desires were less clearly stated. Herein lies the great paradox of Communist rule in Estonia, Latvia and Lithuania: how could a state that was considered illegitimate by the majority of its inhabitants, and that pursued policies considered antithetical to Estonian, Latvian and Lithuanian national identities, build some measure of support and legitimacy? Occupation was possible through the barrel of a gun, but rule, even if supported by those guns, needed more.

Already in 1940 the Estonian, Latvian and Lithuanian Soviet Socialist republics went to great lengths to convince their own constituents and the international community of the legitimacy of Soviet rule; they foisted Potemkin republics upon Estonians, Latvians, Lithuanians and the world alike. The most often cited example of the fabrication of local support for Soviet rule is the claim that the Soviet regimes released official election results for the staged elections of July 1940 before the tallies were completed. Gregory Meiksins's *The Baltic Riddle: Finland, Estonia, Latvia, Lithuania – Key Points of European Peace* presented a more detailed defence to the international stage of supposed Soviet legitimacy in the Baltic Republics.[19] His book's re-publication by the National Council of American–Soviet Friendship in 1944 exposed its partisan content, as did derisive reviews in such leading publications as *The Nation* (5 February 1944). Such campaigns to garner international support and recognition of Soviet annexation recurred for nearly five decades.

The Soviet regime expended even more resources to convince the populations of Estonia, Latvia and Lithuania that Soviet rule was legitimate and preferable to any other option. Even during Stalin's rule, when mass repression was commonplace and few checks to Soviet power existed in the Baltic, carrots accompanied sticks. The Soviet regimes staged massive national song festivals (albeit with hymns to Stalin, Russian songs, and songs and dances from other Soviet Republics) and institutionalized an ethnic cultural and linguistic edifice in each republic. This seems to contradict the commonly accepted view that Soviet rule in the contemporary Baltic states was akin to genocide. Instead Soviet rule in the Baltic followed the pattern of Soviet rule throughout the Soviet Union. With a few significant exceptions (Germans and Tatars), mass repression did not target ethnic groups per se, but rather classes within ethnic groups (the bourgeoisie, the nobility) and those that advocated national deviation (nationalist intellectuals). The small number of Estonians, Latvians and Lithuanians that eagerly embraced a Soviet version of their ethnic identity enjoyed considerable state support for their work, much of which also fulfilled a propaganda role. Violence and subsidies directed at ethnic groups were not mutually exclusive events. As Amir Weiner has succinctly summarized, the

> twin pillars of Soviet population policies [were] the application of state violence anchored in political rationale and the simultaneous cultivation of ethno-national particularism. Without them, one could hardly understand the simultaneous eradication of entire national elites and intelligentsias along with the persistent delineation of particularistic identities.[20]

After the death of Stalin, the initiative for the 'cultivation of ethno-national particularism' came from within the ranks of the Estonian and Latvian (and to a lesser extent Lithuanian) Communist Party leadership and threatened to upset the Soviet balance between particularistic identities and autonomous, political decision-making.

Following the end of the Second World War, the ongoing mass deportations in Estonia, Latvia and Lithuania, and the concomitant heavy-handed Sovietization of these three states, made clear that no meaningful change in the manner of Soviet rule would emerge until after the death of Stalin. Even if Stalinist Estonians, Latvians and Lithuanians placed their unique stamps on the general orders emanating from Moscow, no party official dared contradict or challenge Stalin. In March 1953 this era ended when Stalin collapsed in his private apartment in the Kremlin and over the next four days slowly expired. Lavrentiy Beria, a fellow Georgian who headed internal affairs from 1938 through the Second World War and after, was one of the clear frontrunners to replace Stalin. Beria's ascent, at first glance, may have seemed like a continuation of Stalinist rule with his heavy participation in the NKVD, his participation in the Katyn massacre of Polish officers, and his decision to deport Chechens, Ingush, Crimean Tatars and Volga Germans en masse as ethnic groups that collaborated with the Germans.[21] Yet in the first weeks after Stalin's death, Beria agreed to a limited amnesty of non-political prisoners and suspended the anti-Semitic purge (following the aforementioned Doctors' Plot) that had begun in January 1953. He signalled a reformist campaign that may have included more real power for non-Russian nationalities in their respective republics and throughout Eastern Europe. His rivals for power understood the East Berlin Uprising of 1953 as a by-product of Beria's proposed reforms and imagined a more widespread challenge to Soviet rule. The rest of the Politburo turned suddenly on Beria in June 1953, dismissed him from the Party and his posts and arrested him. He was tried and executed by the end of the year, along with many of his supporters. The victor in this struggle for power and the successor of Stalin was Nikita Khrushchev, who would embark on his own reform agenda in 1955.

In the Soviet Baltic Republics the death of Stalin was met with relief, trepidation and anticipation. It was also, however, met with grief and bewilderment as a vocal minority had believed fervently in his infallibility. For most, however, Stalin's death signalled an end to mass repressions, and what was left of a partisan command structure in each republic advised its fighters to give up the violent, active fight and to return to legal life. Some ignored this advice, but the partisan movement, as an organized mass movement, ended with the death of Stalin. Estonians, Latvians and Lithuanians who had been deported and administratively exiled to Siberia and elsewhere hoped for a speedy return to their homelands. Ultimately they waited until after Khrushchev's Secret Speech in 1955 to take advantage of widespread amnesties. To the majority of the population Stalin's death also signalled the gradual end to such draconian measures as absenteeism from work being treated as a criminal offence. The populace also hoped for increased attention to consumer needs. Artists and intellectuals gingerly tested the waters of official Soviet censorship to see if more would be allowed or tolerated in artistic expression. Most immediately, however, the death of Stalin, the succession struggle and the potential upending of the networks of patronage that stretched to the Communist leaders most associated with Stalin and his successors affected the political elites of Estonia, Latvia and to a lesser extent Lithuania.

Traditionally the period from the death of Stalin to the fall of Khrushchev in the Soviet Baltic Republics has been labelled the period of 'National Communism'. Conventional wisdom describes a brief, tentative period wherein primarily Latvian Communist Party leaders pushed the limits of reform in Khrushchev's Soviet Union to assert more local control over decision-making about party matters, the economy and in-migration.[22] These 'National Communists' enjoyed limited, largely symbolic successes before provoking Moscow's anger. An eleventh-hour visit by Khrushchev to Riga touched off a purge of National Communists and their support-ers and ushered in the kind of torpor and stagnation that would define the Brezhnev era of the 1960s and '70s. This understanding of the 1950s, however, was based on what little could be gleaned by Western academics (largely of Estonian, Latvian or Lithuanian descent) from official sources and dissident reports. Over the last ten to fifteen years open access to archival collections in Latvia portrays a far more active and aggressive campaign of reform initiated by the National Communists and an equal counter-offensive waged against them from within the Latvian Communist Party.

The 'National Communists' is a phrase used to describe the first group of com-mitted Communist activists that challenged the existing status quo of governance in the post-Second World War Soviet Baltic Republics. They did not champion a return to the pre-war Baltic states; rather, most had been instrumental in the Sovietization of these states in 1940–41, and had served the USSR loyally through the Second World War and in its aftermath. They remained true believers in Socialist construction, but they became disenchanted with the Russian face of this construction in the Stalinist period. In some respects these sentiments had existed within the ranks of the Communist Party in each republic well before Stalin's death. After his death, however, party leaders expressing these ideas gained traction and influence and began to assert autonomous decision-making and control. The clearest case was in Latvia with the rise and fall of Eduards Berklavs and the econ-omist Vilis Knoriņš. Both rose through the ranks of the Latvian Communist Party to a fairly high level by the mid-1950s. They used the political confusion after Stalin's death to push for more decision-making at the republic level, a concept popular in local circles. As they consolidated their power in economic circles and in city government, they pushed for stronger enforcement of laws that called for Latvian language fluency. They also questioned new waves of immigration by Slavic workers and Soviet army pensioners. To the All-Union political contest, these National Communists posed a dilemma to the cautiously reformist Khrushchev. On the one hand, the mass repression of the Baltic Republics highlighted Stalinist excess, but on the other the National Communists' leanings towards autonomy placed them ideologically close to the recently deposed Beria. Khrushchev's representative raised this latter charge when scolding Berklavs in a dramatic *coup de grace* to the National Communists in 1958. He allegedly reminded Berklavs that 'Beria was shot for similar views. What do you suggest we do with you?'[23]

In the Soviet Republics of Estonia and Lithuania 'National Communists' were far less influential. In Lithuania Antanas Sniečkus, the all-powerful First Secretary of the Lithuanian Communist Party, pre-empted many of the Latvian National Communists' policies without antagonizing Moscow. Sniečkus remained blindly loyal to Moscow in All-Union affairs (regardless of who ruled in Moscow) and in return he ruled with a freer hand in Lithuania. As a result there was considerably less immigration and mass industrialization in Soviet Lithuania and a concomitant lack of ethnic tension. His rule, however, also ran counter to reform tendencies in Moscow; he apparently refused to allow amnestied Gulag prisoners the right to return to Lithuania. Sniečkus' long rule also more quickly ossified Soviet party and governmental affairs in Lithuania. His successor, Petras Griškevičius, followed in the mould of loyalty to Moscow and exemplified the Brezhnev era in the Soviet Union in its local, Lithuanian incarnation. In Soviet Estonia, on the other hand, the National Communist movement was somewhat stillborn due to Stalinist repressions in 1950. These repressions targeted many of Estonia's local Communists and the party leadership was largely placed in the hands of Soviet Russian-born or Russian-educated Estonians with few roots in the republic. These Moscow loyalists did not lead a charge for republic level control, as had happened in Latvia. Instead Estonia's slow indigenization of the party would begin in the 1960s. The loosening of mass repression and/or concessions to the public in Soviet Estonia and Lithuania were not a result of direct, local lobbying. As a result Moscow and its supporters did not need to move against them, as they had against Berklavs and the National Communists of Soviet Latvia.

Still, even with Khrushchev's and Moscow's heavy-handed threats to the National Communists, their ultimate downfall seems equally due to revanchists within the Latvian Communist Party, most notably Arvīds Pelše.[24] Pelše was the stereotypical 'Moscow Latvian'. He was born into a peasant Latvian family in 1899, and joined the Bolsheviks as a teenager in 1915. He was active in the Russian Revolution and was sent to Latvia in 1919 to work for the aborted 1919 Bolshevik regime. When the regime collapsed, Pelše returned to Soviet Russia and worked as a political commissar in the Soviet Army for more than a decade. He was sent back to Latvia after its incorporation into the Soviet Union and then again after the German defeat in the Second World War. The great majority of his adult life up to that point had been spent in Soviet Russia, within the embrace of the Communist Party and the NKVD. Interwar Latvia was foreign to him. His assignment as Secretary of the Central Committee of the Latvian Communist Party for propaganda and agitation (he served in this post from 1941 to 1959) was a conscious decision to place a Moscow loyalist in a position to Sovietize the state. Berklavs and his allies' attempts to establish greater national autonomy were anathema to Pelše's close Moscow orientation. He meticulously gathered evidence of Berklavs and company's political and economic decision-making and used them to full effect when Khrushchev and Moscow moved to curtail the National Communists' ambition. Pelše's attack and careful portrayal of Berklavs' policies as counter to Soviet and Leninist principles forced Moscow's hand in purging the National Communists. More than 2,000 party members tied to Berklavs were dismissed from the Party and from their positions, and Pelše and his supporters rapidly filled the void. Pelše became First Secretary of the Latvian Communist Party in 1959 and used his conservative, hardline reputation as a springboard into the All-Union Central Committee in 1961, and to the Politburo in 1966. Pelše died in 1983 and was given full Soviet honours, including a state funeral, countless eulogies and a place in the Kremlin wall for his ashes.

Pelše's meteoric rise set the pattern for future First Secretaries of the Latvian Communist Party: close and loyal service and orientation to Moscow, away from local particularism. Pelše's rise, however, was equally due to familial connections. Pelše's wife was Mikhail Suslov's sister-in-law. Suslov, variously described as the 'Red or Grey Eminence', was the foremost hardline ideologue of the Soviet Union from Stalin's rule until his death in 1982. In many respects, Suslov played a kingmaker role within the Politburo: he was instrumental in the fall of Khrushchev, and in the rise of Leonid Brezhnev, Yuri Andropov and Mikhail Gorbachev. Suslov's own Baltic experience included planning deportations and executions in Lithuania from 1944 to 1946. In this respect Pelše's assault on Berklavs provided Suslov with ammunition in his eventual assault on Khrushchev. As was often the case in the Soviet Baltic Republics, initial allegiances based on ideological conviction often masked deeper familial bonds and an almost caste-like nature within the ruling elite of the Communist Parties.

Pelše, however, did not stay in Latvia long, at least not in a governmental or Party capacity, and moved on to All-Union politics in Moscow. His successor, Augusts Voss, even more closely approached the stereotype of the 'Moscow Latvian'. Voss was born in Soviet Russia to Latvian parents, but had no personal experience in the country until he was assigned to Latvia in 1945. Although he understood Latvian, he did not use the language in public, a stark statement about the use of the Latvian language in the political sphere in Soviet Latvia in the 1960s, '70s and early '80s. He rose through the ranks and replaced Pelše in 1966 as the First Secretary of the Latvian Communist Party, a position he held until 1984. His long reign over Soviet Latvia most mirrored the gross generalizations of Brezhnev's rule of the USSR. As with Pelše, Voss translated his long service to Moscow in Soviet Latvia into an esteemed position in Moscow; he was the Chairman of the Soviet of Nationalities of the Supreme Soviet of the USSR from 1984 until 1989. This post drew him to Moscow and he did not return to Latvia after the renewal of independence in 1991. He passed away in Moscow in 1994. His most lasting impression on Latvia may be the construction of the Vanšu tilts (Shroud Bridge, originally the Gorky Bridge) across the Daugava river, which was opened in 1981. Voss's successor, Boriss Pugo, followed the same mould and trajectory. A Latvian born in Soviet Russia, he rose through the Communist Party apparatus, focusing on work in the KGB, to become the First Secretary of the Latvian Communist Party in 1984. He remained in the post until 1988, whereupon he moved to All-Union politics in Moscow. His conservative and hardline pedigree was amply demonstrated in his work as minister of the interior from 1990 to 1991, and more specifically by his participation in the August Coup of 1991. He committed suicide in the aftermath of the coup's collapse.

In Soviet Estonia and Lithuania the Communist Party political elite mirrored Soviet Latvia's Pelše, Voss and Pugo. In Lithuania, after Sniečkus' death, Petras Griškevičius echoed the career of Voss in his longevity and loyalty to the Brezhnev All-Union mould. He ruled as First Secretary until his death in 1987. In Soviet Estonia Johannes Käbin, an ethnic Estonian raised in Soviet Russia, reigned as First Secretary of the Estonian Communist Party from 1950 until 1978. Like Pelše, Voss and Pugo, Käbin translated his long, loyal service to Moscow to a prestigious appointment in Moscow. He was the Chairman of the Supreme Soviet of the USSR from 1978 until 1983. Käbin's successor in Soviet Estonia, Karl Vaino, stayed in his post until 1988, when new, popular forces of discontent removed him in favour of a perceived liberal, Vaino Väljas.

In all three cases, in Soviet Estonia, Latvia and Lithuania, very little momentous change occurred in the higher realms of political life after the purge of National

Communists in Soviet Latvia in 1959. Politics would stay frozen until the late 1980s. First Secretaries were most notable for their close ties to Moscow, for their own comfort in Soviet Russian circles (often established from their childhood or youth), and for their reflection of Brezhnev-like rule in the Soviet Baltic Republics. Many finished their august years of Soviet service in prestigious yet largely ceremonial positions in Moscow. If these politics belie little change or development, much was happening below the commanding heights. Soviet Estonia, Latvia and Lithuania were radically transformed from the 1960s to the '80s.

The bulk of the Sovietization of Estonia, Latvia and Lithuania occurred during Stalinist rule. Private businesses and property were nationalized, the ruble introduced, agriculture collectivized, and a command economy revolving around broad outlines decided in Moscow for five-year economic plans implemented. The command economic decisions stressed the rapid and heavy industrialization of Estonia and Latvia particularly. As a result there was massive investment in infrastructure to build, service and transport newly created industrial enterprises. Hundreds of thousands of workers moved into Soviet Estonia and Latvia (less so to Lithuania) to man these enterprises and tens of thousands of Estonian and Latvian citizens who either resisted these transformational changes to their states or were seen as potential resistors were repressed or deported. All of this happened as the bookends to the Second World War, which included death, destruction and population displacement in Estonia, Latvia and Lithuania on a nearly biblical scale. After all this, however, in the period from 1953 to 1983, these massive changes were digested, processed and continued. The Soviet Baltic Republics of the 1980s were far removed from either the independent interwar states or the traumatized Stalinist republics.

The most pronounced, fundamental socio-economic change for Estonia, Latvia and Lithuania from the 1940s was the radical transformation from relatively traditional, agriculturally focused economies (and all that implied for social relations) to modern, industrial economies, albeit on the Soviet model of modern and industrial. There were, of course, fatal flaws to this Soviet model: economic infrastructure was built into a larger, controlling entity, the Soviet Union, and the lack of political freedoms and representation meant that local populations could not influence, alter or successfully oppose economic plans imposed upon them from Moscow. The decades of Soviet occupation bore witness to much more than repression and terror; the radical socio-economic changes affected everyone. In 1939 agriculture had dominated the economies of Estonia, Latvia and Lithuania. Most people lived in the countryside and most worked in some sector of agriculture. Industrial production in urban centres collapsed during the First World War and never fully recovered. Most industrial concerns were small enterprises, and most were tied to food products or consumer goods. Cities were more administrative centres than industrial oases, particularly the capital cities of Tallinn, Riga and Kaunas. Soviet rule changed all of this. Decades of planned economic investment built massive factories across a wide variety of sectors, including heavy industry, the automotive and chemical industries, the military industrial complex and more. The Riga Automobile Factory in Latvia, for example, produced many of the Soviet Union's vans and minivans (it moved to Jelgava in the 1970s). The Valsts Elektrotehniskā Fabrika or State Electrotechnical Plant in Riga produced many of the USSR's telephones and telecommunications equipment, much of it for the Soviet military. This enormous economic construction demanded equally large investments in providing energy – hence hydroelectric power stations, shale processing plants and a nuclear power plant in Lithuania – and transportation: there was development of rail, highways and ports. Most raw materials were brought to the new industrial concerns from far afield, and most finished goods were equally removed to far removed destinations.

The demands for labour (in the industrial concerns, in power stations, in the transportation infrastructure and in construction) far outpaced available local populations already diminished by deportations and war losses. Tens of thousands of Soviet citizens moved to Estonia, Latvia and to a much lesser degree Lithuania to fill these jobs. These workers radically altered the ethnic composition of Estonia and Latvia. Estonia, which had been a primarily ethnic Estonian state in the interwar years, saw the most pronounced change in its ethnic composition. The non-Estonian population ballooned to almost 40 per cent. Latvia, which historically had included sizeable populations of Russians, Germans and Jews (as well as smaller groups of Estonians, Lithuanians, Poles and Gypsies), saw the Latvian ethnic share of the state plummet from roughly 75 per cent to nearly 50 per cent. Furthermore the vast majority of the massive influx of immigrants moved to urban and industrial centres, where all the recent industrial development had occurred. Estonian and Latvian towns and cities had always been the most multi-ethnic parts of these states, but now they became ethnically Russian. In the most Eastern districts and cities the Russian-speaking population dwarfed the ethnic Estonians and Latvians. In Lithuania a combination of factors limited this massive influx. Lithuania's population was considerably larger and able to provide more manpower from within its borders; there was less industrialization in Lithuania, thereby requiring fewer workers, and the enigmatic Lithuanian Communist boss, Antanas Sniečkus, seems to have played a part as well in limiting immigration.

73

The massively transformed nature of society and the economy in Estonia and Latvia (again, less so in Lithuania) seems to have no equal; it seems a break from the past. However, even if the repressive nature of Soviet occupation and governance was new. Estonian and Latvian society in the midst of Socialist transformation in broad brushstrokes mirrored the industrial transformations at the end of the nineteenth and beginning of the twentieth century. The initial industrialization of the Baltic Provinces was part of a broad, sweeping plan for all of imperial Russia. In this plan, Baltic ports connected to a Russian and imperial hinterland moved resources out of imperial Russia into the international market and also welcomed finished products and modern technologies into the Empire. The rapid growth of Ventspils during Soviet occupation, which at one point would rank one of the world's largest ports, for example, was anticipated by tsarist planners in the late nineteenth century concerned about supply bottlenecks and the limits of the Riga port. All in all, the industrial boom demanded far more labour than local peasant communities could supply and a steady stream of migrant industrial workers swelled the multi-ethnic mosaic of Baltic cities and towns. The First World War brought the almost complete evacuation of industry, the flight or conscription of working masses and ultimately the dissolution of the Russian Empire. The independent states of Estonia and Latvia could not entertain even the idea of maintaining the previous industrial activity – they possessed almost no natural resources for such economic activity. Cut off from its former economic hinterland, now an ideologically hostile Soviet Union, Estonian and Latvian transport systems withered and the industrial nature of the cities (let alone the industrial workforces) left almost as quickly as the machines were evacuated. As a result, the independent nation-states of Estonia and Latvia began their existence and catered to a far more ethnic homogenous and rurally located population than had been the norm ten years previously.

There is, however, a crucial, glaring difference between imperial Russia's haphazard industrialization and its concomitant multi-ethnic cities of the Baltic Provinces and the Sovietization and the centrally planned industrialization of the Soviet Baltic Republics in the second half of the twentieth century: the political space in which each of the transformations occurred. Although imperial Russia was an autocratic state with a virtually omnipotent tsar, local politics were variegated and contested. Electoral lists based on ethnic composition and social placement contested city council elections. Even if the franchise or the representative nature of these elections were not fair and equal, they still provided a public space for different voices and agendas and different avenues for mass mobilization. National elections to the Duma (never quite as powerful as a parliament) extended this principle to a state scale. The Baltic German community, long the unquestioned elite of the Baltic Provinces, was forced to use divide and rule tactics to keep their political power. Ethnic and social hostility and/or rivalry existed. In the Soviet Union politics per se did not exist; there was official, near unanimous support for the Communist Party. As a result the pressures of rapid industrialization and Sovietization were forced under the lid of a rapidly boiling pot. Those few cases that saw an eruption of steam were quickly dealt with as counter-revolutionary enemies of the state. Disagreements and resentments over decision-making on a grand and minute scale remained hidden for decades. When the lid was finally removed, and political speech was allowed, not surprisingly, dialogue boiled over quickly and has been difficult to contain since.

As a result, in Soviet Estonia, Latvia and Lithuania, politics as an open and contested forum ended by the late 1950s at the latest. Even at this late date, debate was limited within the framework of the Communist Party (other forms of political voice and space were exterminated in 1940 and 1941). The purge of the National Communists in Latvia in 1959 signalled the end of politics for nearly four decades. As a result Soviet Estonia, Latvia and Lithuania experienced schizophrenic development; the massive transformations of society percolated into the open in almost all forums but politics. The Soviet Baltic Republics were alive with changes through the 1950s, '60s, '70s and '80s, but the ossified political system reflected none of these. For our purposes, therefore, we have a natural break in our analysis. Political changes were stunted until the 1980s, when the full force of the transformations of the previous decades burst through old confines in a heady twenty years that radically changed Estonia, Latvia, Lithuania and the Soviet Union. The next chapter will examine those political changes.

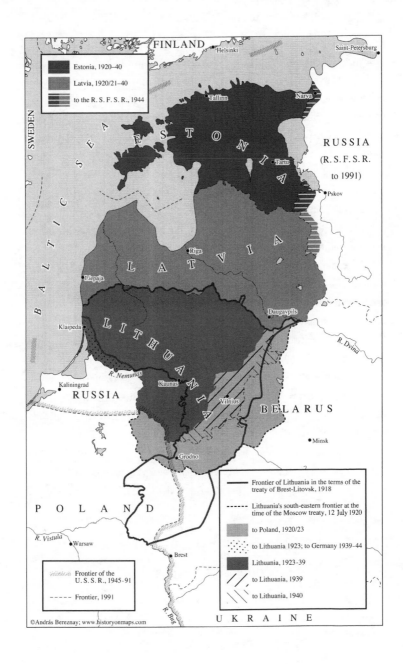

Estonia, 1920–40

Latvia, 1920/21–40

to the R. S. F. S. R., 1944

FINLAND

Helsinki

Saint-Petersburg

SWEDEN

B A L T I C   S E A

E S T O N I A

Tallinn

Narva

Tartu

RUSSIA

(R. S. F. S. R.

to 1991)

Pskov

L A T V I A

Riga

Liepaja

Daugavpils

Klaipeda

L I T H U A N I A

R. Dvina

Kaliningrad

RUSSIA

R. Nemunas

Kaunas

Vilnius

B E L A R U S

Grodno

Minsk

Frontier of Lithuania in the terms of the
treaty of Brest-Litovsk, 1918

Lithuania's south-eastern frontier at the
time of the Moscow treaty, 12 July 1920

to Poland, 1920/23

to Lithuania 1923; to Germany 1939–44

Lithuania, 1923-39

to Lithuania, 1939

to Lithuania, 1940

P O L A N D

R. Vistula

Warsaw

Brest

Frontier of the
U.S.S.R., 1945-91

Frontier, 1991

©András Bereznay; www.historyonmaps.com

R. Bug

U K R A I N E

CHAPTER 3

Soviet Union to European Union

Resistance to Soviet rule in Estonia, Latvia and Lithuania began within the first hours of occupation, continued through annexation and existed throughout nearly five decades of Soviet rule. In Latvia, for example, as a Soviet armoured column lumbered past Latvia's border guards, the wife of an officer opened fire and continued to shoot until wounded and subdued. During the campaigns for rump parliaments, Estonians, Latvians and Lithuanians resisted through attempting to field alternate electoral lists to the Soviet-sponsored ones. During the Second World War violent resistance resurfaced as Soviet troops retreated (particularly in Estonia). Central councils staked principled, non-violent resistance against Soviet and Nazi occupations as well. Likewise flight, collaboration with Nazi rule and desertion were in some regards other forms of resistance. After the end of the Second World War resistance took to the woods as partisans fought desperate, occasionally heroic, yet ultimately doomed wars against Soviet troops. On the death of Stalin the Soviet Union ceased to employ mass terror and repression and Estonian, Latvian and Lithuanian partisans suspended active resistance. At this point, in Soviet Latvia, resistance to Moscow dictates emerged from within the Communist Party by Eduards Berklavs and the so-called National Communists. Their ultimate purge essentially ended autonomously generated campaigns for meaningful reform from within the Latvian Communist Party for almost 30 years. From this point until the mid-1980s resistance to Soviet rule continued, mostly in a muted and individual form, with a few notable exceptions. Soviet repression targeted individuals, not classes or nations, and observation and prevention became the more frequently used weapons against dissent.

Through the 1960s and '70s, dissent in Soviet Estonia, Latvia and Lithuania followed a similar pattern to that of Soviet dissidents more generally. Individuals who stated opposition views, often through typed declarations passed around circles of friends and confidants, were quickly identified, pestered and harassed by an efficient and omnipresent Soviet security system. The nature of a centrally controlled command economy and the power and might of official innuendo forced dissidents from academic and career opportunities. The weight of the state was expertly used to isolate most dissidents and render them largely impotent. The threat of the state was sufficient to keep most from dissenting too publicly or too frequently. The few exceptions, the hardened and principled dissidents, found themselves to be frequent targets of KGB surveillance, interviews and prison sentences. On occasion the regime used institutionalization as well to punish and isolate dissidents. The standard story involved an early warning and arrest; limited economic and social advancement opportunities; recurring, sporadic opposition; repeated surveillance; and ongoing political harassment.

More serious, to Soviet security personnel, were attempts to make contact with other circles of dissidents and most heinously with sympathizers outside the Soviet Union. The 'Letter of 17 Latvian Communists', smuggled to the West in 1972, is a perfect case in point. The long, meandering letter outlined Russification and Sovietization in Latvia and suggested immediate changes in policy.[1] The leading dissident behind the letter was the same Eduards Berklavs who had attempted to change these policies while in a commanding position within the Communist Party in the 1950s. At that time he had been purged, but not imprisoned. He continued to press his case, but to a smaller and more distant audience. The Letter of 1972 had little to no impact in Soviet Latvia at the time of its writing even though it caused a minor flurry of attention in the West and provoked a Soviet rebuttal (in the London-based *Soviet Analyst*) as well.

The attempted defection of the Lithuanian sailor Simas Kudirka in November 1970 was another internationally famous act of dissent, but one which had little impact on events in Soviet Lithuania. Kudirka famously attempted to seek political asylum aboard a US Coast Guard ship off the coast of Martha's Vineyard. Confused by the process of granting asylum, a Coast Guard commander ordered the ship to allow other Soviet fishermen to retrieve Kudirka, beating and bounding him in the process. Kudirka was tried for treason in May 1971 and sentenced to ten years in the Gulag. Unrepentant in the dock, Kudirka lambasted Soviet policy toward Lithuania. In 1974 Kudirka was allowed to emigrate to the US due to a citizenship claim through his mother. The Kudirka case, which was splashed across Western newspapers and magazines, and resulted in several books and a made-for-television movie (with Alan Arkin as Simas Kudirka), helped further harden Western perceptions of the Soviet Union and of its treatment of dissenting nationalists.[2] The case also spurred changes to asylum procedure in the US, but it had little impact in Lithuania. Defections were embarrassing internationally to a Soviet regime eager to prove its legitimacy in the occupied republics, but internally the result was the removal of a dissident.

Most dissidents, however, did not have the Party pedigree or reach of Berklavs or the fifteen minutes of fame of Simas Kudirka. Most calls of opposition to Soviet rule in Soviet Estonia, Latvia and Lithuania came from individual, often conscientious, objectors. Religious faith played a particularly important role in the opposition of many. The Soviet Union was an avowed atheist state that placed great restrictions on religious practice. Resistance to state-sponsored atheism came from established (although heavily restricted and monitored) religious clergy and from believers roughly following an evangelical Christianity. In Estonia and Latvia Bible-smuggling from the West was one of the more common methods of anti-regime activity. In predominantly Catholic Lithuania the Catholic clergy and those sympathetic to it worked to document Soviet repression and restriction. They clandestinely published the *Chronicle of the Catholic Church in Lithuania* and shared information with the most widespread Soviet samizdat source, the *Chronicle of Current Events*, which frequently included a section on 'Lithuanian Events'.[3] Illegal publishing and maintaining contacts with the outside world, however, provoked intense KGB responses. Samizdat publishers or distributors were routinely arrested, sentenced to hard labour in the Gulag and/or institutionalized.

Even more common forms of dissent came from individuals or small groups and were characterized by their sporadic, almost spontaneous nature. Émigré communities grasped at each anecdote of anti-Soviet graffiti or vandalism as a tonic to their fears of national destruction in their homelands. Most of these cases, if discovered by authorities, seem to have received some punishment, followed by further observation, but did not incur the full weight of the state. Deviant, apolitical behaviour was given even more leeway. Tiny but active hippie communities sprang up in the Soviet Baltic Republics, most famously in and around Riga. As long as these longhaired, bearded individuals stayed clear of a political message and did not commit any other crimes, they were watched, but ignored (also by the general populace). Only after the Riga community produced a short film, complete with an orgy and a Michael Jackson song on the radio, did the KGB step in to interview many of the participants.[4] The interview was enough to put the kibosh on the young hippies. The film director cut the film into each of its frames and hid the dissected film around Riga, only to reconnect it well after the collapse of the Soviet Union. To the

KGB, although paranoia and alarm ran deep, sporadic incidents of graffiti and petty vandalism, and the incomprehensible activities of hippies, did not threaten Soviet order.

Hippies did not scare the KGB, but student restlessness did. On 14 May 1972 a nineteen-year-old Lithuanian, Romas Kalanta, set himself on fire in a public square in Kaunas. He died of his injuries and student unrest in Lithuania followed. Kalanta has been remembered as a political hero and martyr and his self-immolation is regarded as a defiant act of national resistance.[5] He seems also to have been a severely troubled young man. Ultimately his own motives became irrelevant to those that rioted in the wake of his death for greater Lithuanian national rights. The student unrest was quickly suppressed, but it highlighted the growing political dilemma for the Soviet regime and dissidents alike. The regime itself was under no immediate threat from any opposition movement. State control of the economy and the massive scale of the police network enabled the state to limit and marginalize dissent. Still, the regime also realized that there was little genuine support for the regime itself, and even less among the titular nationalities of Soviet Estonia, Latvia and Lithuania. Opposition was not an immediate threat, but the possibility of a threat always loomed in the future. Throughout the 1960s and '70s party congresses and internal reports frequently cited 'individualism' and 'nationalism' among the youth, or 'nationalist tendencies', or 'remnants of bourgeois nationalism'. The KGB and the Communist Party remained vigilant, although neither had expectations of imminent, widespread opposition. To the opposition the Soviet regime seemed too monolithic and impregnable to breach. All that was left to dissidents were intellectual exercises of opposition that were quickly crushed and had little penetration into the wider public, isolated cases of petty vandalism, or spectacular and short-lived suicidal events like Kalanta's. Through the 1970s the Soviet edifice remained intact and this cycle continued.

The first cracks in the Soviet edifice came from the realization by the highest-ranking members of the Soviet regime that the economic principles of the centrally planned, command economy were failing. Industrial productivity and efficiency were stagnant or slumping, and the leader of the Soviet Union continued to demand an economy that could deliver the resources needed by a superpower engaged in worldwide competition (through proxy wars, competing aid and subsidy campaigns with the West, and ever more elaborate, technologically sophisticated arms and space races). The dilemma was how to enact tough economic measures – which would result in short-term economic misery for the populace – without provoking political and social unrest. In the era of Stalin brute force and state terror had oiled the machinery of economic performance. Khrushchev's tentative steps at reforms included a repudiation of this terror in the hope of making the Soviet system more legitimate and acceptable. After Khrushchev's fall the state resorted to threats of force against political dissidents and economic bribery for the great majority of the population. The state provided a great many services to its population free of charge, from universal healthcare and education to heavily subsidized food, goods and services, subsidized travel through the workplace, and state-guaranteed pensions. The massive cost of such expenditures handicapped the state's continued economic development and simultaneously limited its ability to meet all of these guarantees. Many of these incentives were of poor quality and infrequent delivery and rationing of basic goods became commonplace. In the age of Brezhnev the black and grey markets defined much of the Soviet Union's economic activity. A common joke of the time was that Brezhnev may have been a thief, but he lets everyone else steal too. His successors faced the alarmingly difficult task of reforming the economy without losing political control, all before the rotten economy imploded upon itself. His immediate successors, Yuri Andropov – who was interested in such reforms – and Konstantin Chernenko, were octogenarians in bad health. Neither ruled for more than fifteen months before dying in office. The comparatively sprightly Mikhail Gorbachev, a protégé of Andropov, came to power in March 1985 eager to radically reform the USSR.

Essentially Gorbachev hoped to reinvigorate the Soviet economy in order to compete successfully on an international scale.[6] The obstacles to economic change and reform were the vested interests entrenched in the economic system as it had existed for the previous two or three decades. The Soviet economy was notoriously slow to respond to change, largely due to the straitjacket of five-year economic plans on the macro- and microeconomic level, and was additionally inefficient and corrupt. Economic life revolved around a complex web of patronage, graft, bribery, influence-peddling, obsessive conformity to regulations, black and grey market transactions and other agreements and measured usage of contacts. The catch-all phrase for such activity was *blat* and it was equally integral to personal life and industry. An individual would use all of the abovementioned strategies to move his or her name up a waiting list for an apartment, just as a factory manager would use them to procure needed supplies or a minister to cover up the shortcomings of his work. Gorbachev's desire to create a more responsive, streamlined and efficient economic system challenged this network and all who benefited from it. Not surprisingly, new directives from Moscow alone were unable to accomplish change and Gorbachev turned to promoting greater citizen involvement in economic and political life and to using a more open and critical press to dislodge intransigent foes.

Early press campaigns focused on corruption and encouraged citizens to come forward to unmask guilty parties, but Gorbachev faced a reluctant populace who were cynical of occasional state-sponsored media campaigns against corruption. In order to jump-start economic reform, perestroika, Gorbachev unleashed more open public debate, glasnost. The simple idea was that if the public saw that previously taboo items could be discussed and criticized, then the campaign would gain sufficient momentum to push aside conservative forces unwilling to make reforms and would simultaneously transform Soviet citizens into shareholders in the new Soviet Union. In Gorbachev's view only this type of campaign could produce a society willing to radically reform itself and to tolerate the economic pain and deprivation that would accompany reform in its early stages. Gorbachev's gamble was that open public debate would still be limited to ideas of reforming the Soviet state; what was less clear was how the state would respond to discourse and demands against the Soviet state *in toto*. In Soviet Estonia, Latvia and Lithuania public dialogue quickly moved from uncovering corruption to unmasking the nature of the Soviet Union's occupation and annexation of its Baltic Republics. The next logical step was to question their future in a reformed Soviet Union.

The first tentative stirrings of public debate in Soviet Estonia, Latvia and Lithuania came from the small groups of principled dissidents whose voices had been unheard in the wilderness for decades. Initially the public reception of such dialogue was not particularly tolerant or welcoming. Dissidents that had rallied around the Helsinki Accords' guarantees of human rights (signed by Brezhnev in 1975) had long claimed that the Accord provided them official permission to dissent. The KGB and Soviet courts had largely disagreed, but in the mid-1980s dissident groups sought to combine the Helsinki Accords with Gorbachev's implied guarantees of more open discussion. In particular, three Latvians in the port city of Liepaja, Linards Grantiņš, Raimonds Bitenieks and Mārtiņš Bariss, founded Helsinki-86 in July 1986.[7] Helsinki-86 considered itself to be the first openly anti-Communist organization in the Soviet Union. The organization attracted intense police scrutiny, but still led a small demonstration on 14 June 1987 to the base of the Freedom Monument in Riga to commemorate the deportations of 1941. Within a year many of the organization's most active members had been expelled from the USSR, but the opposition movement and the idea of calendar demonstrations had taken root. Demonstrations marked the anniversary of the Molotov–Ribbentrop Pact on 23 August, and Latvia's Independence Day on 18 November. By 1988 the calendar demonstrations had taken on an entirely new dynamic as established Communist Party officials and leading lights from the cultural world joined in calling for Latvian autonomy.

Nationalist dissidents at the fringes of Soviet society were not the only individuals and groups to take full advantage of Gorbachev's trumpeted campaign of glasnost. Public sentiment rallied considerably around environmental issues, although the environmentalist label is not exactly that of Western Europe. Environmentalists most vocally rallied against shale exploitation and the proposed phosphate mining in Kabala-Toolse in Estonia, raised concerns about the safety of Lithuania's nuclear power plant at Ignalina (which was of the same model as the Chernobyl plant), and organized against the proposed construction of a hydroelectric dam and metro system in Latvia. The campaigns in Latvia used petitions, letters to the media and government officials and mass demonstrations to stop planned construction projects. This success emboldened Latvian environmentalists, and more generally dissenters, to believe that public protest could change policy in Gorbachev's Soviet Union. The environmental campaigns, however, were largely covers for voicing nationalist grievances against the Soviet Union at a time when political dissent was still a dangerous undertaking. Each of the projects attacked as environmentally dangerous was also a symbol of Soviet planning and disdain for local cultures and opinions. The exploitation of shale resources and the generation of nuclear power underlined an All-Union energy policy that did not seem to adequately benefit Estonia and Lithuania. Likewise, in Latvia, the construction of the dam and the metro would have needed another influx of labour and again raised the question of immigration and the dilution of the ethnic Latvian composition of the republic. Furthermore, to many of these activists, environmentalism included a defence of man and nation in their 'traditional incarnation', a decidedly anti-modern strain of thought. To some, modern industrial society did not damage the environment with pollution alone, but sullied a 'natural human environment'. Some of the earliest campaigns by these 'environmentalists' were aimed at preserving old farmsteads and churches from advanced disrepair, collapse and decay. Their anger was fuelled as much by the consequences of Soviet industrial plans to the supposedly 'natural' state of Estonians, Latvians and Lithuanians as it was by habitat degradation and pollution. These were some of the underlying concerns of environmental action, but protesting openly about them was too dangerous politically. When the nationalist dissidents were able to demonstrate without incurring absolute repression, the environmental campaigns began to change their political discourse as well: environmental concerns receded and nationalist grievances surfaced with more clarity.

Through 1988 and 1989 popular opposition movements in Soviet Estonia, Latvia and Lithuania observed the opening up of political space in the Soviet Union and across Eastern Europe and pushed at the boundaries of what would be tolerated and accepted.[8] As events in one republic (or in Eastern Europe) redefined and expanded the parameters of political discourse, each of the other republics' opposition movements recalibrated their demands and tactics. These two years, 1988 and 1989, were also the crucial watershed years when mass Popular Fronts began by tentatively and gingerly asking for greater autonomy before ultimately demanding the reestablishment of independence lost. On reflection this process seems to have gone at a dizzying pace, but it was a slow, tortured process at the time, defined by astonishing successes and an undercurrent of 'what now?'

Ultimately a kind of political calculus tipped the scales and the bulk of the ethnic Estonian, Latvian and Lithuanian political and cultural elite sided with protest. Opposition to Soviet rule and demands for national interests became commonplace in 1988, although demands for outright independence were still the preserve of the few. In Latvia, for example, while the nationalist opposition prepared for the next calendar demonstration, to commemorate the mass deportations of 1949, some of the established political and cultural elite tentatively joined this process. The nationalists' demonstration centred on the Freedom Monument built by the Republic of Latvia in the 1930s. The chosen site was a demand for independence in itself. The established political and cultural elite, however, still hedged its bets and organized the founding of Latvia's Popular Front (Latvijas tautas fronte) at a less confrontational but still symbolic site, the Cemetery of the Brethren, which served as a cemetery of honour in Latvia and Soviet Latvia. The commemoration of the 1949 deportation was also potentially more ambiguous than commemorating dates directly tied to the pre-war Republic. The 1949 deportation, for example, could be portrayed as a Stalinist excess that highlighted the need for the reform of the USSR, whereas commemorating Latvia's independence day clearly showed irredentist views. These demonstrations were also notable for the heartfelt and impassioned speeches given by leading cultural figures, suddenly reformed Communist Party leaders and eyewitnesses to the events surrounding Soviet occupation in 1940. In Soviet Latvia, for example, the public and televised confessions of Mavriks Vulfsons stunned the nation. Vulfsons described his own participation in the events of June and July 1940 as part of a designed, external takeover and occupation of a sovereign state. Vulfsons's speech was electric not so much for its groundbreaking allegations – he said what many already believed – but because he was the first to blatantly make them publicly and as a source from the inside.

Soon national flags became commonplace at mass gatherings. By the summer of 1988 the Communist Parties of Estonia, Latvia and Lithuania were split between reformists involved in the Popular Front movements and a reactionary minority loyal to conservatives within the All-Union Communist Party in Moscow. Government adopted reformist laws (including official language laws that raised the position of Estonian, Latvian and Lithuanian) and issued demands and ultimatums for greater republic-level control and autonomy. Although the Popular Fronts in Soviet Estonia and Latvia tested the early limits of political discourse, by 1989 the Lithuanian Popular Front, Sajūdis, had charted the most radical and confrontational course with the Soviet Union by pushing for full independence through the course of 1989. The Popular Fronts in Estonia and Latvia shared this ultimate goal, but were more circumspect in declaring it or moving towards it.

The leadership of the Popular Fronts is indicative of the origins of part of the new political and economic elite of Estonia, Latvia and Lithuania. In Estonia and Latvia two prominent members of the local Communist Parties became the leading lights of the Popular Fronts. In Estonia Edgar Savisaar helped found the Popular Front and used his position within it to catapult to positions within Soviet Estonia's Council of Ministers. On the eve of independence in 1991 Savisaar was the chairman of the Council of Ministers and hence became the first prime minister of Estonia after independence. He did not stay in office long, but has remained central in Estonian politics. In Latvia Anatolijs Gorbunovs, often mocked for his fastidious haircut and charismatic appeal, exemplified the members of Latvia's Communist Party, who performed a seeming about-face in their political beliefs. Gorbunovs was also a careerist in the Communist Party; among the many posts he had held was being in charge of ideology. By 1988 Gorbunovs had broken publicly with the Moscow loyalists and led a schism within the Communist Party. His faction supporting greater autonomy worked closely with the Popular Front and Gorbunovs became the Chairman of the Presidium of the Supreme Soviet. Ultimately he became Latvia's first Speaker of Parliament (Saeima) with independence and remained one of Latvia's most popular politicians into the mid-1990s.

The easy and seamless transition of many Communist Party officials and Communist state-supported intellectuals to a more nationalist cause in the heady days of the Popular Fronts has raised an open question on the nature of transition in post-Soviet Estonia, Latvia and Lithuania. Critics dismiss the quick conversions of these figures and see the entire process as either opportunism or, in the conspiracy theories always near the surface in Estonia, Latvia and Lithuania, as a part of a nefarious plot to keep the levers of the new states in old hands, with only cosmetic alterations. Frequently political opponents raise these officials' Communist Party pasts to suggest that their true and ultimate loyalties are with Moscow. The above-mentioned Gorbunovs, for example, was endlessly referred to as the former Secretary of Ideology for the Communist Party of Latvia.

On a more regional and local level, the debate about the frequent returns of Soviet-era apparatchiki to positions of local government and to central roles in economic life mirrors the national debate. Opposition politicians bitterly resent that these opportunists 'stole' the revolution and turned a popular movement into gross economic gain and small political fiefdoms. There are clearly many examples of this phenomenon, since the skills learned and honed during the Brezhnev era could be employed to take full advantage of the dismantling of Soviet planned economies and their subsequent privatization. To those that profited most, charges of ultimate loyalty to a Communist creed are the most hollow: if anything their political mooring is a simple convenience that allows them to keep local, political and economic power. For a great many other Party members that converted to nationalism at the end of the 1980s and into the '90s, the radical change in orien-tation says more about how necessary and expedient Communist Party membership was through the 1970s and '80s. A great many administrators and public officials were likely motivated on a personal level to take on these roles, but they had to belong to the Communist Party to reach these goals in the Soviet Union. For many such individuals, joining and leading popular movements for greater national rights was a cathartic and cherished personal metamorphosis, but after the fact they still wanted most of all to be public officials and administrators.

In Soviet Lithuania the rise of Popular Fronts that were closely aligned with reformist elements within the Communist Party, government and economic and cultural elite was tempered by the rise of Sajūdis. Sajūdis played much the same organizational role as Estonia's and Latvia's Popular Fronts, but its origins and leadership differed substantially. Sajūdis' origins were in the Soviet Lithuanian Academy of Sciences where, in the summer of 1988, 35 academics and artists (seven-teen of whom were members of the Communist Party) formed a group to generally support Gorbachev's reform plans. Through the summer of 1988 Sajūdis-inspired and/or -organized events drew large crowds and the organization radicalized its political dialogue. In October Sajūdis held its founding congress and elected a professor of musicology, Vytautas Landsbergis, its chairman. After this republic-wide televised event, Sajūdis grew rapidly into a political mass movement with nationalist aspirations, a direction that led some of its initial creators to abandon the movement. Still, these cultural figures were on the outside of common, popular sentiment, which grew increasingly confident and demanding of greater ethnic Lithuanian power. Algirdas Brazauskas, a reform-minded Communist minister, found frequent common ground with Sajūdis and used its popular legitimacy to springboard to the post of First Secretary of the Lithuanian Communist Party, also in October 1988. As a result, in Soviet Lithuania by the end of 1988, a large popular organization, Sajūdis, more removed from a web of Communist ties, had pushed a reform wing of the Lithuanian Communist Party towards greater Lithuanian autonomy. In Soviet Estonia and Latvia, on the other hand, the nationalist and reform movements had been co-opted into umbrella Popular Front organizations that were led by reformists from the elite. In Soviet Estonia and Latvia the evolution of political demands from 1989 through to 1991 tended to be slightly less confrontational and less determined by principles than in Lithuania. Although the majority of ethnic Estonians, Latvians and Lithuanians favoured a more complete break with the Soviet Union, in Estonia and Latvia the Popular Fronts spent much more time and energy looking for compromises with Gorbachev's vision of a new, reformed USSR. In Lithuania Sajūdis more closely voiced the grass-roots feeling of the popular movement and dragged the reformist Lithuanian Communists with them towards full independence.

Throughout 1988 mass calendar demonstrations mobilized hundreds of thousands to the Popular Front movements. Emboldened by such popular support, the Popular Fronts pushed for greater demands and in turn saw even larger crowds at the demonstrations. The lack of systematic state oppression lifted the general public's veil of fear. In all three republics the calendar demonstrations included the anniversaries of the peace treaties in which the Soviet Union recognized independence in 1920, the independence days of the pre-Second World War republics, and the anniversaries of Soviet mass deportations. Republic song festivals also played a unifying role and often showcased the mass singing of long-banned national anthems broadcast on live television. The prevalence of song in subsequent demonstrations led some to name the movements 'singing revolutions'.[9] Most of the other long-banned symbols of independence, prominently including the national flags, emerged throughout 1988.

The staggered nature of these calendar demonstrations created an environment in which Popular Fronts, in either Estonia, Latvia or Lithuania, were almost continuously organizing or successfully holding a mass rally that pushed the political envelope further. If one Popular Front succeeded in rehabilitating a national flag, for example, the other two would quickly follow. In this manner the successes of each Popular Front were quickly adopted by the others and all three encouraged each others' confidence in pushing for more authority. As a result the popular movements in Soviet Estonia, Latvia and Lithuania, although always focused on local developments, also took on the character of a Baltic movement, perhaps for the first and only time in their history. All three Popular Fronts reacted to slights against any one of them. The three movements shared information and tactics and clearly saw their ultimate successes or failures as linked. Moscow at times attempted divide and rule tactics between the three organizations, rewarding one while chastising another, but Baltic unity remained largely intact. The most successful demonstration of this unity centred on the calendar demonstration to mark the fiftieth anniversary of the Molotov–Ribbentrop Pact on 23 August 1989. Unlike many of the other calendar demonstrations, the Molotov–Ribbentrop anniversary united all three Popular Fronts because it signified the beginning of the end of independence to Estonia, Latvia and Lithuania in 1939. All other dates in the calendar of Soviet occupation and repression grew out of this Soviet-Nazi division of Eastern Europe. To mark the fiftieth anniversary of this event, the Popular Fronts of Estonia and Latvia and Sajūdis organized a human chain from Tallinn to Riga to Vilnius. The three movements were united behind nearly two million people who formed a human chain that stretched for more than 600 kilometres. The Baltic Chain was a wildly successful event, mixing a mass unified message with the telegenic imagery needed to capture international attention and sympathy. After the Baltic Chain, international opinion firmly believed in the legitimacy of the Popular Fronts and foresaw only two potential outcomes in conflict with the Soviet Union: real concessions to the Baltic Popular Fronts or violent repression and the restoration of minority rule and foreign occupation.

The official Soviet response within Soviet Estonia, Latvia and Lithuania included conciliatory gestures, such as decreeing the Estonian, Latvian and Lithuanian languages official, mixed with a frantic attempt to define the limits of accepted political dialogue. The contradictory messages reflected the schism within the Communist Parties of Soviet Estonia, Latvia and Lithuania; a reformist faction made common cause with the Popular Fronts while a conservative faction looked despairingly to Moscow for a repressive response. Lacking such a response, the hardline Communists began belatedly to organize Popular Fronts of the Slavic-speaking people of Estonia, Latvia and Lithuania. These alternate Popular Fronts became known as international fronts or Interfronts, but they failed to generate equally massive enthusiasm and support, even if some of their concerns and demands represented the interests of Russians, Belorussians, Ukrainians and others. These ethnic groups worried about the rise of political nationalism and about their place in republics dominated by the increasingly nationalistic Popular Fronts. The Interfront organizations, however, were too transparently tied to the heavy-handed Soviet security apparatus. Initially supporting Interfront seemed more like supporting the old ways of governance and administration in the Soviet Union. Rising nationalism among Estonians, Latvians and Lithuanians may have been a concern, but the greater threat initially was the repressive regime of the USSR.

The years 1988, 1989 and 1990 demonstrated the enigmatic relationship between Popular Fronts in Soviet Estonia, Latvia and Lithuania and the power struggle in the greater Soviet Union revolving around Gorbachev's reformist plans. Gorbachev's glasnost campaign enabled Estonians, Latvians and Lithuanians to voice ever more overt political demands. In this sense Gorbachev seemed a natural ally and his plans for economic restructuring were generally supported throughout the three Baltic Republics. However, Estonian, Latvian and Lithuanian demands for a complete re-evaluation of Soviet rule as forced annexation and occupation threatened the integrity of the entire Soviet Union, something Gorbachev never desired nor could entertain. Baltic Popular Fronts could arise only with Gorbachev in power; yet if they were to achieve their ultimate aim they would likely topple him from his position in the process. If Gorbachev were toppled, the ensuing reaction would probably crush the Popular Fronts as well.

Two other factors greatly complicated matters. Hundreds of thousands of Soviet troops were stationed across Soviet Estonia, Latvia and Lithuania. Many of these bases were considered vital to Soviet security. If the troops refused to leave, how could Estonia, Latvia and Lithuania evict them? Finally the Popular Fronts, which appealed to the ethnic sentiments of ethnic Estonians, Latvians and Lithuanians, still had to define their relationship with the hundreds of thousands of Slavic-speaking people that had settled in the Soviet Baltic Republics following the Second World War. Even if the abovementioned Interfronts could be written off as agents of Moscow, the Popular Fronts needed to confront the interests of the hundreds of thousands of Russians and Russian-speakers living in the Baltic region.

This process of establishing unquestioned legitimacy at home while pressuring Moscow and appealing for international attention and influence began in earnest throughout 1989. The calendar demonstrations, and most spectacularly the Baltic Chain, showcased the Popular Fronts' abilities to put hundreds of thousands of people into the streets in protest. Increasingly the question became: could the Popular Fronts provide government and administration without losing public support? They had already proven their merits in opposition, but could they govern? Through 1989 and '90 the Popular Fronts moved into this forum by participating in, and contesting, a bevy of increasingly open elections. Elections to local, republic and All-Union Soviets had been commonplace throughout Soviet rule, but the electoral list consisted of a single, party-chosen and approved candidate. The Communist Parties of Soviet Estonia, Latvia and Lithuania, desperately divided between reformist and hardline factions, now held contested elections with competing candidates, although these were still limited to Party members. In these elections the Popular Fronts threw their support behind the reformist Communist candidates, who swept to victory. These elected candidates moved up through the hierarchy of Soviet legislative and governing bodies to put reformists in control of Soviet Estonia, Latvia and Lithuania. Once in power, reformists altered electoral laws to allow for future multi-party elections and adopted the political platform of the Popular Fronts. In each republic, from the very halls of the Supreme Soviets that had rubberstamped fiats and decrees from Moscow for decades, came calls, demands and laws establishing the intent to claim autonomy and eventually reassert independence.

Still, independence needed to be more than declared: it needed to be realized. This proved exceedingly difficult when the Soviet Union simply refused to negotiate. Through 1990 and '91 the Popular Front governments of Soviet Estonia, Latvia and Lithuania played a cat-and-mouse tactical game against Moscow by endlessly asserting and reasserting independence and control in countless little ways. All the while, the threat of Moscow's use of concerted force against the Popular Front governments dangled over the entire scenario.

In Soviet Lithuania confrontation between the Popular Front and Moscow was most acerbic, with the least room for a negotiated compromise. The elections to the Lithuanian Supreme Council held in March 1990 (in all three republics, the Supreme Councils began referring to themselves as councils, as opposed to the longstanding Supreme Soviets, to show the growing distance between themselves and all things Soviet) returned an overwhelming majority of Sajūdis -supported candidates. On 11 March the newly elected Supreme Council declared the restoration of Lithuania's independence. This was a far clearer declaration than Soviet Estonian and Latvian council declarations of intentions to restore independence on 30 March and 4 May respectively. Moscow initially responded by not responding. In May, however, Moscow began an economic blockade of Lithuania to force its Supreme Council to rescind the 11 March declaration. No such blockade was declared against the more cautious Estonian and Latvian governments. Still, the crisis mostly simmered through 1990. The three Popular Front-supported governments took symbolic and small steps to appear like the governments of sovereign states while

Moscow refused to consider the option. Gorbachev seemed more preoccupied with the negotiations for a new All-Union treaty and did not want Baltic developments to scuttle a tenuous negotiation.

By the end of 1990 hardliners in Moscow and their loyalists in the union republics had pushed Gorbachev to rein in dissent and opposition across the Soviet Union, most specifically in the Soviet Baltic Republics. Moscow, it seemed, had given up its earlier policy of largely ignoring Baltic demands and began considering the imposition of direct presidential rule. In January 1991 'National Salvation Committees' called for the immediate suspension of the Supreme Councils and their governments, and for the introduction of Gorbachev's direct rule. In Lithuania these calls reached their zenith on 11 January 1990 when a Lithuanian National Salvation Committee announced its assumption of political control and authority. Soviet armed forces surrounded the press centre and the television and radio tower. A coup attempt was clearly in progress and the Supreme Council was obviously a target. Tens of thousands of people quickly came to the defence of the symbols of the Popular Front government. A massive human cordon surrounded the Supreme Council, and no assault was attempted against this manifestation of people power. At the television and radio tower, however, Soviet tanks and troops clashed with the public and fourteen people were killed.

A week later similar assaults targeted Latvia's Popular Front government. Soviet paramilitary and armed forces stormed government buildings and press and communication centres. Five people were killed during these assaults: two police officers that defended the Ministry of the Interior, two documentary film-makers who broadcasted this assault to an international audience (the broadcast included the dying gasps of the cameraman, Andris Slapiņš, and of the filmmaker Gvīdo Zvaigzne), and a student caught in the crossfire. As in Vilnius, people rushed to defend the Popular Front government. Makeshift barricades were built across Riga, around government buildings and on bridges. The human barricade was more significant; tens of thousands of people gathered across Riga to defend the government and to make a statement of defiance. The crowds stayed for days, a period remembered as the barricade days, to guarantee the failure of the attempted coup. Although the coup attempt failed in Lithuania and Latvia (no such violent clash occurred in Estonia at this date), reformers were unable to assert sole authority. Soviet forces kept control of the media and communications buildings captured while the Popular Front governments continued to attempt to act as sovereign state authorities. Most dangerously, armed police units loyal to Moscow and units loyal to the Popular Front councils coexisted uneasily on the tense streets of Vilnius and Riga. Nevertheless the public's defence of the Popular Front institutions in Latvia and Lithuania in January 1991, and the Baltic Chain, are popularly remembered as the most cherished accomplishments of the struggle for independence.

The use of force against the public rekindled immense anger about and distrust of Soviet intentions and practices throughout Soviet Estonia, Latvia and Lithuania. The Popular Front movements were able to channel this displeasure into strong returns in the campaign of competing referendums in the spring of 1991. In Estonia, Latvia and Lithuania a majority voted for a locally sponsored referendum, which asked: do you want the restoration of independence? In each republic most people boycotted a Moscow-sponsored referendum on the future of the USSR. In Estonia and Latvia particularly, this electoral result demonstrated that support for independence also existed among the Slavic-speaking populations of each republic. This lukewarm support, however, was more a denouncement of Soviet rule than a vote in favour of the nationalist programmes of the Popular Fronts.

Through the summer of 1991, as before, the Popular Fronts' quandary was how to translate electoral success and popular support into Soviet capitulation. The continued presence of pro-Moscow paramilitary forces exacerbated tensions. In Lithuania and Latvia attempts at building customs and border guard posts resulted in the forced destruction of several of these makeshift symbols and the killing of several border guards. The tense environment could easily have run out of control and led to more generalized violence.

In August 1991 hardliners in Moscow attempted the coup tactic in the heart of the Soviet Union. Renegade politburo members (including the Minister of the Interior, the Latvian Boriss Pugo) declared themselves a National Salvation Committee while Gorbachev holidayed in the Crimea. The coup stumbled badly due to poor planning and execution and popular opposition in Moscow led by Boris Yeltsin. Sensing the magnitude of the moment, all three Baltic Republics declared their immediate and complete independence. They had little choice. If the Moscow coup had succeeded, a crackdown on the Baltic movements would have followed. If the coup failed, as happened, the defeat of the hardliners would give the Baltic states their window of opportunity. Yeltsin declared his support for Baltic independence and recognized it as President of the Russian Federal Republic. Denmark and Iceland became the first states to recognize Baltic independence. Gorbachev acquiesced in September 1991 and more general international recognition followed. On 21 September 1991 the republics of Estonia, Latvia and Lithuania were admitted to the United Nations. Improbably, almost miraculously, independence was achieved in less than five years, with only a few dozen people killed. Creating and governing independent states, however, proved a longer and more difficult process.

The morning after the sudden return of independence was a massive hangover. Almost overnight, the rallying point that could draw hundreds of thousands of people together – opposition to the old-style Soviet Union – disappeared. Instead the governments of the republics of Estonia, Latvia and Lithuania were faced with truly governing their states. The challenges before them were immense and countless: from the mundane points of creating government policy, even staffing government, to huge challenges such as negotiating the withdrawal of hundreds of thousands of Soviet troops from a web of Soviet military bases, defining the citizenry of the new states, and building a new economy from the ruins of a collapsed, central command economy devoted to Moscow's directives and needs. Among political elites there was a fear that popular support for the new states, particularly regarding economic transformation, would not last long without some immediate, material improvements. All the while, hardline politicians remained recalcitrant in their support of the Soviet model and ethnic minority communities were suddenly faced with a new locus of decision-making in their lives. If, during the previous year, their greatest concern had been the return of an oppressive Soviet Union, that was no longer the case. Suddenly ethnic minority communities worried about potentially discriminatory policies which might be adopted by Estonian, Latvian and Lithuanian governments. Furthermore Estonian, Latvian and to a lesser degree Lithuanian extreme nationalists demanded that these ethnic minority communities be treated as former occupiers with few legal rights to reside in the newly independent Baltic states. Some even floated ideas of forced repatriation. The governments of Estonia, Latvia and Lithuania also had to position themselves in a new Europe that had been radically transformed by the collapse of Soviet hegemony in Eastern Europe and the development of the European Union. Ultimately the three governments also had to solve the security conundrum that had besieged the states between the wars: how could Estonia's, Latvia's and Lithuania's independence be guaranteed?

The potential solutions to all these myriad challenges were hopelessly intertwined. For example, the Soviet government and its successor the Russian government quickly linked the removal of army bases with the treatment of Russian and other Slavic minorities in the newly restored states, specifically in Estonia and Latvia. As a result the dilemma of defining the state's citizenry developed around the perceived extortion of the removal of a foreign state's military bases. Likewise, until relations between Estonia, Latvia and Lithuania with Russia and other Soviet successor states were clearly defined, economic transformation wavered between reconstructing economic ties with the East or with the West. Finally, in all three states, the existing governments faced legitimacy issues, since they had enjoyed immense popular support as Popular Fronts against the Soviet Union, but had not stood for election to office in free, democratic, multi-party elections around the specifics of proposed government policies. Even before the attempted coup of August 1991 the Popular Front governments, or the governments they supported, were under increasing strain from a public who were disaffected with their day-to-day administration as opposed to their general support for the lofty goal of independence. As the governments of the three newly restored states made policy decisions that directly and detrimentally affected the public – or, worse yet, detrimentally affected some and benefited others – their public approval ratings plummeted. With each controversial and difficult policy decision, the disaffected accused the governments of overstepping their bounds. This line of thought suggested that the remnant Supreme Councils were caretaker governments whose most important goal was to make way for new, democratically elected, multi-party parliaments. Until a citizenship law was enacted, however, new elections could not take place since the question of who would be eligible to vote in such elections was still bitterly contested. If, on the other hand, the governments did not act, the disaffected attacked them for acting as lame duck regimes that were too timid or too illegitimate to take action when it was desperately needed. This transition period lasted from 1991 (even before the failed coup of August) until the autumn of 1992 in Estonia and Lithuania, when the Riigikogu (Estonia's parliament) and the Seimas (parliament in Lithuania) were elected. In Latvia this transition phase lasted longer, since the Saeima (parliament in Latvia) was not elected until the summer of 1993. The lengthier interval in Latvia was also reflected in the greater unpopularity of its ruling Popular Front, which failed to win any seats in the new parliament.

Defining citizenship marked the beginning of politics in the newly restored states. The options ran from the so-called 'zero option', which would grant citizenship to everyone who had resided in the republics at the renewal of independence, to more restrictive citizenship laws based on ethnicity and/or the citizenry of the interwar republics. In Lithuania Soviet immigration had not seriously altered the ethnic composition of the republic, which remained overwhelmingly Lithuanian and considerably rural, and therefore a law close to the zero option was quickly introduced and accepted. Lithuania did (and does still) have difficult relations with some ethnic minority communities, but these are confined to a few cities and geographic regions and play a much smaller role in national politics. In Estonia and Latvia, however, immigration during the Soviet occupation radically altered the ethnic composition of the states, most sharply in Estonia, where the ethnic Estonian majority of nearly 88 per cent in 1935 had dropped to 61 per cent by 1989. In Latvia, where the ethnic Latvian majority had hovered around 75 per cent in the interwar period, by 1989 Latvians were almost reduced to a plurality with just over 52 per cent of the population comprised of ethnic Latvians. In each of these countries much of what fuelled anti-Soviet protests in the late 1980s was the sense of an impending demographic catastrophe; many believed that if Estonians and Latvians did not reacquire independence at this critical moment, hope would be lost as the ethnic nations would slip into minority status in their own homelands and eventually extinction (such fears of ethnic extinction had a long history and were often exaggerated). As a result, in Estonia and Latvia, the ethnic Russian minority and other Slavs were viewed with suspicion as a potential fifth column or with outright hostility as remnants of an occupation. During the Popular Front period overtures of ethnic reconciliation wooed ethnic minorities to support and vote for Estonian and Latvian independence. Some activists suggested that the reward would be a citizenship law best described as the 'zero option plus one'; or, in other words, one that recognized the interwar past but quickly reconciled all the current residents. With independence achieved, however, these overtures became less essential to the Estonian and Latvian political elites.

Gradually a far more restrictive concept of citizenry developed. This idea originated with nationalist extremists and with the émigré communities who argued that Estonian and Latvian independence had not ceased with Soviet occupation and annexation, but had existed in a kind of ethereal form personified by the still extant diplomatic representatives in the USA and by the surviving citizenry and their descendants. This line of reasoning continued that only these people were entitled to automatic citizenship in the newly restored republics and only they would be entitled to vote for the countries' parliaments.

If this approach disenfranchised hundreds of thousands of people overnight, this was either a legal necessity that could then be addressed by newly elected parliaments or a disingenuous way of disenfranchising the dreaded, and suspected, Russian minority communities. Not surprisingly the affected ethnic minorities complained bitterly, as did the Russian Foreign Ministry, a range of officials from across Europe and others throughout the international community. The common rallying call was opposition to Estonian and Latvian discrimination against

Russians. In fairness, neither citizenship law disenfranchised Russians or Slavs per se. In each case those Russians (and their descendants) that had been citizens of the interwar Republics were entitled to automatic citizenship, as were all other interwar citizens. In practice, however, the new citizenship law meant that most Russians and Slavs were not granted citizenship in Estonia or Latvia in 1992. If anything, the decision to use the day of Soviet occupation in 1940 as the defining point of Estonia's and Latvia's legal political body disingenuously disenfranchised the Baltic Germans (and their descendants) that had been forced to 'repatriate' to the Reich less than a year before Soviet occupation. This historical community was essentially kept out of the current political landscape and away from potentially lucrative restitution claims.

Once citizenship was narrowly defined, this predominantly ethnically homogenous citizenry became the electorate for the first parliaments. The politicians that had already begun to shy away from the ethnic conciliation of the Popular Front days had no reason to appeal to people that could not vote them into office. Even more importantly, many of the political elite had had political, administrative or professional careers in the Soviet Union, and were now vying for political office by appealing to a narrow ethnic electorate suspicious of their past loyalties to the ethnic nation. As a result, there was no immediate political gain to be had from reaching out to ethnic minority communities, and indeed there was political capital to be had in appealing to exclusionary Estonian and Latvian nationalism.

If the Popular Front governments took the legalistic explanation that citizenship was not meant to be disenfranchising, but rather a precise continuation of the interwar republic's political and biological legacy, they still felt authorized to tamper with the mechanisms of parliamentary voting by decreeing a 4 per cent threshold for election to parliament. This prudent and logical step was meant to avoid the apparent political instability of the interwar experience when dozens of parties or electoral lists were regularly represented in parliament. As a result governments had been fragile coalitions in near constant peril of collapsing. The Supreme Councils' electoral threshold laws limited the number of parties that could contest elections and win seats in parliament. The laws have also slowly encouraged the consolidation of political parties, although they have not eliminated the frailty of coalition cabinets. As such the decisions were prescient and commendable, but the logic behind their implementation and the implementation of citizenship was inconsistent. If the Supreme Councils were only restoring the states that existed prior to Soviet occupation, and thus limiting citizenship, they must also have returned to the electoral laws as they existed as well. Essentially, in the period between the struggle for the restoration of independence and the elections of new parliaments, the Supreme Councils in Estonia and Latvia chose to disenfranchise Soviet migrants. There may have been many reasons, some of them defensible, behind this decision, but the explanation given was one that hid behind the idea that the state had been restored. That restoration, however, was never intended to be complete and consistent. As a result, once citizenship was defined as limited, a longer divisive struggle about non-citizens, the process of naturalization and language policy became inevitable, particularly because politicians targeted the electorate that mattered and not those who were disenfranchised.

Estonia and Latvia enacted their citizenship laws in the face of considerable opposition from Russia and displeasure from other international quarters, including non-governmental organizations. They also followed economic policy counter to most international and expert advice, although with far better results. In the wake of the collapse of the Soviet Union and its massive economic aftershocks, many Western experts counselled the Baltic states to stay within a Russian ruble economic zone to keep access to established markets and resources. These experts understood that Baltic commodities would not immediately be competitive in Western markets and advised this economic policy to minimize economic collapse. In all three states, however, governments and the mostly independent Central Banks that they created steadfastly followed a policy of reintroducing the currencies of the 1920s and '30s. A staggered transition included an initial release of republic rubles on a one-for-one exchange rate, followed in due course by the introduction of the krona, lats and litas in Estonia, Latvia and Lithuania respectively. The process of exchange and the rates of exchange were fair and gradual, a break from the extractive and sudden monetary transitions that had accompanied Soviet and Nazi occupation. Most anticipated chaos and the sudden devaluations of the new currencies, but with a strong commitment to keep them pegged to baskets of Western currencies, the state money proved strong and enduring. Although the exchange rates continued to be debated (and over different circumstances), the monetary transition from 1992 to 1994 was an unqualified success. More than any other policy, the monetary change removed Estonia, Latvia and Lithuania from the tight economic orbit of Russia. Although each state had considerable economic difficulties throughout the 1990s, they were not Russia's economic difficulties. This economic break also enabled a process of moving the Baltic Republics entirely away from Russia's gravitational pull into the European Union's expanding heavens (for more a more detailed discussion of the economics of Estonia, Latvia and Lithuania, see chapter Four).

Within the defined parameters of the citizenship laws, all three republics organized free and fair multi-party elections in the autumn of 1992 and the late spring of 1993. In all three countries what has followed has been the unfolding parliamentary history of independent states. The political events and developments can be examined either in close and thorough detail of each parliamentary election in each state or with an eye to the broad brushstrokes that define politics in the Baltic states after Soviet occupation. The two approaches do not contradict each other but bring different issues to the fore.

If, for example, the chosen approach is a close examination of politics, more often than not the commentator will get drawn into the partisan battles waged in Estonia, Latvia and Lithuania. In each state the commentator will likely find themselves supporting or criticizing one or many of the highly divisive, polemical politicians. Is the wealthy businessman in Latvia, Andris Šķēle, a Machiavellian manipulator of all political decisions or is he a hard-nosed businessman that brings the same acumen and style to politics? Can Edgar Savisaar present a leftist alternative in Estonia or is his platform old Soviet wine in new bottles? Is Rolandas Paksas's political career entirely based on corruption or does he bring a new style to politics? These debates are seemingly constant, with one cast of politicians replacing another in each election, while a few prominent kingmakers in each state survive through successive parliaments, governments and scandals. Estonian, Latvian and Lithuanian politics have largely been defined by scandals and the competing egotism of the political elite. At times Baltic democracy seems to sink to the lows of 'football politics', where the electorate loyally supports a side and gloats and benefits if they win in elections or complains and regroups anew if elections are lost.

The close survey of Estonian, Latvian and Lithuanian politics follows political developments chronologically through each successive elected parliament. In Estonia, for example, this approach describes the tension surrounding the eventual election of Lennart Meri to the post of State President in 1992. Meri's personal history seemed to encapsulate the history of the Estonian nation in the twentieth century. Born to a prominent and successful interwar Estonian family (a diplomat father and an Estonian-Swedish literati mother), the young Meri grew up speaking many languages, and attended school in Paris as well as in Estonia. With Soviet occupation and the onslaught of the Second World War, the extended Meri family split between those supporting the Soviet and Allied cause and those resisting Soviet occupation. These 'nuances' meant little, as many were deported to Siberia in 1941. Meri returned to Soviet Estonia, earned a degree as a historian with high honours and worked as a writer for theatre and film. Throughout the long Soviet occupation Meri's career showed both high achievement within the Soviet space and a constant chafing at Soviet restrictions. He published and directed with accolades, but also struggled to establish links with Finland and the Estonian émigré community. His international cultural contacts served Estonia well in the early days of environmental protest against Soviet development plans and brought him naturally into the founding circle of the Estonian Popular Front. In the transition years of Popular Front rule he was minister for foreign affairs and ambassador to Finland. Still, his nomination to the presidency was opposed by Estonian nationalists who saw his years of relative success in Soviet Estonia as indicative of potential ties to the KGB. Once in office Meri's presidency was almost universally acclaimed. His death in 2006 of a brain tumour, almost five years after leaving office, was an international event that recognized his contributions to post-Cold War Europe.

In Latvia a close political survey would catalogue the rise and fall of political elites through the 1990s and into the 2000s in a merry-go-round of established parties and popular reformists with a smattering of local oligarchs. This all began with the electoral list, Latvia's Way. The majority of the politicians that would become the nucleus of Latvia's Way (it was not initially a political party) were closely aligned with or a part of Latvia's Popular Front or the reform wing of Latvia's Communist Party. As the parliamentary election of 1993 approached, these politicians understood their unique position: they remained popular, but the Popular Front was doomed to electoral defeat. They abandoned the Popular Front to electoral ignominy and crafted a new list of candidates with leading figures of the Latvian émigré community. Quickly dubbed the 'dream team' of Latvian politics, with the popular and photogenic Anatolijs Gorbunovs as its electoral 'locomotive', Latvia's Way won more than a third of the seats to the fifth Saeima. Although seemingly weakened with a minority government, Latvia's Way became the kingmakers of Latvian politics through the 1990s. Their representatives regularly claimed the most important and lucrative ministers' portfolios and they personified the unabashed political elite of a new state. Despite renegade politicians almost literally offering free bananas for votes, and the chaos of the 1995 electoral returns that saw nine, nearly equally weighted parties dividing parliament between themselves in an almost ungovernable mess, Latvia's Way seemed to be the floating political centre most concerned with staying in power. Their ultimate challenger and successor, Andris Šķēle, was the 'non-partisan' brought in to mediate the chaos of the 1995 elections. He in turn, became a political force, ultimately creating a new political movement, the People's Party (1997), as a counter to the status quo elitism of Latvia's post-Soviet political life. Latvia's Way fought a successful rearguard campaign against

Šķēle's People's Party in the 1998 elections, ultimately pulling out all the stops to keep Šķēle from office. The short-lived Krištopans' government (dominated by Latvia's Way) gave way to a short-lived Šķēle government. The ultimate compromise between the warring satraps was another Latvia's Way-dominated government led by the popular mayor of Riga (from Latvia's Way), Andris Berziņš. Although popular, Berziņš presided over the ultimate collapse of Latvia's Way in the 2002 parliamentary elections to a new pretender, the New Era Party, headed by the widely regarded former head of the bank of Latvia, Einars Repše. Repše and his party fashioned themselves as the latest crusaders against the political elitism, cronyism and corruption of high offices in Latvia, but soon ran aground on political obstructionism and poor management. Another new party, Latvia's First Party, led by a brash anti-intellectual 'man of action', Ainārs Šlesers, and with the promise of a new blend of politics that merged social conservatism, populism and a hint of rapprochement with Russia, announced itself as the next pretender to the throne. Latvia's First Party's alliance with the remnants of Latvia's Way either represented the continued influence of Latvia's Way or its turn as a lame-duck political force. Either way, both supported the return of the People's Party to political power under the stewardship of Aigars Kalvītis. His ultimate fall, the caretaker government of Ivars Godmanis (the leader of the Popular Front reborn as a member of the People's Party/Latvia's Way alliance), and the return of the New Era to power under Valdis Dombrovskis owe more to Latvia's beleaguered navigation through the recession of 2008–10 than to a new political landscape in Latvia. Over all these political realignments dangles the legal fate of the former mayor of Ventspils, Aivars Lembergs. Lembergs rose to national political significance as the mayor of the port city that oversaw the transit trade of Russian gas, oil and ammonia. His deep pockets influenced Latvian politics for years, and his arrest for alleged corruption offences has unsettled, but not derailed, his political influence. His most favoured and supported party, Latvia's Green and Farmers' Union, seems as interested in ameliorating the legal standing of Lembergs as in achieving any specific legislative goal. The media outlets within his thrall seem equally committed. Although Lembergs' long-term standing may be fatally compromised, his impact on elections in the short term remains a wild card in Latvia's politics. Not surprisingly, given all of the aforementioned events, popular trust in parliament, elected officials and in government is at a historical ebb. The 2010 elections returned Valdis Dombrovskis and the New Era to the premier's office, but with a similar divided and combative coalition cabinet.

In the spring of 2011, when Parliament refused to sanction a police search of prominent politicians' offices and apartments in an ongoing corruption case,

Latvia's state president, Valdis Zatlers, surprisingly used his constitutional power to call for a national referendum on dismissing the parliament. In response parliament did not re-elect the generally popular Zatlers to a new term in office and chose the unexpected former banker Andris Berziņš. In the summer Latvia's electorate voted to dismiss parliament by a staggering 95 per cent of the vote. Popular disaffection with the political elite has become almost super-saturated. Elections in the autumn of 2011 brought more of the same. Zatlers formed the latest new political force claiming to represent a break from the status quo. His Zatlers' Reform Party jumped to parliamentary preeminence but without a majority, government was little more than a reshuffling of the faces, positions, parties and platforms that brought more of the same.

In Lithuania the most dominant political story to grab the attention of the close, detailed examination of recent events is the greater power of the state president. In Estonia and Latvia governing power resides in the cabinet of ministers and its head, the minister president or premier, is the head of government. The state president is head of state, whose authority resides more in stature than in legally defined powers. In Lithuania, on the other hand, the state president is considerably more powerful and in many ways rules over the larger political scene. The state president is popularly elected and he or she in turn nominates a prime minister. The Seima in turn votes on the president's choice and can also vote to remove a prime minister. As a result, much of Lithuania's political history has revolved around the power-sharing arrangements between the state presidents, their prime ministers and parliaments. The rise and fall of prime ministers has primarily revolved around scandals and loss of confidence, and less so around the collapse of fragile coalition governments. The greater power and position of the president has also focused many of the most noticed political developments within the office. The first two presidents, Algirdas Brazauskas and Valdas Adamkus, each served a single term and each term included a regular shuffling of the prime minister's post. Adamkus's successor, Rolandas Paksas, however, brought political scandal directly to the presidency. Paksas had been a popular, conservative mayor of Vilnius and vaulted to the prime minister's office in 1999. His government was short-lived and he resigned in October of the same year. Over the next several years, Paksas returned to the mayorship of Vilnius and to the post of prime minister as well. In 2003 Paksas was the surprise run-off victor in the presidential elections, foiling Adamkus' attempt at reelection. His term began in February 2003 but was quickly sidetracked by frequent allegations of his ties to the Russian mafia. Stories swirled about his extortion of construction firms and his decree granting Lithuanian citizenship to a prominent Russian financial backer that was later ruled unconstitutional by Lithuania's Constitutional Court. Lithuania's Department of Security investigated the President and the Seima began impeachment procedures against him in 2004. On 6 April 2004 Paksas became the first European head of state to be impeached by parliament. Paksas's impeachment led to a second term for Adamkus, followed by the recent election of Dalia Grybauskaite in the summer of 2009.

Prior to winning the presidency, Grybauskaite excelled in the European Commission, serving as commissioner for education and culture and as commissioner of financial programming and the budget. Grybauskaite remains a popular and strong president, but the strong president and the weaker government and parliament is a characterization that continues to define Lithuania's politics.

The broad overview of political developments, however, suggests an entirely different course of political development in Estonia, Latvia and Lithuania, a course of remarkable stability within the parameters of incessant political infighting between ultimately very similar politicians. The broad overview also highlights key accomplishments and lasting challenges in the political developments of each state. Not surprisingly the great challenges facing Estonia, Latvia and Lithuania are intricately intertwined. The first and most pressing issue at the moment of restoring independence was establishing real national independence and security. First and foremost, this entailed the negotiated withdrawal of hundreds of thousands of Russian troops from Estonia, Latvia and Lithuania. In Lithuania's case the curious geographic challenge of Kaliningrad (formerly Königsberg), a part of the Russian republic blocked by Lithuanian territory, created an additional wrinkle. Beyond the removal of foreign troops, all three states needed to resolve the security of their international sovereignty. The interwar republics were unable to resolve this central, vital state interest. Part of resolving this issue included the second great challenge facing Estonia, Latvia and Lithuania in the 1990s: the geographic orientation of foreign policy and international relations and the nature of relations with neighbours, most crucially with Russia. The third great challenge involved defining the citizenry of each state. The most pressing part of this challenge consisted of the legal definition of ethnic minorities and Soviet-era migrants. With time, however, the state's relationship to its citizens has become the focus, with ethnic minorities emerging as only one potentially aggrieved party along with sexual minorities, racial minorities and others. This challenge reduces to the great debate about the role, relationship and responsibilities of state and citizen. This debate, however, has unfolded in the midst of the fourth great challenge, massive and complete economic transformation. The winners and losers of economic transformation almost inevitably influence discussions of citizenship and vice versa. Finally, the fifth great challenge revolves around the state's and elite's estrangement from society more generally. Systemic, endemic corruption is the most notorious example of this challenge, but it speaks of a more general malaise.

The removal of Soviet armed forces from Estonia, Latvia and Lithuania follow-ing the restoration of their independence in August 1991 was not a simple manner. All three republics were vital to Soviet security defences of their western border. Hundreds of thousands of troops were stationed in the Baltic region as well as an enormous amount of equipment. Further complicating the logistics of removing troops was the very real question, for Russia, of where to put them. Already hundreds of thousands of troops were returning from East Germany, Czechoslovakia, Poland, Hungary and Bulgaria. To the Russian military high command, the logistical inabil-ity to bring every soldier home quickly while stationing and provisioning them in new quarters made it an order that was impossible to carry out. In addition the high command was loath to lose the strategic importance of troops on the Baltic Sea for their defensive or – if needed – offensive capabilities to deal with war with Western Europe. Key naval bases were in Liepaja, Latvia, and in Paldiski, Estonia. Lithuania was key to the defence of Kaliningrad. Furthermore the Soviet armed forces' forward radar defences centred on bases throughout the Baltic, particularly in Latvia at Skrunda and along the northern shores of Kurzeme. The rapid removal of troops was also politically difficult for the government of the Soviet Union and then for Yeltsin's government in Russia. The rapid loss of influence in Eastern Europe was difficult for many to stomach, but the loss of influence in republics that many considered integral parts of the USSR was unfathomable. This sense of salvaging something of the USSR's might and territorial expanse reached its absurd end with the likes of Vladimir Zhirinovsky championing a return of Alaskan territories as well as all of Eastern Europe and all Soviet Republics. More influential policy makers developed and championed the idea of Russia's 'near abroad'. The term came to denote the former republics of the Soviet Union that were still considered to be of vital strategic importance. Furthermore Russia, without being asked, assumed a mantle of responsibility and protectiveness over the Russian and Slavic populations residing in these states. Most were free to return to Russia if they wished (or if they had ever come from Russia), and/or adopt Russian citizenship. From these asser-tions the Yeltsin government began to link the treatment of the Slavic populations of Estonia and Latvia particularly with the removal of Russian troops.

This linkage of troop removal and rights for Russians residing in Estonia and Latvia was unabashed extortion, but it was ineffective and counter-productive. If the old adage is that if someone pulls a gun, they should be willing to use it, it was never entirely clear if Russia was willing to use the gun, or if it had even been drawn. Some of the linkage debate was posturing and grandstanding. The Russian army was weak, demoralized and in a state of general collapse. The Russian state was equally weak and financially exhausted. If challenged Russia would have been hard pressed to mount and sustain an aggressive campaign against even the small republics of Estonia and Latvia without massive destabilizing effects in the international community and throughout Russian society. Ultimately international pressure and clear diplomatic language, specifically from the USA, refused to recognize the legitimacy of any linkage and forced the Russian government to accelerate and complete withdrawal. By 1994 (in retrospect a very short period of time) the great majority of troops had been withdrawn. The last troops left Estonia at the end of August 1994. Most left Latvia in 1994 and the Skrunda Radio Complex was destroyed in a controlled explosion on live television in 1995, but the very last handful of Russian troops did not leave until 1999. The slow withdrawal and the attempted blackmail further failed in that it reinforced the belief among many Estonians and Latvians that the Russians and Slavs in their midst were a fifth column. In Lithuania, where the issue of linkage was not central, troops left in 1993.

In the aftermath of independence restored, some Western analysts and local businessmen counselled Estonia, Latvia and Lithuania to continue to orient themselves to the East, at least economically. They argued that the markets of the former Soviet Union were familiar and that Estonian, Latvian and Lithuanian commodities had healthy 'brand awareness' in these markets. Correspondingly Western markets seemed impregnable due to the high cost of increased quality control and the massive amounts of resources needed for advertising and for breaking into new markets. Businessmen and politicians that reflected the interests of these businesses argued that good relations with Russia were needed to maintain the transit of resources, most notably oil and gas, through Baltic pipelines and out from Baltic ports. The transit lobby in Latvia became synonymous with 'Ventspils' interests', named for the port city on the Western coast that had been one of the USSR's most important ports for the export of oil, gas and chemicals. As long as Russian trainloads continued to race towards the port, Ventspils was almost assured of wealth beyond the standard Latvian town's dreams. The city's mayor, Aivars Lembergs, translated the wealth and importance of the city's transit trade into nearly unlimited political influence. If, however, the tap ran dry, then Ventspils's economic boom could turn to bust. As a result Lembergs's and Ventspils's interests were caricatured as a foreign relations posture that would do anything to maintain steady Russian transit trade. For most, however, the promise of wealth was weighed with the threat of past behaviour. The Russian market may be known and conquerable, but conquering armies were most likely to come from Russia as well. National security and guaranteed sovereignty trumped immediate economic rewards and Estonia, Latvia and Lithuania steadily charted a course away from the Soviet past and Russian present to a future in the European Union.

If the focus of a survey of the political history of Estonia, Latvia and Lithuania following the collapse of the Soviet Union is local and immediate, the constant string of scandals and personality clashes dominate the narrative. If, however, we move away from the immediate, we are presented with a stunningly quick evolution into full membership of the EU and the North Atlantic Treaty Organization (NATO). Estonia, Latvia and Lithuania broke finally from the Soviet Union in August 1991, at a time when there were only twelve members of the EU, most recently Greece, Portugal and Spain in 1981 and 1986. Reunification brought East Germany into the fold along with Austria, Finland and Sweden by the end of 1995. For the countries of Eastern Europe the Copenhagen criteria of 1993 seemed difficult and time-intensive. Yet Latvia and Lithuania, and most specifically Estonia, moved government policy to meet the requirements of EU membership. If almost all Warsaw Pact countries began negotiations in the 1990s to join the EU, Estonia did so with singular drive and purpose. Despite political squabbles and scandals at home, the Estonian delegation negotiating with the EU simply asked what needed to be done, and did so immediately. As a result Estonia was rewarded with a favourable decision to officially join the EU in December 2002. Latvia and Lithuania were less successful early on, and were initially rebuked with their progress towards EU accession, but they too joined the EU as full members in 2002. In the same year, at NATO's Prague Summit, Estonia, Latvia and Lithuania were invited to apply to join NATO, a process that was completed on 29 March 2004.

The complicated path to full membership in the twin pillars of security and prosperity in Europe varied considerably in the three states. When the first post-Soviet parliaments were elected in 1992 and 1993, although closer ties to the European Economic Community (the precursor to the EU) were almost universally declared in almost all political party platforms, almost none would have expected to successfully negotiate full ascension in ten years time. In negotiations with the EU Estonia took the clear lead. The Estonian delegation repeatedly impressed EU negotiators with their drive and determination to pass needed laws and regulations and to meet all the economic criteria of the Maastricht Treaty. The results were so laudable that the EU moved Estonia into the top tier of states most ready to join the EU, together with nations such as Hungary, the Czech Republic, Slovenia and Poland. At that time the EU gently rebuked Lithuania and particularly Latvia for not matching Estonia's pace. Changes to citizenship laws and the process of naturalization seemed particularly affected by EU lobbying and linkage between reform and membership. The most recent push for further integration into the EU is an ongoing attempt to enter the Eurozone and adopt the Euro as the official currency of each state. The economic crisis of 2008–10 slowed progress toward this goal, but Estonia again was the first to meet the established criteria and introduced the Euro in 2011. In Latvia and Lithuania the Euro is more likely to arrive in 2015, if not later.

Joining NATO was a more difficult transformation politically, but was perhaps less difficult to actually achieve. If almost all parties at least claimed to support closer economic ties with Western Europe and ultimately also supported, in some cases, tepid negotiations to join the EU, NATO was not so widely supported. Politicians that supported closer ties to Russia were vocally against NATO expansion along the eastern Baltic Sea. Furthermore Russia expended considerable energy on voicing their constant opposition to NATO expansion eastward. Mikhail Gorbachev claimed that the Western powers, while negotiating about the reunification of Germany, had promised that NATO would not expand further eastward. Russian political leaders viewed NATO expansion into the Czech Republic, Poland and Hungary in 1999 with indignation, but expansion into Estonia, Latvia and Lithuania was something even worse. To the Russian government and much of its public, NATO expansion into Estonia, Latvia and Lithuania was seen as a humiliating display of NATO power and its disregard for Russian sensibilities. Too often the Russian government continued to see the Baltic states as former republics of the Soviet Union and therefore interpreted NATO expansion as Russian defeat. They attempted to mobilize international opinion against the further expansion of NATO, but their efforts failed (and fed further into Baltic suspicions of Russian intentions). Still, NATO expansion was influenced considerably by a different external political factor: the USA. Unlike with the EU, the list of demands that Estonia, Latvia and Lithuania needed to meet to secure NATO membership was far simpler. The largest sticking point was the size of the military budget in each state and a demonstration of Baltic cooperation. The Baltic Air Surveillance Network, the Baltic Naval Squadron, the Baltic Defence College and the Baltic Battalion stand out as the most integrated and successful collaborative efforts of Estonia, Latvia and Lithuania since united Popular Front action against Soviet occupation. If Estonia led the charge into the ranks of the EU, Lithuania did so with NATO.

Still, NATO expansion into the Baltic region was most championed by the Clinton state department. When George W. Bush became president of the USA, many analysts assumed that the Bush administration would not champion Baltic membership in NATO so forcefully. Instead Condoleezza Rice, who taught as a political scientist specializing in the USSR at Stanford, pushed forcefully for NATO expansion into the Baltic states as quickly as possible from her position as National Security Advisor. Within a month of full membership, NATO air forces began policing Baltic air space, which therefore concluded a shocking transformation in a little more than a decade from being the western edge of the Soviet Union to the eastern perimeter of NATO.

Membership in NATO has not come without sacrifice; all three Baltic states have contributed forces to NATO and UN missions in Afghanistan, Iraq, Bosnia, Kosovo and Georgia, and these forces have experienced casualties. Currently the largest concentration of soldiers and casualties is in Afghanistan. Eight Estonian, three Latvian and one Lithuanian soldier have been killed in Afghanistan (a Lithuanian soldier was killed in Bosnia in a UN peacekeeping mission) through 2011. These numbers may seem very small, but their impact grows when wounded casualties are factored in to a mission force numbering no more than a few hundred soldiers from armed forces of no more than several thousand troops; 3 per cent of the active armed forces of Estonia, for example, are stationed in Afghanistan. The mission in Afghanistan is not particularly popular, although there is little organized anti-war activism at home. Most see the mission as the price paid for NATO membership. Extremist nationalists and provocateurs frequently complain on Internet message boards about Baltic troops taking part in an occupation when they themselves have been occupied, but the thread seems to have little popular traction. More ironic, although less discussed, is the return of Estonian, Latvian and Lithuanian troops to a land where troops from these countries conscripted into the Soviet army had fought more than two decades before.

Although Estonia, Latvia and Lithuania are full member states of the EU and NATO, and although many Estonians, Latvians and Lithuanians serve in high-ranking positions in each organization, there remains uncertainty about each organization on a public level. Some are not convinced that NATO would provide military aid in case of attack. They doubt that the initial treaty's declaration that 'an armed attack against one . . . shall be considered an attack against them all' will apply to Estonia, Latvia and/or Lithuania. Others question the economic advantage of EU membership and complain about Brussels' intervention in all aspects of life. The common slogan is: why fight so hard to get out of one union to rush into another? On any given day the number of Eurosceptics in Estonia, Latvia and Lithuania threatens to be a majority. Opposition to the EU cannot be simply dismissed. Many are distrustful of EU provisions, obligations and regulations as a piecemeal strangulation of Estonian, Latvian and Lithuanian particularism. This unease swells with each policy decision that seems detrimental to Estonia's, Latvia's or Lithuania's interests. Furthermore opposition politicians (and those that like to present themselves with opposition-like credentials) have become particularly adept at mining hostility towards the EU. They lambast the EU's perceived byzantine power structure as far removed from the realities of everyday Estonia, Latvia and Lithuania while presenting themselves as local engines of change and reform. More often than not, however, their accusations are saturated with artful condemnations and lack the substance of actual policy. Still, particularly in the light of the recent economic crisis, the EU provides the economic resources and capital without which massive infrastructure improvements would be exceedingly difficult. Furthermore the EU guarantees a place in a massive free market extending across Europe. NATO provides the guarantee of sovereignty that neither Estonia, Latvia nor Lithuania could ever secure in the interwar years.

Although Estonian, Latvian and Lithuanian nationalists remain sceptical of the foundations of sovereignty, continue to fear renewed Russian aggression (although the longer history of the region suggests paranoia is often substantiated), and see political developments within their states as moves in a great chess match waged by forces aligned against Baltic independence, qualitatively and quantitatively Estonia, Latvia and Lithuania have never been as safe as they are on the eve of 2012. They are full members of the world's most powerful military alliance and of the world's most wealthy economic union (as defined by GDP or purchasing power parity calculations). Yet this relatively unparalleled degree of security and sovereignty has not lessened Baltic, and particularly Estonian and Latvian, fears about long-term survival. Relations with Russia continue to be strained at the best of times (in no small part due to the demonstrative actions of Russia, even if their ability to act is massively tempered by the EU, NATO and Russian weakness). More crucially, internal relations with ethnic minorities have shown few signs of improvement, although there have been relatively few signs that relations have worsened considerably. As material, international and statistical conditions have buoyed the standing of Estonians and Latvians, the lack of movement in redressing ethnic grievances is increasingly disturbing.

The question of the treatment of ethnic minorities has been less acute in Lithuania, where the great majority of the population is ethnically Lithuanian and a 'zero plus one' citizenship policy was adopted at the end of Soviet occupation. Still, Lithuania struggles with accommodating sizeable ethnic minorities (primarily Russian) in its largest towns and cities and with Polish communities south and east of Vilnius. Relations with Polish communities hearken back to interwar ethnic and international tensions revolving around the occupation of Vilnius. The iconic place that Vilnius has in Lithuanian and Polish memories guarantees that the perception of how minorities are treated outstrips the actual policies of governments. Citizenship has not been a focal point, but questions of language, language instruction in schools and the associational rights of ethnic minorities will likely continue to fester for the foreseeable future. Ultimately state policy will likely evolve into a pattern that neither accommodates the harsher demands of Lithuanian nationalists demanding assimilation, nor grants sweeping rights to a vocal Polish minority that is particularly small on a national scale.

In Estonia and Latvia however, accommodation with ethnic minorities has been a far more difficult path; one that has offered few lasting solutions and continues to simmer mass-based ethnic discontent with the status quo. The ethnic issue, meaning the possible likelihood of Estonians and Latvians becoming ethnic minorities in their titular republics, played a central role in the mass mobilization of the late Soviet period. This starting point, however, did not guarantee that the majority of Estonians and Latvians wanted to disenfranchise the bulk of the Russians living in their midst. These Russians and Slavs generally supported Estonian and Latvian demands for greater autonomy and independence from Moscow. The decision to base citizenship on the population of the pre-war republics, and to defer any changes to this basis for the foreseeable future, cast political discourse in an ethnic vein that far exceeded realities on the ground. As politicians continued to vie for predominantly ethnic Estonian and Latvian votes, while largely ignoring (if not presenting themselves as hostile to) disenfranchised Russian, Belorussian and Ukrainian communities, politics became increasingly ethnic. Slavic-speaking communities became increasingly alienated from the official politics of the states within which they lived (but were not citizens of), and Estonian and Latvian politicians continued to build political communities largely devoid of a sizeable portion of their real states.

Through the middle of the 1990s a hard ethnic political line shaped legislative decision-making. Former Communists needed to prove their nationalist mettle and agreeing with restrictive citizenship laws was the path of least resistance. In Latvia, for example, citizenship was quickly fixed to the pre-war Republic's population, but the rights of non-citizens were less quickly determined. Hundreds of thousands of residents were thrown into a legal grey area concerning property rights, employ-ment rights and the right to re-enter the state. As these shortcomings came to international attention and were generally addressed fairly, the looming issue of the legal process for naturalization remained unresolved. Latvia placed itself temporarily in the curious position of disenfranchising a sizeable minority of its population overnight without providing a process for those people to acquire citizen-ship. Ultimately, currying nationalist votes, Latvia's parliament passed a quota- or windows-based naturalization law. The law allowed non-citizen residents to become citizens after passing a battery of exams, and meeting residence requirements, but this was not enough. The quota system determined that the number of new citizens must stay within a prescribed ethnic percentage for the state as a whole. To Latvian nationalists this provision guaranteed a considerable Latvian ethnic majority after decades of Soviet occupation. To everyone else this law enshrined the collective over the individual, an idea fundamentally at odds with Western thinking. In other words, even if an individual absolutely qualified for citizenship, she or he would wait indefinitely for collective demographics to allow their citizenship. To almost everyone else this law was a fundamental perversion of legal practice and received considerable criticism. Ultimately parliament buckled under withering interna-tional pressure and liberalized citizenship and naturalization laws. The new law automatically granted citizenship to everyone born and residing in Latvia since 1991 and lifted the quota system from the naturalization process. The amendments satisfied EU concerns, but their introduction and adoption seemed dictated entirely from abroad; Latvia was shaping its policy to meet the standards of a foreign body and not of its own volition. Nationalist politicians responded with a signature campaign that generated a constitutionally mandated referendum on the citizen-ship law. EU representatives subtly suggested that membership in the EU hinged on the vote, but still with a limited electorate and a crest of anti-EU sentiment, the vote seemed in doubt. In the autumn of 1998 Latvia voted narrowly to accept the looser citizenship laws. Soon after, with the procedure for citizenship defined, a small wave of residents applied for and obtained citizenship. Since this defining moment, however, the acquisition of citizenship has slowed to a trickle and the further liberalization of citizenship policy has not been entertained.

To become naturalized in Latvia, an individual must pass a language exam and a test on Latvia's history and constitution and fulfil a residency requirement. The requirements are not excessively onerous and are more liberal than the naturaliza-tion process of many of the 27 members of the European Union. A considerable number of Latvia's non-resident population seem likely to meet these qualifications, but current patterns rule out a quick naturalization of Latvia's non-citizens. Instead demographics will slowly whittle away the number of non-citizens, since everyone born in Latvia after 1991 qualifies for citizenship and year after year a greater number of non-citizens become elderly. Slowly, year by year, the non-citizen population will decrease. By 2011 fewer than 320,000 people, roughly 14 per cent of the total population, were non-citizens. Furthermore the majority of Russians living in Latvia in 2011 were citizens. The percentage of inhabitants that are citizens has climbed to more than 83 per cent in 2011. Yet the steady drop in the number of non-citizens has hardly ameliorated ethnic divisions in Latvia. The nationalist discourse that accompanied the reforms to the citizenship law shifted to new political arenas after the once thorny issue of citizenship was largely settled. After 1998 language and education laws became the new battlegrounds of ethnic politics.

To ethnic Latvian and Estonian nationalists the root cause of unrest against Soviet rule in the 1980s was the struggle to preserve the ethnic Latvian and Estonian nation. The Soviet Union was a mortal threat to survival, and the migrants that Soviet occupation brought into Estonia and Latvia were an ongoing threat. New citizenship laws and fragile coalition governments suggested that Slavic political power and clout would increase with time, an idea greeted with great alarm. The only defence against this new threat to national survival was using the power of the state to guarantee the fundamentally Latvian and/or Estonian nature of the state. Education policies and the usage of language in public spaces became the preferred tools in a new rush to integrate and/or assimilate Russians. The approaches in both spheres lacked necessary components of negotiation and consensus-building. As a result Latvian nationalists' concerns to ensure the general understanding of the Latvian language came across as dictates to Russian schools to quickly expand the numbers of hours taught in the Latvian language. Likewise, moves to maintain an ethnic Latvian character in cities included signage laws that demanded the dominant usage of the Latvian language, even for commercial and social events in overwhelmingly Slavic communities. The government haphazardly moulded a social integration programme. The overall result was a heated discussion about integration and assimilation. Ethnic Latvians imagined a process in which Russians and other Slavs would become more familiar with the Latvian language, become citizens and ultimately develop a greater allegiance to the Latvian state. This entire process would unfold in Latvian. To many Russians, however, this description sounded more like a policy of assimilation than integration. What, they asked, was being integrated into the state from their community? Social integration was looked upon with suspicion, particularly in light of the difficult development of citizenship rights, and many responded by choosing neither integration nor assimilation. They demanded an entirely different option, or saw themselves as alienated from the state in which they lived.

In Estonia the political division is similar, although in key ways it is far more potentially explosive (while in other ways it is less so). In June 1993, when the Riigikogu, drew up legislation to define the legal rights of non-citizens, its 'Law on Aliens' suggested the dawn of an era of divisive and potentially combative ethnic politics. The Law gave few rights to non-citizens and did not differentiate between recent migrants and those born and raised in Soviet Estonia. The most ominous provisions outlined a process by which non-citizens would have to apply for residence and work permits. Initial permits would be temporary and permanent ones would be dependent on sources of income. Alarmists saw this law as the first legal step towards state-sanctioned repatriation of Slavic residents to Russia. In Narva, an industrial city in northeastern Estonia bordering Russia in which Russians make up more than 80 per cent of the population, the 'Law on Aliens' was seen as an opening salvo in a concerted Estonian ethnic political campaign. While international bodies, most importantly the CSCE (Commission on Security and Cooperation in Europe), pressured the Estonian government and parliament to soften or clarify provisions within the law, the city council of Narva provocatively announced a local referendum on territorial autonomy. Ultimately the Narva City Council overplayed its hand and many of its leaders became marginalized as last-minute compromises averted a further escalation of the crisis. The compromises included a revision of the 'Law on Aliens' in line with CSCE recommendations and a slate of local candidates and politicians in Narva keen for better relations with the national government. The historian David Smith sees this victory for peaceful resolution as 'a testament to the political culture of restraint in Estonia . . . not just for the Estonian government, but for the local leaders in Narva'.[10] Through the 1990s revisions and amendments to citizenship and language laws (most notably in 1995) and spikes in naturalization rates kept ethno-political relations tense. As with the resolution of the 'Law on Aliens', compromise in practice ameliorated each situation, but the legal status of non-citizens was slower to change. Similarly attempts at social integration have been half-hearted in implementation and acceptance.

Although the Slavic populations of Estonia and Latvia are primarily located in the largest cities and in the east, in Estonia ethnic division is more pronounced throughout society. Even during the Soviet years sociological studies suggested that Estonians and Russians lived in two solitudes, seldom crossing the social boundaries between them. They were less likely to work or socialize with each other. As a result Estonians and Russians stereotypically are portrayed as being largely foreign to each other. This greater social distance between ethnic communities can fuel ethnic violence when it erupts, as it did during the riots around the moving of the Bronze Soldier, a monument to Soviet Second World War casualties. In Latvia, on the other hand, Latvians and Russians tend to know each other more on an individual level. The conflicting sentiments of anger/distrust of Russian (or Latvian) political parties with more positive evaluations of individuals can soften or diffuse more widespread ethnic violence.

Ethnic divisions remain central to politics in contemporary Latvia. Eventually a political party that draws its electoral support from the Russian community will gain power or win influential portfolios in a coalition government. Latvian nationalists and their politicians forecast this scenario as doomsday and equate it with a loss of Latvian sovereignty. If these nationalists continue to see a Russian party in power as the greatest threat to Latvia, they will form coalition governments with ever more contradictory parties by working with all ethnic parties to keep a Russian party at bay. This in turn will continue to fuel Russian suspicions of Latvian designs against them. The very real threat is that these divisions will ossify and politics will be distilled to ethnic concerns first and foremost. Through the 1990s and 2000s disingenuous politicians manipulated fears and perceptions to move into and remain in power as the new political elite. This elite is largely the political face of a handful of oligarchs who campaign to preserve economic power. Not surprisingly, with power as the prime goal, systemic corruption has grown almost unchecked. This in turn has led to a different divide in the political life of Latvia: between the state/political elite and the populace at large. Although not entirely absent, corruption and the overwhelming power of oligarchs seems less developed in Estonia than in Latvia. To more thoroughly understand the new politico-economic elite and endemic corruption, we must turn to a more detailed discussion of the economic development of Estonia, Latvia and Lithuania over the past century.

CHAPTER 4

Economic Developments

The massive political transformations endured by Estonia, Latvia and Lithuania over the past 150 years are equalled by revolutionary economic transformations. The two have almost always been inextricably intertwined. Late nineteenth-century industrialization, modernization and urban growth tore apart traditional, tsarist and Baltic German institutions. War and revolution devastated economies and people alike. Independence involved state-building and entirely new economic models. Soviet occupation brought deportations and terror, but also socialist transformation. Nazi occupation brought the Holocaust and more terror, together with an economy completely subservient to the war effort. The return of Soviet rule introduced five-year plans in a central command economy, collectivization, heavy industrialization and migration of workers. The collapse of the Soviet Union also meant the collapse of this economic order. The Baltic states' aspirations to join the European Union included a fundamental reordering of all economic life, and momentary, fleeting success brought euphoria and new expectations. The most recent economic calamity, and the slow, painful recovery that has followed, has simply reinforced the common theme of economic development in the Baltic region: massive, violent economic disruptions have come with dizzying regularity and, as with states and populations, no general system has remained in place for more than a few decades. If economic analysts crave stability, there has never been any in Estonia, Latvia or Lithuania.

Early economic history

Estonia, Latvia and Lithuania suffered acutely from the distorted, convoluted 'iron laws' of economic development professed by Soviet leaders and theorists.

Nevertheless, more basic and fundamental laws of economic development have shaped the region (and the world) for millennia. The first and foremost of these is that a society's capabilities are defined and limited by the productive capacities of said society. Second, long-term economic development is incremental and sustained (not a boom harvest), whereas economic calamity and collapse can be almost instantaneous, and often is often entirely extraneous to immediate, local developments. Estonia, Latvia and Lithuania have repeatedly experienced each of these phenomena.

For the bulk of settled human history, in the Baltic region as well as everywhere else, the length of the growing season, temperature and precipitation, and a crop's yield, defined prosperity or poverty more than any other factors. Despite its northerly latitude the Baltic Sea region has relatively moderate temperatures and sufficient, yet not overly abundant rainfall. Still, the eastern littoral of the Baltic Sea is decidedly disadvantaged in two ways: the growing season is relatively short, allowing for only one harvest, and that of generally hearty, cold-resistant crops; and, until the late nineteenth century, agricultural yield was very poor. Some staples of the modern Estonian, Latvian and Lithuanian diet, such as the potato, were introduced only in the last 200 years. As a result societies in modern-day Estonia, Latvia and Lithuania, all overwhelmingly agricultural, were restricted by relatively poor agricultural production. With agricultural productivity so low, most people were tied to agricultural production for their livelihoods. Agricultural yield and production simply could not support many other people devoted to other professions. Many of the supplemental sources of food so common to the region, mushroom- and berry-picking to name the two most popular, became desperate survival skills when unpredictable harvests failed. Vestiges of this necessity survive to this day, as witnessed by the author, who listened in as two elderly Latvians discussed at length the way in which poisonous mushrooms could be made edible (primarily through hours of boiling in vinegar), although still very unpalatable. The conversation's setting, at a funeral, added to the sense of the macabre. Even the ever present sea and the ability to hunt were of limited value. Baltic Sea fishing remained dangerous and returns meagre (fishing villages remained some of the poorest until very recently), while hunts were difficult in thick forests and potentially risky with hunting privileges reserved for the nobility. Latvians, Lithuanians and particularly Estonians are fond of drawing parallels between their states and societies and the Nordic countries. Perhaps the closest resemblance is in the extremely difficult agricultural conditions prior to the nineteenth century and the frequent accompanying rural poverty, want and misery.[1]

This harsh description of pre-modern agriculture and thus pre-modern life for almost everyone in pre-modern Estonia, Latvia and Lithuania is, in part, an exaggeration. The economic history of the region included long-distance trade contacts and times of relative prosperity. Even in the late Neolithic period, when agriculture was at its most primitive, the archaeological record shows dazzling ornaments, shards of pottery and vestiges of clothing that speak of a diverse and prosperous society. Baltic amber made its way to the Mediterranean world; the rivers of the Baltic were the highways of Nordic–Slavic trade (and conquest). After the twelfth century, when the local inhabitants of modern-day Estonia and Latvia gradually became tied to conquering German nobles and priests, ultimately as serfs, and when the Lithuanian peasantry sunk into greater domination from a Polish and Lithuanian nobility, pockets of agricultural ingenuity or mercantile success remained. Several Baltic cities were vibrant members of the Hanseatic League and Vilnius became a centre of trade and learning. Still, for the bulk of the peasantry (which made up most the population), and for the greater part of settled human history in the Baltic region, survival was very difficult because of relatively poor agricultural conditions. Nobles and clergy that relied upon the surplus taken from these poor peasants were restricted in their luxury and excess. Economic progress, when it existed, was slow and incremental.

If progress was slow, catastrophe was often immediate and long-lasting for individuals and societies alike. Sickness, injury and death were constant threats to pre-modern peasants that could unravel the most prosperous family into despair and abject poverty. The death of a family member or a draught horse needed for agricultural labour could be a handicap. Disease and injury could be even worse: a chance broken leg could become a hobbled lifetime and tip the difficult scales against even a prosperous peasant family. For society, an outbreak of disease (most spectacularly the plague, which devastated all of the Baltic lands), repeated poor harvests, war or any combination of the above could overshadow the slow, incremental progress of generations before. This was the most common economic picture before the mid-nineteenth century: most people depended on local crops produced in relatively poor local conditions. These conditions produced painfully little in the way of development and progress and were always in danger of being overwhelmed by extraneous circumstances.

Through the eighteenth and early nineteenth centuries the condition of peasants arguably became worse. The aspirations and appetites of ruling elites, be they local noblemen desperate for grander palaces and more opulent lifestyles (all needed to maintain prestige and position) or rulers of state eager for more power and/or more territory, squeezed more of the meagre surpluses from their overburdened peasantry. Apparently peasants rebelled more often, but the gap between their tools of resistance and the oppressive force of near-modern armies doomed these acts of rebellion out of hand. Far more influential was the revolutionary change of state and society elsewhere and its effect on the power of states. Across Western Europe agricultural advancements and the first stirrings of the Industrial Revolution created exponentially more wealth and hence power for some states. If the Russian tsar (in control of the entire eastern Baltic littoral by the end of the eighteenth century) wanted to keep pace with the modern European states, his society and its economy had to provide on this new level. This seemed only possible through a radical transformation of society and its economic foundations across the Empire. This transformation began in the Baltic Provinces of Estland, Livland and Courland (most of the territory of modern Estonia and Latvia).

The fundamental social impediment to modernization seemed to be serfdom and its myriad restrictions on peasant labour and agricultural production. Serfdom, however, was also the social underpinning of the state and hence was very difficult to transform. Nevertheless, in the Baltic Provinces at the beginning of the nineteenth century, Tsar Alexander I and a group of relatively progressive Baltic German nobles authored legislation that freed serfs across the Baltic Provinces. By the 1820s serfdom was abolished in the Baltic Provinces, but with disappointing immediate results. Former serfs were denied possession of land (as private or communal property), did not receive freedom of movement, and continued to carry many obligations to their former lords, who still controlled the administration of law and order in the countryside. For the first few decades conditions may well have become worse for most peasants. Revisions to the laws in the 1840s and after, however, gradually allowed for peasants to purchase land and to move from the countryside to urban areas. These important changes would fundamentally alter society and its economy through the latter part of the nineteenth century.

As previously mentioned, the second half of the nineteenth century was a cauldron of social fermentation throughout modern-day Estonia and Latvia (in Lithuania, emancipation of the serfs came in the 1860s and the timeline of developments was significantly skewed later), which saw the rise of extreme need and misery for a landless poor and the roots of radical revolutionary sentiments, but also material progress that ushered in the first great era of modernization, urbanization, and industrialization to the eastern Baltic region. In the countryside the dire conditions were further compromised by an apparent baby boom – the population began to expand considerably, although a precise causal reason is difficult to pin down.[2] As population increased in the countryside, but opportunities and capacity there decreased or remained stagnant, urban migration acted as a stopgap release valve for discontent in the countryside. Urban migration provided the needed manpower for the radical transformation that was happening in the cities of Imperial Russia.

Broadly speaking, the modernization and industrialization of tsarist Russia in the late nineteenth century is referred to as the Witte System, after the minister of finance and, later, prime minister Sergei Witte, who championed these reforms.[3] Witte saw the rapid modernization and industrialization of Russia as essential if it were to remain a great power. The dilemma was that in Western Europe the private sector provided much of the stimulus for industrialization through investment and entrepreneurship. The private sector in Russia, by comparison, was weak and Witte believed that the Russian Empire could not wait for the private sector to develop. Instead, presaging a strategy that would be common in post-colonial states, Witte championed the role of the state as a necessary replacement for the private sector. If private enterprise alone would not build railway systems across the empire, the state would have to take its place. Equally important to the 'Witte system' was attracting foreign, direct investment for the modernization and industrialization of Russia on lucrative terms, more or less guaranteed by the state. The nexus of much of the industrialization and modernization of imperial Russia was in the Baltic Provinces of Estland, Livland, Courland and Finland. Mass investments in railway-building and port improvements were central to this larger empire-wide plan. The railway lines built across modern-day Estonia and Latvia were meant to transport goods from the interior of Russia to the rapidly expanding ports of Riga, Helsinki, Liepaja, Ventspils and Tallinn, to name just a few. Finished industrial goods from Western Europe needed for the continued modernization of Russia entered the empire through these very same Baltic Sea ports. Much of the industrial development of the urban centres of Finland, Estland, Livland and Courland made up the second steps in the Witte system for transforming the economy. Railway car and wagon manufacturers in Riga, for example, eliminated the need to import these goods and new textile factories produced more valuable semi-processed goods, such as cloth, for export as opposed to raw materials. Across the board, from the rise of a chemical industry to banking, the modernization and industrialization of the urban centres of the Baltic Provinces and Finland was the vanguard of an empire-wide plan. The rapid pace and massive scope of the changes would have been impossible to imagine from within the Baltic Provinces alone;

there was neither the needed capital for investment, the supplies for production, the energy resources for power nor the market for finished goods.

By the end of the nineteenth century the urban centres of the Baltic Provinces and Finland were prominent industrial centres on a par with many similar centres across Europe and North America. Modernization followed closely behind industrial development, and urban towns saw the rapid development of streetcar systems, telephone and telegraph networks, modern plumbing, sanitation and electrical power. As elsewhere early industrialization created huge disparities between wealth and poverty. The chasm between social classes was further exacerbated by the restrictive political system of tsarist Russia and the paucity of equal civil rights across society. Political power remained overwhelmingly in the hands of the tsar and his representatives in the Baltic Provinces, including the Baltic German nobility.

Still, individual Estonians, Latvians and to a lesser degree Lithuanians amassed great wealth through real estate development, lumber, publishing and consumer goods and services. Among the working class considerable variation existed between skilled and unskilled workers and there was an ever growing number of 'professionals', be they lawyers and bureaucrats or teachers and physicians. In the countryside, where the pull of labour for factories siphoned off some of the rural poor, land hunger was the dominant driving resentment of the rural economy. Most land belonged to the entrenched Baltic German nobility, although increasing numbers of Estonians and Latvians succeeded in becoming smallholders, owning their farms outright. Some were even nicknamed 'grey barons' for amassing holdings and wealth on a par with the hereditary nobility. The majority of agricultural workers did not own the land they worked. They either sold their labour to other farms or worked in a kind of sharecropping economy where some of their produce went to the legal owners of the lands they worked. Not surprisingly among the rural landless poor, the majority of the rural population, simple slogans such as 'land for the landless' and 'land to those who work it' were immensely popular. Still, year after year in country and city, socio-economic patterns became increasingly more variegated and complex. This complexity, however, tended to break down and simplify during crises and conflict, most violently during the Revolutions of 1905, 1917 and 1918.

As stated, the industrialization and modernization of the Baltic Provinces was an integral part of the so-called Witte Plan for modernizing all of Imperial Russia. The benchmark study of this system referred to the plan as the 'Witte gamble'. By using the power and resources of the state to kick-start industrialization, with a heavy reliance on direct foreign investment, Witte gambled that an economic boom would take hold before investments needed to bear significant returns and before the resentments and grievances of the disenfranchised and downtrodden boiled over into active rebellion. The gamble was played for high stakes in the Baltic Provinces and the economic grievances of workers and peasants fuelled the Revolution of 1905. After the revolution was put down, society and the economy continued to develop at its earlier dizzying pace. Whether wealth and modernity could take root throughout the Baltic Provinces through this non-violent transformation remained an open question. What is clear, without a doubt, is that the path taken up until 1914 was one shared with the modernization and industrialization of the entire Russian Empire.

The First World War ended the tsarist Witte plan for industrialization just as it ended the tsarist state. In the Baltic Provinces and in Lithuania the war's impact was no less extensive. Ultimately the First World War led to a series of wars that produced the independent states of Finland, Estonia, Latvia and Lithuania, but also terminated the modernization and industrialization of the Baltic Provinces within a larger Russian context. This end was all the more final with the actual evacuation of most of the industry of the Baltic Provinces.[4] Most workers also fled or were conscripted into the tsarist army. The pre-war economic infrastructure ceased to exist and the once booming centres, such as Riga, became silent ports with a fraction of their pre-war population and less of their industry. Wars triumphantly brought independence, suddenly a 'long-cherished' goal of Estonian, Latvian, and Lithuanian nationalists, but they also brought complete economic collapse and a deep identity crisis in terms of what would be the economic basis of the newly independent states. The new states faced the Herculean task of repairing war damage (almost total in the hardest-hit regions) and building a new economy from nothing.

In the truest example of political economy, where economic and political decisions intertwine, all three newly independent republics decided to support the creation of hundreds of thousands of smallholder agriculturalists. There was little hope of an industrial revival; even when short-lived, socialist governments in power negotiated trade deals with the Soviet Union, there was no return to the industrial character of the pre-First World War-era Baltic Provinces.[5] Without a market to the East, the newly independent Baltic Republics similarly struggled to break into markets for finished goods in Western Europe. The three states turned increasingly to an agricultural identity. The major urban centres of all three states, belying their earlier industrial credentials (which were least developed in Lithuania), became primarily administrative capitals and not industrial centres. Instead the Baltic Republics relied upon the currency of smallholders, dairy and bacon, and the exploitation of forestry resources, as the underpinnings of new economies. Government subsidies to agriculture or to new farmers became common political talking points, and to some degree agricultural advances came on the backs of urban dwellers. State support went as far as supporting and establishing wide-arching agricultural reform that expropriated land (with no real compensation) from the Baltic German nobility and assigned it to primarily ethnic Estonian and Latvian smallholders. In absolute economic terms some have questioned the foresight of such reforms, arguing that large-scale farms may have produced more profitable goods (specifically wheat and other cereals). Still, in the larger view, it seems likely that agricultural reform – even if supporting less efficient smallholding agriculture – successfully transformed the bulk of the rural population into shareholders of the new state. Other forms of agriculture may have produced better immediate short-term market results, but the rise of smallholding agriculture invested the previously explosive and radical landless rural poor in the new Baltic states.

Throughout the interwar years political calculations trumped economics in setting the new states' economic foundations. The heavy investment in and government support of locally grown sugar beet for domestic sugar needs in Latvia is a clear example. Encouraging sugar beet production supported farmers and seemed a sound policy of import substitution; in other words, Latvia could produce its own sugar rather than buying from abroad. The political logic was overwhelming and most political parties and politicians wholeheartedly supported the plan. In later years the popular anecdote was that Kārlis Ulmanis, Latvia's dictator, drank his coffee with three spoons of sugar, one from each of Latvia's factories that processed domestic sugar beet into sugar. The symbol remained strong through the Soviet era and into independence in the 1990s. In the 1990s, however, as well as in the 1920s and '30s, sugar production was not profitable. In the 1920s one of the few voices raised against the sugar beet project came from the wealthy, conservative nationalist newspaper mogul Arveds Bergs. Bergs often championed using the state to improve the lot of the Latvian nation, but he also had a keen financial sense. He pointed out that the final cost of sugar produced in Latvia from Latvia's sugar beet was higher than the price of better-quality sugar from sugar cane on the world market. Domestic sugar would only be viable if it was forced upon the population with tariffs and other restrictions (thereby forcing the population to pay excessively for the commodity), or with massive government subsidies, also ultimately paid for by taxpayers.

Political influence impeded economic activity in many other damaging ways as well. Corruption permeated society and political favouritism and patronage ran through the financial institutions of the new states. Foreign affairs also impinged upon economic decision-making. A Social Democratic government in Latvia in 1927 and 1928 signed an economic treaty with the Soviet Union to rebuild the industrial sector of the economy, more from their conviction that such a development would create more industrial workers that would then vote for Social Democrats than from any greater appreciation of how such a treaty would impact Latvia's economy. A host of trade wars over tariffs and regulations marred relations between Estonia and Latvia, and Latvia and Lithuania, as well with Germany.[6] These disputes were as defined by national, political posturing as by firm economic principles. Finally, in Lithuania, where the Vilnius question determined everything else, the hostile relations between Poland and Lithuania seriously hampered economic development.

Nevertheless the interwar era witnessed great economic development on a small, local scale, repeated endlessly through the three states. The reconstruction after the devastation of war and the construction of hundreds of thousands of farms, hundreds of schools, local government offices, hospitals, clinics, train stations and more was revolutionary. The impetus was from within local communities, the resources were often from local communities, and the end results served local communities. With hindsight some of these developments may have been counterproductive or could have been better managed, but the democratic principle of economic decision-making invested the citizens of the three states in the new states. Decades later, after countless years of occupation and loss of control, the simple fact that Estonians, Latvians and Lithuanians had once been their own masters coloured their recollections of independence with nostalgia about ever greater accomplishments. The cherished memory was that the physical infrastructure of the independent states was once decided upon and built by their citizens.

By the mid- to late 1920s, war reconstruction was largely complete in all three states, and national and local economies were settling into some routine. To be sure, disputes about economic policy were as commonplace as endemic malfeasance, graft, corruption and financial scandals, but the states witnessed slow economic development and year on year growth. Using most economic indicators Estonia, Latvia and Lithuania's economic growth accelerated away from the USSR example, but closing the economic gap with the industrialized states of Western Europe was still a distant ideal. Gaps remained, particularly in the mechanization and electrification of production.[7] Further economic development would require considerable capital investment to build infrastructure. Access to capital emerged as the Achilles heel of economic development. There was simply too little domestic capital to invest, particularly with competing popular demands for capital in a democratic system. Furthermore foreign capital was aloof, uninterested or hostile. German capital particularly could have been a natural source, but Baltic German bitterness over land reform fuelled a strong anti-investment lobby in Germany as well as ongoing legal challenges at the League of Nations. Municipal economic development could be similarly hamstrung. The city of Riga, for example, refused to honour a pre-war loan from Lazard Brothers of London for the construction of the Riga tram system. Lazard Brothers, in return, pressed other financial institutions to refrain from lending money to the Riga municipal government until the outstanding debt issue was resolved. These concerns about the inability to attract foreign investment were less significant when the economies of Estonia, Latvia and Lithuania shared in the post-war boom of much of Europe, but the global depression highlighted the weaknesses and limitations of economic development.

The depression in Estonia, Latvia and Lithuania had several components. Banks in all three states were, in modern parlance, leveraged to banks across Europe. As banks in Austria and Germany collapsed, ripples were felt in the Baltic area as well. Runs on banks, although not commonplace, existed, and the private banking industry suffered considerably. The close ties between banks and political parties heightened public anger at the cozy relationship between wealth and power at the expense of the people. As the depression settled across Europe, orders for Estonian, Latvian and Lithuanian products, primarily lumber and agricultural goods, dropped. With fewer products sold, Estonians, Latvians and Lithuanians could not afford to purchase so many European manufactured goods. Finally, on a state scale, the drastic decrease in economic activity and the difficult economic straits experienced by many citizens led to a marked drop in tax revenue. National and local governments often pursued the shortsighted immediate policy of pursuing delinquent taxes and raising the taxes of those that were still solvent to bring some needed resources into state coffers. These policies, however, often drove more people into debt. The extent of the depression in Estonia, Latvia and Lithuania has received too little attention in the scholarly field. A common, yet incorrect, view holds that the depression was not as severe in Estonia, Latvia and Lithuania as elsewhere. On the contrary, bread lines, debtors' auctions and mass unemployment existed across all three states. More significantly, the relative political peace in Estonia and Latvia was shaken. Sessions of parliament and municipal councils alike degenerated to name-calling and accusations. Communist sympathizers challenged the merits of the existing economic system more vocally. The most difficult years were 1930, 1931 and 1932. By 1933 economic indicators suggested the beginnings of recovery, but the political moods of Estonia and Latvia were still toxic. In 1934, in Estonia and Latvia, the democratic system did not survive to see the clearer signs of economic recovery. Authoritarian coups led by founding political fathers in each state dissolved parliaments, suspended constitutional laws and ushered in authoritarian rule. In the Latvian case Kārlis Ulmanis, who as the minister president in March 1934 sat in on cabinet meetings that discussed the clear end of the economic crisis, disingenuously used the perception of ongoing economic crisis as one of the defining reasons for grabbing dictatorial powers in May 1934.

The economic repercussions of the end of the democratic systems of government in Lithuania (1926) and Estonia and Latvia (1934) were not immediately clear. Most would have anticipated that economic rewards would flow to regime supporters and that more corruption would ensue. Still, initial rapprochements between the new regimes and economic leaders suggested that common ground could be found between them. As the regimes became more firmly entrenched, however, they began to attempt to use the power of the state to mould the economies to their liking, although with mixed results. Generally, in each state, a slow slide to state capitalism trumped the prior primacy of the market. The growing state dominance of the economy reflected similar ideas across most of Europe. Each state attempted to direct economic activity towards the regime's more general national goals. This pattern was most developed in Latvia, where the state controlled almost all facets of the economy by 1940 through state-controlled cartels that determined industrial activity, and through state-controlled agricultural cooperatives that determined agricultural prices.

Fitfully and periodically the Ulmanis regime employed the power of the state to transform the country into a more 'Latvian Latvia'. In the realm of the economy this included the dispossession of economic wealth from primarily Baltic German and Jewish owners of businesses and real estate. The programme was not thorough or systematic, but the power and wealth of the state attempted to limit the economic importance of ethnic minorities in the new regimes. State acquisitions were not passed on to ethnic Latvians, but rather became the property of the state. The growing power of the state in all economic aspects had the unintended consequence of easing some Soviet and Nazi economic policies during their initial occupations. The markets and autonomous, individual economic activity had already been severely compromised and the state already gripped many of the commanding economic levers of society. All that remained to occupying powers was to take the helm and accelerate the course while changing who would benefit.

There is no general consensus about the economic balance sheet of the authoritarian regimes. Apologists and those looking for a gilded age repeat the propaganda claims of the three regimes without closer inspection. The most thorough critiques strongly suggest that the economic policies of the authoritarian regimes were seriously flawed, and that economic crisis would have been imminent if not for the more general, and more imminent, crisis of the Second World War. Despite public calls for economic self-sufficiency in the face of an increasingly hostile European world at the end of the 1930s, the three regimes understood the acute dilemma of small states in terms of economic development. Development fuelled by domestic investment would be slow and piecemeal; would this satisfy the population, particularly considering the bravado of regime propaganda? Massive foreign investment in the late 1930s seemed possible only by becoming a protectorate of Nazi Germany or Soviet Russia. Foreign capital from other sources seemed highly unlikely. Some notable exceptions existed, such as the role of Swedish capital in building the hydroelectric dam at Ķegums in Latvia. The dam highlighted the need for more development. It met much of the electrical power need of Latvia, but only because Latvia was still relatively un-electrified. The economic quandary of the interwar years remained. How could Estonia, Latvia and Lithuania modernize? How could modernization be rapid enough to meet public demand, and from where would the capital come?

The Soviet occupations offered a solution to the latter question, but not a popular one. The Soviet Union intended to provide the resources for massive transformation, modernization and industrialization, although many of those resources would be forcibly extracted from the population. The public's involvement, from input to acquiescence, was irrelevant to Soviet economic decision-making. The Soviet Union would build dams and infrastructure across Estonia, Latvia and Lithuania, but the fruits of development would benefit Moscow first and foremost. Long-term Nazi economic policies for Estonia, Latvia and Lithuania are more difficult to discern. Different Nazi ministries competed for resources and offered plans for a post-war OstEuropa, but these were little more than rough sketches for future consideration, and at times figments of feverish imaginations. The Nazi occupation was also much shorter and took place entirely during years of war. Nazi wartime economic policy, like that of the Soviets, was overwhelmingly driven by the need to extract vital resources for the war effort. In this regard there were occasional similarities between both regimes' wartime economic policies. In each case these policies quickly alienated the great bulk of the populations of Estonia, Latvia and Lithuania, and effectively obliterated the private wealth and savings that had been carefully accrued over the previous two generations. Once again the economic foundations of each society shifted radically, which in itself was detrimental to economic development.

As previously discussed, the summer of 1940 witnessed the military occupations of Estonia, Latvia and Lithuania, sham parliamentary elections and unconstitutional requests from these rogue parliaments for independent states to be incorporated into the Union of Soviet Socialist Republics. After the theatre of the process was complete (by early August 1940), the more grim, sometimes violent and often mundane task of actually incorporating independent states into the Soviet Union began. The process was still in its infancy when interrupted by the Nazi invasion of June 1941. Still, the broad brushstrokes of the Sovietization of the three states became apparent. Ideologically private wealth was anathema to Soviet sensibilities, and realistically it was needed to fund massive industrial development. As a result private wealth was expropriated by the state. Private real estate holdings were confiscated, although small farms and homes and the notion of private property were maintained. Private savings accounts holding relatively small amounts were likewise confiscated and the introduction of the Soviet ruble at disastrous rates of exchange effectively wiped out the savings of most people. Wage increases for workers and very small-scale land reform for landless agricultural workers attempted to build some popular support among recipients rather than acting as bulwarks of a new economic order (neither the wage increases nor the small farmers were economically viable). The confiscation of private industrial and mercantile wealth was considerably aided by the previous regimes' policies of state economic intervention. The standard bearers of the Soviet economic system, massive, rapid, centrally planned heavy industrialization and the collectivization of agriculture, did not figure prominently in the first year of Soviet occupation, although they were almost certainly part of a plan to minimize popular resistance to regime change. The introduction of model collective farms in 1941 with benefits and propaganda fanfare signalled an oncoming wave of forced collectivization. The Nazi invasion, however, pre-empted this more complete Sovietization of the Estonian, Latvian and Lithuanian economies.

Nazi economic policies were even more one-sided and blindly driven by war needs. The mass murder of the great majority of the Jews of Estonia, Latvia and Lithuania was accompanied by the theft of the victims' possessions (either by the state or by those involved in killing victims). Despite constant propaganda against the Soviet state, the Nazi occupation did not rescind the economic policies of the Soviet Union in Estonia, Latvia or Lithuania, but rather used them to Nazi benefit. Vague promises of a return of property were never seriously considered, while the conversion of currency to Reichsmarks at disastrously unfair rates eliminated any residual savings among the populations of the three states. Throughout the war economic production was dictated by war needs at rates that bordered on legalized state theft. Rationing and shortages were commonplace as all local resources were funneled into the war effort. Even labour was seen as a resource to be exploited for the war effort, with thousands sent to the Reich as labourers (often forcibly) and tens of thousands sent to work for the war effort locally (undertaking tasks ranging from digging ditches to providing portage and cartage for the German army). The destruction of war was further exacerbated when retreating Nazi forces destroyed much of value that could not be evacuated in order to deny the resources to the Soviet army. The same drafting of labour and supplies for the war effort continued under new masters with the return of Soviet occupation during wartime. Not until after the Nazi surrender did economic planning and the resumption of Sovietization commence.

As in the aftermath of the First World War, the immediate economic task in the reoccupied Estonian, Latvian and Lithuanian Soviet Socialist Republics was reconstruction. All three republics witnessed great material destruction, massive population displacement and the complete breakdown of infrastructure. Most ports, railway hubs and urban centres had been repeatedly bombed and rendered inoperable. The Soviet regime dealt with each of these challenges with characteristic brutality. In all matters the reestablishment of political control was paramount. Top German officers and administrators and Estonian, Latvian and Lithuanian collaborators were executed, but prolonged partisan warfare kept military operations active for more than five years. This partisan warfare was, however, mostly diversionary and a nuisance, not a real threat to the reestablishment of Soviet rule. Reconstruction, the effects of population displacement and extreme material want – including short periods of famine – were far more acute problems for the Soviet republics. Conscripted labour and prisoners of war carried out the initial tasks of reconstruction by removing rubble and so on. Their conditions were particularly brutal and often lethal. The more skilled tasks of reconstruction, however, were complicated by the great loss of the majority of the most educated, trained strata of Estonian, Latvian and Lithuanian society. Many of these people had fled the approach of Soviet troops and were quartered in displaced persons camps across occupied Germany, or had been previously arrested and deported by Soviet authorities in 1940 and 1941. The great lack of skilled engineers, doctors and so on throughout the professions hampered reconstruction efforts. To resolve this absence, Soviet authorities pursued several occasionally contradictory policies. Soviet propagandists attempted to woo displaced persons from camps back to the Soviet Union, while Soviet officials tried to convince Western powers to agree to mass, forced repatriation. Relatively few displaced persons returned to the Soviet Union (not counting those in camps in Soviet-occupied Germany) out of fear and loathing made all the more acute by the presence of Soviet security personnel, who accompanied the propagandists. In many cases Estonian, Latvian or Lithuanian refugees who did return were promptly arrested and deported to Siberia; a clear case of perceived state security interests trumping economic necessities. With few returning Estonian, Latvian and Lithuanian specialists, the Soviet Union began to bring in migrants from the reaches of the Soviet Union. This immigration had political as well as economic affects.

The ongoing legacy of the Soviet-orchestrated immigration of labour into Estonia and Latvia (and to a lesser extent Lithuania) bears closer examination and analysis. Hundreds of thousands of Slavic-speaking workers (Slavic-speaking has become shorthand for an ethnic mix that is predominantly Russian, but also Ukrainian and Belorussian) moved into Estonia and Latvia in the first two decades following the Second World War. This migration followed the politically induced exodus of tens of thousands of Estonians and Latvians during the Second World War, and coincided with the ongoing war against Estonian, Latvian and Lithuania partisans who resisted the re-imposition of Soviet rule and the deportation of hundreds of thousands of Estonian, Latvian and Lithuanian farmers during the collectivization of agriculture beginning in 1948. The two phenomena, moving hundreds of thousands of Slavic workers in while simultaneously shipping hundreds of thousands of potential Estonian, Latvian, and Lithuanian workers out, seems either to make no economic sense or to be clear proof of a Soviet attempt at genocide in Estonia and Latvia, or at the very least a heavy-handed example of state-sponsored ethnic gerrymandering to dilute the ethnic strength of Estonians and Latvians. Neither explanation, however, is satisfactory, although each contains elements of truth and fabrication. As to the economic sense of such population transfers, economic planners were aware of the seeming absurdity of such movements and when possible spoke out against them. This became a central plank of the reform agenda of the National Communists of the mid- to late 1950s. Economic concerns, however, took second billing to political control. The Soviet state, by past experience and by natural inclination during the Stalinist era, dealt with opposition or the possibility of opposition with a heavy hand that targeted classes and tens of thousands of people. To the Soviet state deportations were a political necessity. But heavy industrialization was also an economic necessity and the backbone of the idea of a Soviet state. To the Stalinist regime enemies were to be deported first, and if workers were needed to fulfil economic plans, they would be moved where needed. If the changing ethnic makeup facilitated Soviet rule and weakened Estonian and Latvian ethnic strength, this, to the Soviet regime, was a fortunate side effect. There is little to suggest that Soviet planners specifically brought in Slavic-speaking workers with this intention. If so, there would have been equally aggressive population transfers into Lithuania, which was the most violent in its resistance of the re-imposition of Soviet rule. Lithuania, however, did not figure so centrally in economic plans for rapid and heavy industrialization. The primacy of the needs of the economic plan remained even after the Stalinist excesses of political control waned; or, in other words, when opposition figures were no longer deported en masse, Slavic-speaking workers continued to move into Estonia and Latvia as labour for planned economic development. Still, Estonians and Latvians remembered and understood the previous experience of massive ethnic dislocation as a political tool. They were further constantly reminded of the primacy of the Russian language and understood a threat to ethnic survival as a planned agenda. Throughout the Soviet era, and particularly in the 1980s, there was considerable public apprehension about and opposition to new, large economic developments that would require the import of labour for construction and operation. The Slavic-speaking workers that moved to meet the economic opportunities in Estonia and Latvia were not generally aware (at least at first) of this narrative. To them, they were moving to another part of the Soviet Union, while to Estonians and Latvians they were outsiders, foreigners, that were a threat to ethnic survival. These seeds of enmity would return with greater force after independence was restored in 1991.

The overwhelming economic priority for the Soviet Union in Estonia and Latvia, and to a lesser degree in Lithuania, was rapid and heavy industrialization. Key sectors included the electronics, automotive and chemicals industries. The Soviet military industrial complex featured significantly in each of these sectors. To develop these industries, the Soviet regime invested heavily in creating the necessary industrial infrastructure: power plants to provide power, rail and road networks to bring raw materials and remove finished products, ports for international trade, and the subsidiary needs of the rapidly growing labour force (housing, hospitals, schools and rudimentary consumer services). The economic blueprint for much of this development mirrored economic plans for the same territory during the industrialization of late tsarist Russia. In the rail and port system, for example, tsarist planners had already identified the likely bottleneck created by using Riga as the principal and sole international port in the region. Tsarist railway development extended rail networks to the small towns of Liepaja and Ventspils in modern-day Latvia and laid the framework for a similar extension to Klaipeda in modern-day Lithuania. Concurrent with these plans were the proposed long-term development of these towns as ports (Liepaja was also developed as an important tsarist naval port).

The massive development and expansion of the port of Ventspils is the best example of this trend. Ventspils was historically a small provincial town with a small mercantile and fishing port. The tsarist rail network extended Riga's booming international trade to the town as a port for overflow. Ventspils was further preferred for mostly being ice-free all year round. The port atrophied during the two decades of interwar Latvia as international trade dropped precipitously, but during the Second World War it played an important role in German transportation of troops and supplies. After the war the port of Ventspils featured prominently in Soviet industrial plans, particularly owing to the Soviet decision to export huge amounts of natural resources (oil and gas) and ammonia to the West for hard currency to fund further heavy industrial expansion. By the late 1980s the Ventspils port, as the primary conduit of Soviet trade (in petroleum, petroleum products, metals, salt, ammonia and chemicals), was the busiest port on the Baltic Sea and the twelfth largest in the world. Although the construction and development of Primorsk in Russia has eclipsed and dwarfed Ventspils, the port remains the second largest on the Baltic Sea in terms of tons of goods moved. The development of Tallinn as an international port mirrors Ventspils's trajectory. Tallinn was a historic Hanseatic port, but its use remained largely small and mercantile. In the nineteenth century imperial Russian economic plans for railway and port development also targeted Tallinn. The port's use declined during the interwar years, but resumed at a furious pace after Soviet occupation to vault Tallinn into one of the five most important ports of the Baltic Sea. With independence the Tallinn port has successfully transformed itself into one of the busiest passenger terminals on the Baltic Sea. Klaipeda in Lithuania is another similar case, and remains a busy port today, which belies its more modest history.

The economic health of these ports is central to an entire current of economic thought in Estonia, Lithuania and most significantly Latvia, where it is frequently referred to as 'Ventspils interests'. This line of economic thinking, advocated by its relevant business and political leaders (often the two are synonymous), suggests that the most viable economic model for Estonia, Latvia and Lithuania is the continuation of these ports as conduits for trade between Russia and the West. These interests doubt that domestic trade or trade without a Russian component could maintain this infrastructure and are similarly sceptical of economic development based on anything but transit trade. If this trade is vital for economic prosperity, they argue, the economic interests of Estonia, Latvia and Lithuania demand strong political relationships with its transit trade partners. Others see their interest in rapprochement with Russia as unacceptable acquiescence. This continues to be an open debate and one of the key areas where economic decision-making overlaps with national politics and international relations.

Other than the massive and rapid centrally planned industrialization of Estonia, Latvia and Lithuania, the Stalinist regime revolutionized the agricultural sectors of all three states with forced collectivization beginning in 1949. The decision for collectivization was probably based on the desire to standardize the Estonian, Latvian, and Lithuanian experience with that of the rest of the Soviet Union and was likely as much a political decision as an economic one. The Soviet regime historically saw an independent smallholding agricultural class as a mortal threat to the Soviet state. Furthermore the dogma of Marxist economic thinking defined a diversified agricultural community as one rife with the exploitation of poor peasants by the kulaks or wealthy farming class. The collectivization of agriculture was seen as a tool with which to break the power of the kulaks and bring Soviet rule to the countryside. In Estonia, Latvia and Lithuania, as throughout the Soviet Union in the late 1920s and early '30s, forced collectivization was only accomplished with state terror on a mass scale and spirited, yet ineffectual, popular resistance.

The campaign to collectivize agriculture followed the earlier Soviet example closely. The Soviet regime began gradually with the introduction of model collective farms in the Estonian Latvian and Lithuanian Soviet Socialist Republics. These farms were lavishly subsidized by the state and a propaganda blitz in the regime-produced media (in newspapers, magazines and film reels) trumpeted the advantages of collective life. With this inducement, the regime employed tax codes to make private agriculture untenable. Private farms were taxed incessantly on any and all use of employed labour, and were assigned excessive quotas for agricultural production for the state. Still, as in the Soviet example of the late 1920s, the peasantry in all three states refused to enter collective farms en masse. Mass deportations of kulaks as supporters of Lithuanian partisans (or in Soviet-speak, Lithuanian bandits) began in 1948, but the organized use of mass deportations to aid collectivization extended through Estonia and Latvia in March 1949. Previously these deportations were discussed for their political reasons (see chapter Two), but they also served an economic goal. After tens of thousands of families, identified as kulaks (often on the most spurious of reasons, such as the possession of more than one cow) opposed to collectivization, were deported into administrative exile in the far reaches of Siberia, the remainder of the agricultural population of each state fearfully entered collective farms. Across Estonia, Latvia and Lithuania the found-ing dates of most collective farms are – tellingly – in the first few weeks after the mass deportations of 1949.

Although much of the collectivization of agriculture was motivated by Marxist theory and the need for effective state control of rural areas, collectivization was also a state-driven solution to the economic modernization of the countryside. Despite popular nostalgia for the countryside of the interwar era, rural conditions included widespread poverty (often focused in less developed eastern and south-eastern regions of Estonia, Latvia and Lithuania), and a general absence of elec-trification and indoor plumbing. These amenities of modern life made inroads into the countryside in the 1920s and would have continued to spread through private initiative and local and national governmental programmes. The Soviet regime demonized independent, private initiative and viewed local government as an executor of national decision-making, not as an autonomous, independent decision-making authority. The Soviet dilemma was how to provide modern ameni-ties to the rural population with a minimum amount of investment (since most resources were earmarked for industrial development). In this case collective farms shared a familial resemblance with global state-centric attempts at rural develop-ment as varied as the ujamaa villages in Tanzania or the Tennessee Valley Authority in the southern United States.[8] In the collective farm case the dismantling of private farmsteads in favour of rural apartment blocks made economic sense. Instead of providing a sewage system and electrical grid to many farms spread over a huge geographical area, the state could centre such amenities in a single space and, by bringing people to this space, maximize resources and effectiveness. The same argument applied to the collective use of mechanized agricultural equipment. Providing five tractors to several collective farms through a shared machine tractor station seemed economically more feasible and efficient than providing countless tractors to countless farms. For many there was real material benefit from this transformation of the countryside as Soviet-built housing featured amenities that had been previously unavailable and agricultural work became generally mecha-nized. Likewise the geographic concentration of housing with schools, cafeterias, healthcare and other resources made their use more likely. The primary weaknesses of this scheme, however, were the complete lack of local input in the creation of such rural centres and the lack of ongoing investment in these centres or in collectivized agriculture more generally. If farmers refused to move to newly established rural apartment blocks or criticized details of their establishment, the state assumed that it knew better. Likewise, if Soviet rural centres enjoyed material advantages (or promised such) at the time of their construction, the lack of upkeep, maintenance and improvements diminished their appeal with time. In other words, if at first the Soviet apartment block was better than a private farm because the apartment block had indoor plumbing and reliable electricity, this advantage disappeared when the plumbing suffered constant stoppages, and hot water was provided intermittently at best. The availability of tractors became less relevant if they did not have enough spare parts. To further exacerbate the situation in the countryside, the central regime was slow to respond to local requests and agricultural production slumped and stagnated. Much of Soviet food production was heavily reliant on small private plots within the collective farm structure.

Stalin's death in 1953 saw a shift in Soviet economic policy similar to its thaw in political affairs. The centrally planned, command economy was reformed and more resources were devoted to light and medium industry, but the broad, general goals of rapid, heavy industrial development remained, as did the Soviet regime's monopoly of power and authority. Nikita Khrushchev's rise to power mirrored this same theme. In his de-Stalinization campaign Khrushchev aligned himself with many republic-level institutions to wrest some power away from entrenched central authorities with close Stalinist ties. In the economic case this often meant giving some real decision-making authority to the ministries of Soviet Socialist Republics, including those of Estonia, Latvia and Lithuania, rather than the All-Union ministries based in Moscow. Throughout the remaining decades of Soviet rule the back and forth between republic-level and All-Union-level ministries would become a common feature of economic decision-making. At times republic-level ministries increased their influence, which often included a greater degree of local input and influence, but there were limits to republic level authority. When Estonian and Latvian Communist Party leaders tried to assert greater power and authority in the mid- to late 1950s (these figures are often referred to as the National Communists), the limits of their reforms were defined by their failed attempts to limit new construction projects that would include more immigration of Slavic-speaking workers, and their demands for greater local language competence from those migrants that had arrived since the end of the Second World War. Communist

Party revanchists exploited these economic over-reaches to sweep the National Communists from positions of authority with Moscow's support in 1958 and 1959. Until Gorbachev's reforms of the mid-1980s this incident set the parameters of the economic to and fro between republic level and All-Union level decision-making; some tinkering with the formula always existed, but the supremacy of Moscow's directives became the established norm. In the most vital industries, particularly all of those associated with military production, the centre–periphery struggle was never allowed and these sectors remained solidly in the apparatus of All-Union ministries.

After the tumultuous economic transformations of the Stalinist era, economic development became defined by the vagaries of the five-year plans that ostensibly planned all economic activity across the Soviet Union. After fighting market forces in the early history of the Soviet Union, Stalin introduced the first five-year plan in 1928, well before Estonia, Latvia and Lithuania's incorporation into the USSR. Each five-year plan was an enormous production of bureaucratic control and allocation of resources. In theory the plan would regulate and distribute all economic activity and thus rationalize production and effort to meet specific state goals for development. Overachieving the plan (or meeting the plan's goals in a shorter period of time) became a frequent propaganda claim that demonstrated the economic progress of the USSR. During the height of the Stalinist purges of the 1930s the five-year plan became both more absurd in its claims of success and, more sinister, a weapon in the ongoing battle to unmask and punish 'wreckers and saboteurs' across the USSR.[9] The five-year plan thus claimed fantastic progress in the success-ful building of socialism, and also identified enemies of the state as scapegoats for poor economic performance. Central planners and industry leaders alike perished with regularity throughout the 1930s. Such extremes were less common when the five-year plans were applied to the Estonian, Latvian and Lithuanian Soviet Socialist Republics, particularly after the death of Stalin, but the plan remained an elaborate scheme that wedded a real attempt to direct and control the entire economy with propaganda claims of success. As a result official statistics tied to the five-year plans are notoriously unreliable.

Without the 'invisible hand of the market', central planners relied on the use of quotas to determine production across the Soviet economy. Quotas were set on the macro-level, for example for steel produced in the USSR, on a republic level, on a ministerial level, on a sector level, on a factory level, on a factory shift level and even on an individual's shift level. Incentives were frequently offered for over-achieving quotas, while punishments could be levied if one failed to meet them. In the Stalinist era rewards and punishment tended toward the extreme, with workers that far outpaced their quotas awarded the title of Stakhanovites and even achieving national fame. Punishments could include garnering a label as a wrecker and a potential criminal sentence even for such trivial issues as work attendance. After Stalin, and particularly from the Brezhnev era on, rewards and punishments were more ordinary. Rewards could include vacation time at more prestigious resorts or advancement, while punishment might be occupational stagnation and/or regression. The same principle applied up and down the economic ladder, with enterprise managers put in line for promotion by overachieving quotas, and ministers in line for demotion for failing to. Needless to say, achieving quotas became an all-encompassing obsession complicated by the economic fact that meeting quotas often depended upon matters outside of one's control (such as the steady supply of raw materials, the necessary number of workers or the weather). A vast, complicated grey market emerged throughout the Soviet Union and in the Estonian, Latvian and Lithuanian Soviet Socialist Republics to manage needs associated with filling these quotas. This system included holding reserves for future shortages, cultivating contacts to ensure a needed supply of resources and ingratiating oneself into elaborate systems of patronage. This system, in part referred to with the Russian term *blat*, operated on both the macro- and the micro-level. An enterprise director might cultivate good relations with a party leader through graft while receiving similar favours from underlings. With time, economic activity seemed impossible without this shadow institution, yet the institution shackled economic performance and frustrated the efforts of central planners.

The quota system as an economic incentive was further weakened by the blind adherence to the strict requirements of a quota for success, even if this produced sub-standard products. If, for example, a glass factory was given a quota of producing 100,000 drinking glasses, the factory could exceed the quota by using less glass per item and thus producing 150,000 drinking glasses so thin that they quickly broke with everyday usage. If the quota system was modified to reflect weight produced as opposed to items, a chandelier factory could produce very few, extremely heavy chandeliers.[10] Across the board, the quota systems of the Soviet planned economy relied upon some form of success indicators and the actual economic actors immediately acted to maximize their ability to surpass such set quotas even if the end results were useless. Many of the most cited examples may have a mythic quality to them, but just as many were accurate and explain the slow stagnation and decline of the Soviet economy in the 1970s and into the early '80s. A potential solution to this maddening situation was a degree of quality control across the system that would highlight waste, abuse and absurdities. The author, for example, noticed an odd feature on a Soviet-built dormitory in the small Latvian town of Jaungulbene. The four- or five-storey building seemed little different from hundreds of other such dormitories across Latvia and the USSR, except that the balconies at the ends of each floor were overgrown with weeds and moss. The reason for their disrepair was that there were no access points to them. When the building was constructed, if the plan did not include doors, and if there was no incentive to include them, and if the ability to reform or alter plans at a local level was miniscule, worthless balconies were built as directed.

By the 1980s the rigid nature of the planned economy, widespread graft and corruption and the poor quality of produced goods yielded economic stagnation. The central economy with its five-year plan was also alarmingly slow to respond to the rapid development of technological goods (an issue with profound military implications in the age of a weapons race that relied on ever more technologically sophisticated arms). First Andropov, but more famously Mikhail Gorbachev, ushered in an attempt to restructure the Soviet planned economy (perestroika) by injecting some market forces to create a more responsive economy. Reform, however, endangered all the existing networks of *blat* and patronage that were the motors of the real Soviet economy. Not surprisingly, the reform-minded Gorbachev encountered severe resistance. His solution to entrenched interests was a degree of political liberalization (glasnost) that would tolerate public discussion of the waste, weaknesses and corruption within the Soviet system. Ironically, reformers in the Estonian, Latvian, and Lithuanian Soviet Socialist Republics aggressively embraced perestroika and glasnost, and the resulting weakening of entrenched Soviet interests facilitated the toppling of the entire Soviet edifice.

Many of Gorbachev's economic reforms seemed to bear immediate fruit in Estonia, Latvia and Lithuania in the mid-1980s. Particularly in the Estonian Soviet Socialist Republic, which was often used as a laboratory for proposed economic reforms, the Soviet economic system found individuals eager to offer initiative, accept risk and produce more efficiently and effectively than according to the old plan. The author, for example, remembers watching with great excitement a CNN feature on economic reform in Gorbachev's Russia that featured a barbershop in the Estonian Soviet Socialist Republic. In a major break from Soviet orthodoxy (but admittedly a small case in hindsight), Estonian barbers were able to rent the tools of their trade from the state-operated barbershop, and keep any profits above their achieved quotas. The risk-taking barbers with personal incentives provided better service, learned more hairstyles and serviced more customers than barbers working under the old system. This small case and the more general shift to republic-controlled economic decision-making with slightly more innovation and responsiveness across the Estonian, Latvian and Lithuanian Soviet Socialist Republics suggested that Gorbachev's hopes for economic restructuring could succeed.

The reformers around Gorbachev, however, could not easily replicate these early successes more generally across the Soviet Union due to the great deal of resistance and foot-dragging from the myriad cast of economic actors tied to the pre-existing economic order. Gorbachev then introduced the ability to criticize authority with a campaign of glasnost (openness), hoping to expose the economic opponents of reform. Initially a more free and investigative press produced reports that uncovered criminal misconduct and corruption at various industrial enterprises and in some government offices. If perestroika showed promise in the Estonian, Latvian and Lithuanian Soviet Socialist Republics, the limits and dangers of glasnost were similarly exposed there. The litmus test for the campaign of greater openness was whether more general criticism of the Soviet Union would be allowed. In Estonia, Latvia and Lithuania, timidly at first, people began openly to question the legitimacy of Soviet rule by discussing the nature of occupation, annexation and incorporation into the Soviet Union. As these demands became more strident, vocal and numerous, the political question of Soviet power and the legitimacy of calls for independence crowded economic restructuring from the stage. Gorbachev was never able to balance the demands for immediate political liberalization with the continuation of Soviet rule, first in Lithuania, Estonia and Latvia, and eventually across the Soviet Union.

The lasting impact and value of the Soviet economic experience must be evaluated before moving on to its collapse in Estonia, Latvia and Lithuania. There are several myths and distortions concerning Soviet economic performance in contemporary Estonia, Latvia and Lithuania, and in most cases these myths are more attached to current political agendas than to sober reflection on what transpired. First and foremost, in terms of human capital, the Soviet experience was an utter and devastating disaster. The deportation and/or execution of hundreds of thousands of Estonians, Latvians and Lithuanians (and others living in the region), most of whom were in the prime of their productive adult lives, is impossible to quantify, yet it is exceptionally crucial to recognize it. The introduction of 'replacement human capital' hardly impacts on or ameliorates the scale of the tragedy inflicted on countless families and communities. The loss of highly skilled, experienced professional human capital through refugee flight to the West is also crucial and difficult to express. The sudden near collapse of entire professions (medicine, dentistry, engineering and higher education, to name a few) massively impacted on the scale and quality of post-war reconstruction. Still, to deny post-war reconstruction is equally misleading.

Émigré historians and economists engaged in a battle of ideas with Soviet propagandists during the long decades of Soviet occupation looked to the example of Finland as a barometer of what could have been if not for occupation. The idea, as with several other émigré myths, has been partially adopted in contemporary Estonia, Latvia and Lithuania. The Finland case assumes that the socio-economic conditions of Finland, Estonia, Latvia and Lithuania were relatively similar on the eve of the Second World War and then tracks the divergence between an independent Finland's economic growth and prosperity and the relative stagnation and decline of the Estonian, Latvian and Lithuanian Soviet Socialist Republics. The conclusions are stark and extreme: today Finland is one of the most developed, prosperous states in the world, leading in many quality of life indexes, while Estonia, Latvia and Lithuania are the poorest nations in the European Union and far behind Finland in these indexes. There are several problems with this line of thought; chief among them is the great complexity of events that are reduced to a single, albeit massively important, event in the 'what could have been' rewriting of history. Although counterfactual approaches to history can suggest intriguing divergences, the stretch needed to imagine a plausible outcome of the Second World War without Soviet occupation is too unrealistic: without a Soviet defeat in war the occupation of the Baltic states seems inevitable, in part alleviating the need for an occupied Finland. The Finland case is further weakened by the material differences between Finland and Estonia, Latvia and Lithuania and the difficulties these states would have had in mimicking Finland's development if they had remained independent after war.[11] Finland's transformation from a poor, agrarian state to a diversified, modern economy is generally identified as a post-war phenomenon, and thus invites comparisons with Estonia, Latvia and Lithuania (neighbours that were also poor, agrarian states prior to the Second World War). Finland, however, witnessed more pronounced industrialization and modernization in the interwar years than Estonia, Latvia or Lithuania. Industrial production and foreign trade more quickly recovered and surpassed pre-First World War levels. The industrial workforce and power used in industry also increased far more quickly in Finland. Of particular importance was the expansion of metalworking industries and the discovery and exploitation of copper reserves and other limited metal resources. If agriculture and forestry still dominated the Finnish economy at the eve of the Second World War, they did so to a lesser degree than in its neighbours to the south. Furthermore the Finnish response to the post-war world was exceptional and unique. The Soviet Union forced reparations upon Finland (until 1952) that stimulated the expansion of key industries such as shipbuilding and further spurred industrial transformation. The following two decades witnessed the firm establishment of a modern, industrial economy that reinvested in a strong Nordic-style welfare state. All of the prerequisites were in place for Finland to reap rewards in an age that stressed information, technology-based production and trade. From the 1970s, accelerating in the '80s, investment in Finland and from Finland has further transformed the state. A key factor in the difference between Finnish and Estonian, Latvian and Lithuanian economic development (in the counterfactual model) is the question of capital investment and markets.

The question that has always bedevilled economic development in Estonia, Latvia and Lithuania has been the issue of finding a source of capital to fund development and, to a lesser degree, finding markets for economic production. Short-lived attempts at economic autarchy have underscored the difficulty of a small state with limited natural resources in generating enough capital to 'go it alone'. Throughout the twentieth century, and in anticipation of the twenty-first, Estonian, Latvian and Lithuanian governments have struggled to provide the funding for the massive infrastructural developments and improvements expected by its inhabitants. The Soviet Union provided a massive amount of infrastructural investment and a ravenous market for Estonian, Latvian and Lithuanian goods, but was this relationship desired? Much Soviet investment was primarily for Soviet benefit and had few carry-over benefits to a country independent of the Moscow-centred state. Military installations and military industries, and there were many throughout Estonia, Latvia and Lithuania, are excellent cases in point. Naval bases at Paldiski, Estonia, Liepaja, Latvia, and Klaipeda, Lithuania, consumed huge amounts of infrastructural investment throughout the Soviet era, but with the withdrawal of Soviet forces, the bases were stripped bare. Independent states received little from these former military installations other than the considerable cost of environmental cleanup and redevelopment. Across Estonia, Latvia and Lithuania there were hundreds of such military bases, barracks, warehouses and other infrastructure. The anti-ballistic missile array at Skrunda, Latvia, a massive Soviet infrastructural and military investment, was ceremoniously destroyed on live Latvian television in 1995 as a symbol of the end of Soviet military presence. There is little Latvia could have done with the site, but the array's fate underscores the pointlessness of much of the Soviet Union's military-related investment in all three states. The less symbolic radio installation near Mazirbe, Latvia, on the other hand, lay dormant for years and then was reconstructed and returned to service. This is a case of value from Soviet military investment, and although rare, it is not alone.

Other Soviet industrial investment and development proved to have an equally short life following independence. The automotive, electronic and telecommunications industries, proud staples of Soviet propaganda, withered quickly when cut off from their larger Soviet supply chains. They no longer enjoyed easy access to parts and energy, could not send finished components to Soviet plants for further production, and their goods could not compete in international markets. In some cases, such as the fibreglass factory in Valmiera, Latvia, the factory was able to attract German investment and produce for an international market, but for each of these success stories there were dozens of failures. The occasional attempts to entice a resurrection of the automotive industry is an example of a Soviet skeleton of industrial development hoping to adapt, but with little to no success. The largest infrastructural investments, hydroelectric dams and power stations, the electric grid, ports and the atomic power plant at Ignalina in Lithuania, were all assets of great (but problematic) value inherited by the newly independent states of Estonia, Latvia and Lithuania.

Regardless of the potential balance sheet of Soviet economic policy in Estonia, Latvia and Lithuania, the collapse of the Soviet Union meant the collapse of the existing economic order. This economic collapse was well entrenched even before political collapse. In the final years and months of the Soviet Union, authority was undefined and contested across Estonia, Latvia and Lithuania. In each republic, elected parliamentary bodies declared the intent to restore independence, and later declared independence, while endlessly negotiating with a Kremlin authority that refused to consider the independence option. In the light of this overarching political struggle, economic decision-making was severely compromised. The old jurisdictional battles between economic planning on an All-Union, Republic or newly local level became more intense, but with no clear and immediate victor. The well-worn systems of patronage, graft and corruption teetered on a precipice between a revolutionary change in how all of society (and the economy) worked and the maintenance of the status quo. Uncertainty is one of the great plagues to economic development and activity and it visited all three states throughout the collapse of the Soviet Union. Economic uncertainty would continue to reign through the first years of Estonian, Latvian and Lithuanian independence. Such uncertainty was not firmly resolved until all three states joined the European Union.

Economic orientation and the speed of reform were the overwhelmingly dominant economic themes in the early 1990s in all three countries. The great majority of economists and Western economic advisors counselled Estonia, Latvia and Lithuania to keep economic connections with the former Soviet Union, most exemplified in early advice to remain in the 'ruble zone' or in a broad currency union that covered much of the economic territory of the former Soviet Union, as previously discussed. The reasons for this advice seemed sound: maintaining existing economic networks and building upon established markets would likely be more productive than beginning from scratch and competing on an open international market for goods and services. The steadfast decision to buck this advice in all three states was rooted in a deep-seated belief that any ties with the former Soviet Union could too easily become new shackles that would limit the hard-fought fruits of their restored political independence. All three states moved quickly to reintroduce the national currencies of the interwar era (the Estonian krona, the Latvian lats, and the Lithuanian litas) despite the general international community's belief that the transition would be difficult, if not doomed to failure. Instead the currency reform set a precedent for notable economic policy success. With a staggered conversion timetable, each state introduced temporary currency that traded initially on par with Soviet era rubles. Over several months, Soviet rubles were withdrawn from circulation, and ultimately permanent national currencies were exchanged for the temporary ones. The new currencies were pegged to Western currencies (or to a basket of international currencies) and apparently the foundations of a new economic systems were laid seamlessly in each state; a foundation that was demonstratively separate from the former Soviet Union.

Beyond currency reform, Estonia, Latvia and Lithuania each needed to devise plans to transition from a centrally controlled (previously outside of its borders), command economy to a market-based economy in an international framework. Ultimately, as across Eastern Europe and the former Soviet Union, two schools of thought emerged on the best plan for transition. One plan imagined a quick and radical economic revolution. This imagined quick sales of state-owned enterprises and property and would likely include considerable social costs as hundreds of thousands would suffer with little social safety netting in place. The other plan imagined a more gradual and controlled transition. Those that favoured the second plan believed that the slower pace of transition would ameliorate the social pain attached to such a profound economic transformation. Each plan, however, assumed the need to factor in the tolerance of a newly voting population for economic reform, and in many ways each assumed the worst.[12] Reform needed to be rapid in order to entrench a market economy before an angry electorate derailed it at the next elections. Gradualists assumed that only the slow approach was electorally viable over more than one election.

In Estonia the economic transformation was most rapid, at times dizzying. Perhaps the pace of initial reform was slowest in Lithuania. Still, with twenty years of hindsight, it is clear that the pace of economic transformation from a centrally controlled economy to a market-based system was rapid in all three states. Moreover it is clear that the electorate in each state often punished political parties and politicians at the electoral booth, but in no country did they fundamentally sway from a commitment to a market economy over the course of four or five elections. The citizens of Estonia, Latvia and Lithuania have been firm in their resolve to forge a market economy based on private property and the rule of law. Their political parties and governments, however, have at times struggled with property questions and the equal implementation of the rule of law.

The very notion of private property, with the exception of personal possessions, was severely limited and circumscribed in the Soviet economy. As Estonia, Latvia and Lithuania moved to a market economy, the three states also needed to create systems to move the ownership of personal, commercial and industrial property from the state and collective bodies (such as kolkhozes or collective farms) to individuals (real and fictive). Furthermore the three states needed to consider the existing claims to the properties in question. In all three states the Sovietization of society in 1940 and 1941, and the collectivization of agriculture (primarily in 1949), had seized the property of hundreds of thousands of people. The property rights of these dispossessed – or, in other words, the idea of restitution – dominated the early years of economic transition. There were a great many complications, small and large. For example, some individuals had a legal claim on land, but the Soviet state had confiscated it and built factories or housing developments across a much wider area. How could an individual receive land that was a fraction of a currently much larger – and occupied – plot? Many legal claimants were the descendants of people who had fled during the Second World War. Would the new states grant property rights to an absentee class of property owners with few links to contemporary Estonia, Latvia and Lithuania? Furthermore, establishing legitimate legal claimants required a degree of archival proof and documentation not imagined beforehand as well as a legal system to arbitrate all of these paper trails. And beyond these everyday questions of property ownership, the more existential issue of the legal right of Holocaust victims (where heirs were even more difficult to identify) and the repatriated Baltic Germans of 1939 and 1940 (whose movements were only slightly voluntary) hovered over the debate. The issue of restitution also clashed with the short-term goals of economic transition: to give the citizens of Estonia, Latvia and Lithuania a stake in the new system through relatively easy ownership of real estate and other property. Instead of converting people quickly into stakeholders in housing estates or in former state enterprises, the entire real estate and property market, a cornerstone of a market economy, took shape in fits and starts.

The imperfect solution to restitution and privatizing property was a system of certificates and compensations. With variations across Estonia, Latvia and Lithuania, all three parliaments created a web of certificates available to all citizens (often pro rata to age and/or years lived in the state). These certificates were assigned a monetary value when used in exchange for purchasing state property, although many people leery of the viability of the plan sold their certificates at discounted prices for immediate gain in a shady market for the buying and selling of said certificates. People with claims on property that could no longer be restituted often received compensation in greater awards of such (or similar) certificates. To all others, if proper documentation of prior ownership could be found, and in most cases legitimate descent and inheritance proven, former landowners or their heirs recovered lost property. Not surprisingly the process was long, convoluted, messy and often surrounded with charges of abuse, fraud and corruption. Nevertheless, through the 1990s, the system of complete state ownership of all property came to an end. Private property was securely rooted as the foundation of the new economic order, although the equal dispensation of the rule of law often suffered.

The nature of privatization, primarily of collective farms, factories and large state companies, created a perception of corruption and sowed the seeds of the rise of financially powerful oligarchs who with time would use their wealth and influence to push into the political realm. This phenomenon was not unique to Estonia, Latvia or Lithuania, and replicated itself across Eastern and Central Europe, with dizzying financial success in Russia and other former Soviet Republics. In comparison to the oil and resource tycoons of Russia, the oligarchs of Latvia (and by extension Estonia and Lithuania) seem like poor country cousins, in the commentary of one resident political scientist.[13] Through the 1990s, particularly in the first half of the 1990s, former Communist Party apparatchiki often used their position and connections to benefit most from privatization. Similarly gray marketeers and entrepreneurs jumped into the economic chaos and despair to turn systemic collapse to their own personal gain. Not surprisingly this has fuelled nearly constant conspiratorial threads within Estonian, Latvian and Lithuanian societies about an independence stolen from the masses and the fruits given to a few. There is much grist to this perception, and the ongoing struggle in all three states is combating the confluence of wealth and power where one is used to maximize the other. Still, privatization occurred as should have been expected. Hopefully, with time, the grosser injustices of the process will be righted and the most egregious violators prosecuted.

Against this backdrop of economic collapse and transformation and the emergence of property, the first half of the 1990s was characterized by the collapse of cherished model industrial enterprises from the Soviet era, in a kind of extractive, primal grab for immediate economic gain, aided by an early round of loose financial regulations and the collapse of early private banks. The great symbols of Soviet heavy industrialization in Soviet Estonia, Latvia and Lithuania, such as the State Electronic Factory (VEF – Valsts elektrotehniskā fabrika, created in the 1930s) in Riga, were unable to preserve markets and resources in the former Soviet Union or to compete with Western and Asian products even within the domestic market, and quickly imploded. The extractive model of economic activity centred on the management of many of these once-hallowed enterprises, turning to quick and final profits through the scavenging of machines and supplies, often for their cash value for their weight in international metals markets. The 'coloured metals' mania was the extreme version of this craze, where the physical remains of an industry, down to the last strands of copper wiring, were stripped and sold by weight with most, if not all, of the proceeds benefiting a handful of individuals. Most economic activity seemed geared to transactions that could yield massive returns quickly, with little in terms of longer reinvestment or long-term returns and yields. The first private banks in Estonia, Latvia and Lithuania reinforced this trend.

The bank crises of the mid-1990s were a convergence of the lax financial regulations of a nascent economic sector, and an early skirmish between criminal elements and institution-building. Emerging from the Soviet economic world, Estonia, Latvia and Lithuania had no private banking sector (the only banks with individuals' deposits through most of the Soviet period were rudimentary state savings banks), and creating one that was viable and prosperous proceeded through many fits and starts. To begin with, with economic collapse and rampant inflation, there were few individuals interested in opening accounts in newly created private banks. Yet banks needed depositors to be able to lend money. Lending money was equally risky for new banks, since there was no system to rate an individual's credit reliability and few people had access to collateral. The initial solution revolved around high interest rates (to Western norms, astronomically high) for both returns on deposits and for repaying loans. As loan interest rates dropped slightly, the most likely way in which banks could meet return rates for its depositors was through new deposits. In other words the early years of banking in Estonia, Latvia and Lithuania often looked like an ever-growing Ponzi scheme. The other easy early route for banks to attract depositors was to offer money laundering to criminal groups or to hide other ill-gotten gains. Banks in Latvia, for example, even advertised themselves as being 'closer than Switzerland'. Banks and criminal elements crossed over into each others' territory in both of these schemes. By the mid-1990s state legislation had clarified financial rules and regulations and enforcement had begun to be more serious. Legally required audits from independent, international auditing firms pushed many banks to the brink of collapse.

In 1995 Latvia's largest private bank, Banka Baltija, and a host of others collapsed. Tens of thousands of people lost their savings, the country's GDP declined, and the resulting legal proceedings lasted for many years. The investigations exposed the close relationships between Latvia's political and business elite. More troubling was that the nature of the relationship seemed often to be criminal or at the very least self-serving. Despite the severe impact on public trust in the banking sector and in political parties, Latvia remained committed to the transformation to a market-based economy. If anything, the crisis reinforced a desire to pattern more closely after established norms in Western countries. This became considerably easier as Western banks made inroads into the Estonian, Latvian and Lithuanian markets. The role of banks with considerable foreign ownership (Swedish, German, Norwegian) increased. Furthermore the goal of economic reform became more explicitly stated: it was needed to meet standards for successful entry into the EU. The next major economic crisis began again with banks in 1998 and showcased how much had been accomplished in economic transformation.

The 1998 crisis was caused by 'extraneous circumstances', or in this case the collapse of many banks in Russia followed by a severe economic contraction across Russia and many of the former republics of the USSR. In Estonia, Lithuania and most acutely in Latvia, banks with heavy exposure in Russian banks were under immediate and immense strain, and many did not survive this crisis. Factories, particularly those that processed foods such as fish and dairy primarily for a Russian market, were pinched by the general failure of Russian buyers to pay for goods and a collapse in future orders. On the other hand, the factories and industries that had struggled to change their products to meet Western tastes and demands were far less affected by the 1998 crisis. Almost the entire Estonian economy is the best case in point. Estonia had successfully and aggressively pursued Nordic trade connections and as a result suffered least in the 1998 crisis.

In the immediate aftermath of the 1998 crisis, the economic tea leaves seemed to suggest a watershed moment across Estonia, Latvia and Lithuania. As mentioned previously, in all three states political momentum moved decisively towards inclusion in NATO and economic reorientation moved towards the European Union. If the idea of NATO and EU membership seemed a distant dream in 1991, by 1998 all three states aggressively plotted the needed steps for successful entry in less than a decade. With NATO the path was simpler: a political will and a largely token military investment towards NATO norms. With the EU, a reference book was created. The EU declared economic goalposts for government debts and deficits and an encyclopedia of laws and regulations that needed to be adopted. Again Estonia led the way, with a singularly determined push to meet all EU demands as quickly as possible. In Latvia and Lithuania there continued to be some popular resentment towards EU demands and occasional governmental attempts to negotiate specifics. The EU rewarded Estonia by suggesting it might meet EU requirements in the first round of expansion into Eastern Europe, while rebuking Latvia and Lithuania for delays and inadequacies in their reforms. Nevertheless, Estonia, Latvia and Lithuania became full members of NATO and the EU in 2004. If NATO membership had long been the Holy Grail that would provide security in Estonia, Latvia and Lithuania, the EU was the analogous Holy Grail for prosperity. With membership in the EU, prosperity seemed at hand.

Through the early 2000s Estonia, Latvia and Lithuania were at times referred to as the Baltic Tigers – or at least tiger cubs – relative to the Celtic Tiger of Ireland. Economic growth was impressive and the dream of convergence, the idea that Estonia, Latvia and Lithuania would be economic equals to other members of the EU, seemed close to fruition. In the mid-1990s the governments of Estonia, Latvia and Lithuania all committed to the idea of foreign direct investment as the key to economic development. The ultimate prize was membership in the EU, with its deep pockets, to speed economic prosperity. The first half-dozen years of the twenty-first century seemed to highlight the wisdom of this approach. Capital, both private and from the EU, flooded into Estonia, Latvia and Lithuania. EU funds helped pave the way for road- and railway-building, improvements to sewage, sanitation and ports and new connections to a European electrical grid, as well as reforms and extensions of the social beneficence of the state through funds earmarked for education, public assistance and pensions. Of course, in all of these areas, Estonian, Latvian and Lithuanian governments also contributed financially and local governments and non-governmental organizations designed and managed the countless projects submitted to and approved for EU funding. Still, it seemed as if the old conundrum of locating capital for Estonian, Latvian and Lithuanian economic development had been solved. Naturally parochial nationalists in all three countries griped that bureaucrats in Brussels had as little concern for small nations as bureaucrats in Moscow had had, and that infrastructural improvements were meant to remove wealth from Estonia, Latvia and Lithuania. But although Eurosceptics remained a considerable (at times majority) percentage of public opinion polls, few seriously considered or suggested an alternative method of economic development, particularly when it was rushing ahead at such a pace.

For the governments of each country economic prosperity meant larger public purses through greater tax revenues. Lithuania and to a greater degree Latvia began to reward sectors that had long been ignored during the difficult economic transition. Direct governmental employees (from parliamentary deputies to ministerial bureaucrats) as well as indirect recipients (teachers, professors, healthcare providers and pensioners) received increases in wages and benefits. Cultural events and institutions again noticed an uptick in government support after more than a decade of dwindling support. All of this, which Latvia's Minister President referred to quasi-biblically as the 'seven years of fat' after 'seven years of want', seemed a moral and actual necessity since private sector wages and investments were racing ahead of governmental ones. Estonia avoided some of this largesse by steering closely to the Schengen criteria for introduction of the Euro by keeping down government debt and deficit rates.

Foreign direct investment from private corporations and a suddenly robust private banking sector fuelled a real estate boom from the late 1990s into the 2000s. Rapid returns on real estate investments became such a lucrative proposition that for some buying and selling real estate became a primary occupation. The rapid rise in real estate values even attracted such international investors as the Liberian despot Charles Taylor. To Taylor, purchasing a string of condominiums in a pricey neighborhood of Riga was as good an investment as any other for his ill-gotten gains. Furthermore, in Latvia the source of his foreign investment was of little consequence. Despite the notoriety of investments from African tyrants, to most private investors Estonia, Latvia and Lithuania had much to offer through the early part of the twenty-first century. Governmental regulations could be bothersome, but were not an insurmountable obstacle (particularly with the widespread prevalence of graft and corruption). Most importantly, Estonian, Latvian and Lithuanian banks could quickly move investment in and – if need be – out of the countries.

Through the boom years the need to remove money was curtailed as the over-heating economic picture consistently gave better than expected returns. In an earlier book the author warned that Latvia (and by extension Estonia and Lithuania) could well suffer from the whims and perceptions of international investors. Once a darling, lauded as an unrivalled success story, Estonia, Latvia and Lithuania could just as easily suffer if the international tide of opinion were to turn. By 2008 not only did international opinion begin to sour, but many of the serious weaknesses in the foundations of the rapid economic development of the preceding decade were slowly exposed. As the full weight of the international economic crisis became apparent in the summer of 2008 and throughout the remainder of the year and across 2009, Latvia foremost and Lithuania and Estonia suffered precipitously as some of the crisis' first European casualties. The economic collapse, in many ways as stark as the growth and prosperity of the previous decade, was a perfect storm of real estate bubbles, overvalued assets and a sudden loss of international credit and investment. Well before Greece, Ireland or Portugal were in need of 'bailouts', well before the implosion of private banking in the United States and across the world, these same problems descended upon Estonia, Latvia and Lithuania.

Through 2006 and 2007 the most common red flag from international economists about Estonia, Latvia and Lithuania was that their booming economies were in danger of 'overheating', or in other words that inflation could potentially race ahead of real economic gains, creating a kind of bubble. This, however, was not the most pressing bubble facing particularly Latvia, where a classic real estate bubble grew increasingly untenable. Prices skyrocketed in a country where average annual income remained well below the rising cost of real estate, yet sales continued to accelerate. The real estate market had become a decidedly speculative affair, but few saw the potential for collapse. In the run-up to parliamentary elections only one party mentioned plans to combat a real estate bubble in its electoral platform, and others, including members of the ruling coalition, almost openly mocked the idea of an 'overheating economy', claiming that they would be in favour of overheating the economy for several more years. This was populism at its most popular, yet economically most dangerous. An electorate that had experienced considerable economic deprivation for more than a decade did not want to believe that the current prosperity could be short-lived. After the elections politicians continued to ignore increasingly dire economic indicators.

By 2008 these economic indicators became more ominous. Government deficits were nearly a quarter of GDP and inflation again picked up steam. Government ministers continued publicly to refuse to entertain the thought of an oncoming financial catastrophe and claimed robust economic health. When the real estate market burst, so did a general climate of easy credit. As a result, one of Latvia's largest private banks, Parex Banka, collapsed. The state belatedly stepped into the void to suddenly find a gaping chasm. The Latvian economy quickly reversed course from robust growth to even more startling contraction. Private economic activity, dependent on cheap and easy credit for quick transactions, contracted sharply. Spooked foreign investors pulled out of a suddenly difficult economic climate while others called in loans or restricted access to new ones. As a result Latvia's GDP contracted more than 10 per cent in the final quarter of 2008. Latvia's government, which had enjoyed a period of economic profligacy in return for popular support, did not have the financial resources or authority to decisively step into the brink. The frequent charges of governmental corruption fuelled the discussion of economic collapse and a serious economic depression descended quickly and thoroughly in 2009. Unemployment in Latvia stood near 7 per cent at the end of 2008; within a year that rate was well over 20 per cent. Latvia's government was forced to turn to the International Monetary Fund and the EU for a financial bailout in February 2009, while its credit rating was slashed to 'junk' by Standard & Poors, Moody's and other analysts. Latvia, after years of economic boom, became the 'Argentina' of Europe by late 2008. A change in coalition government in February 2009 did not arrest Latvia's precipitous decline. By the last quarter of 2009 Latvia's GDP had shrunk by almost 20 per cent, at the time the worst contraction in the world.

Initially Lithuania and particularly Estonia were keen to show that Latvia's economic collapse reflected on its specific real estate bubble, and the corrupt relationship between its government and its oligarchs, rather than being a sign of similar weakness in its neighbours. Estonia's offer to help bail out Latvia financially in February 2009, for example, was probably more an attempt to demonstrate the difference between the fiscal health of the two states than a real, viable solution. There is some validity to these claims, but Estonia and Lithuania suffered equally due to their heavy dependence on foreign direct investment and cheap, readily available credit for their economic development. When the global recession of 2008 and 2009 severely restricted liquidity for the Estonian and Lithuanian economies, they crashed as quickly and as precipitously as Latvia's had. Latvia's world-leading decline in GDP in the last quarter of 2009, for example, was bested by a Lithuanian contraction of just over 20 per cent in the first quarter of 2010. Dramatic rises in unemployment, and severe government austerity measures in

Tallinn, Vilnius and Riga, echoed Ilves' earlier quotation that Estonia, Latvia and Lithuania shared traumatic experiences and little more. Each state had charted its own economic boom, most impressively in Estonia, yet they all shared in the collapse of 2008–10.

Throughout 2009 and 2010 economists and politicians fruitlessly looked for solutions to the sudden and dramatic economic contraction in all three states. The devaluation of local currencies, a call that had periodically surfaced ever since the currencies were introduced, seemed the most likely alternate (but not guaranteed) path toward economic revival. In Estonia this option was least entertained, as the country remained remarkably on-target to meet EU standards for introducing the Euro as legal tender, which it achieved in 2011, despite the ongoing affects of a dramatic economic collapse. In no country was the currency devaluation idea adopted, although rumours did touch on short-term currency speculations and bank withdrawals. More significantly the global economic crisis created a moment of doubt among economists and politicians alike through 2009 and 2010. This moment was almost an existential crisis: economists, politicians, businessmen and analysts who had completely accepted the foreign direct investment plan for economic growth and prosperity as infallible for more than ten years suddenly had doubts. Given the aforementioned problem of generating capital for economic growth in small, relatively poor countries, the sudden entertaining of the very idea that the foreign direct investment plan could be bankrupt caused these decision-makers to wonder if anything could be done. Among the general population, many of the young generation had believed in a kind of 'progressivist' view of continued economic growth and prosperity. They knew that there were serious problems of poverty and want in Estonia, Latvia and Lithuania, but believed that these problems could be explained by age, ethnicity or other factors (such as alcoholism and so on). To the young business and governmental elite, a solid Western-based education, knowledge of languages and hard work led to success and prosperity. The idea that unemployment, mortgage defaults and bankruptcy could strike a much larger swath of the population, including themselves, and that recovery could take many years, was a bitter and difficult pill to swallow. This moment of doubt has faded slightly, and has been replaced with a more general narrative that greedy and corrupt politicians and businessmen were to blame for economic collapse, but the once surefire solution to the issue of development, entrance into the EU, has come under more scrutiny.

The loss of the EU's lustre has become more prominent for Estonia, where the hard work and single-minded determination of several Estonian governments bore the Euro as its fruit. Estonian Euro coins became the legal tender of the state on 1 January 2011 as the kroon was withdrawn from circulation. This moment was one of incredible accomplishment, but with a bittersweet potential future. In order to meet EU requirements for the use of the Euro, Estonia had to consistently keep low yearly deficit and debt levels. This accomplishment came at a time of nearly constant need for greater governmental spending. Extraordinary discipline kept Estonian fiscal and economic policy on the Euro prize. The idea that Estonia would share a common currency with the majority of the EU was almost unthinkable in 1991, particularly to outside observers. When the Euro came into existence in 1999 in eleven EU states, the idea that Estonia (not yet a member of the EU) would join these ranks in a little more than ten years would have been equally difficult to fathom. Still, after reaching this apogee, the great irony that has unfolded is that by showing remarkable economic discipline and restraint to get the Euro, this economic prize could be undone by a lack of economic discipline and restraint elsewhere in the EU, which in the worst case could sink the Euro and Estonia's economy with it. Estonia reached the long-sought promised land of the EU and its more exclusive Eurozone at precisely the moment when some of that paradise had lost much of its sheen. Still, with a pragmatic stoicism, the Estonian government and the Estonian electorate has seemingly concluded that there is no other way forward for Estonia. If Estonia is to continue to develop and move up the ranks (Estonia is currently the poorest state in the Eurozone), more capital and investment is needed and the EU is the best option available. Estonia has chosen to be in the economic lifeboat with Austria, Belgium, Cyprus, Finland, France, Germany, Greece, Ireland, Italy, Luxembourg, Malta, the Netherlands, Portugal, Slovakia, Slovenia and Spain.

Latvia and Lithuania as members of the EU are obligated to join the Eurozone once they have met the strict fiscal and economic requirements, and once the EU is eager to include new members. Their eagerness for the fiscal sacrifices or for the common currency are considerably more ambivalent than Estonia's was. Nevertheless, within the next five to ten years, assuming the Euro survives, Latvia and Lithuania will board the same lifeboat as Estonia and forego the recent revival of their national currencies for membership in the Eurozone.

Twenty years after Estonia, Latvia and Lithuania succeeded in freeing themselves from the Soviet Union and the planned Soviet command economy, they have radically transformed themselves into market economies based on private property and enterprise. All three states became full members of the EU in remarkably short order. Estonia already uses the Euro, and it seems but a matter of time before Latvia and Lithuania do so as well. Investment has flooded into all three states and wealth has been created at a pace almost beyond the dreams of the 1990s. Still, Latvia and Lithuania are the poorest countries in the EU, and Estonia is the poorest country in the Eurozone. The idea of convergence with other EU members, once a legitimately anticipated event for the short and mid-term, seems further and further away. There have been great economic achievements, but much remains to be done.

CHAPTER 5

Identity

The study of identity has become a current academic obsession, but it is a topic and theme that bears close examination in Estonia, Latvia and Lithuania. The rise of Estonian, Latvian and Lithuanian ethnic nationalisms in the nineteenth and early twentieth centuries was essentially about refusing a German or Russian identity and nurturing and raising a folk, mostly peasant, identity worthy of the 'family of nations'. The establishment of independent Republics after the First World War (and the collapse of German and Russian empires) was, in part, an extension of this process of creating and defining identity. Resistance to Soviet occupation and rule was largely mobilized on an idea that the ethnic identity of Estonians, Latvians and Lithuanians was under dire threat in a Russian-dominated Soviet system. Ongoing mistrust and resentment of the European Union is also focused primarily on the threat of the institution to ethnic national identities. Throughout this entire timeline, however, multiple alternate trajectories of identity creation and definition coexisted, sometimes acrimoniously, and at other times separately from the dominant ethnic trope of Estonians, Latvians and Lithuanians. Germans, Russians, Jews, Roma, Belorussians, Ukrainians, Poles, Livs, Swedes and more have imagined and worked for either multi-ethnic communities or states dominated by other ethnic groups, or classes in the lands of Estonia, Latvia and Lithuania. Furthermore, even within the titular ethnic national groups of Estonians, Latvians and Lithuanians, there are schismatics still unsure of their relationship with others. The Seto of southeastern Estonia, the Latgalians of southeastern Latvia and the Samogitians of western Lithuania have all historically struggled with their own identity vis-à-vis the dominant ethnic group: are they subgroups, are they separate nations, or are they both? Increasingly, to many others, in the modern world of the twenty-first century sole ethnic identity seems too defined and at times irrelevant or anachronistic. A brief excursion that examines identity in Estonia, Latvia and Lithuania is therefore exceedingly relevant to their pasts and future.

Before the nineteenth century there was little attention paid to the idea of ethnic identity in present-day Estonia, Latvia and Lithuania. Society was ordered by station; people were born aristocrats, merchants and other city folk, or peasants. Careers may have taken individuals into the clergy or into military or government service, and this vocation defined a person. If a peasant managed to leave the countryside and become a tradesman or merchant in a town (a difficult proposition), his identity would migrate as well. The languages spoken by the majority of the people in the countryside were considered simple peasant languages and the idiosyncratic customs, beliefs and practices of these simple peasants were as easily dismissed. Culture and civilization on a higher plane were the exclusive province of a half-dozen refined languages. Along the eastern shores of the Baltic Sea these cultured languages were German, Russian, Polish, Latin and French (with a short period of Swedish and Danish hegemony as well). German and Russian dominated, while Poland became a declining regional power, and by the end of the eighteenth century, a non-existent power. Latin was primarily the religious language in Catholic realms, while French was the fashionable language of the highest ranks. By and large, however, the German language, and by extension the Germanic world and civilization, was the lingua franca of court and the political and economic elite in modern-day Estonia and Latvia. Polish and Latin played a similar role in modern-day Lithuania. In the rare cases in which individuals reached beyond their station in life, either through migration and social mobility in towns or by extreme distinction in the limited educational opportunities available to them, they moved into one of these high cultures. If someone was born a peasant, speaking a peasant tongue, but managed to raise himself to a different social order and speak German, he was no longer a peasant, but German.

Ethnicity as we understand it in the twenty-first century was yet undeveloped, and played even less a role in identity. For most people religion formed the core foundation of identity (Christian first, followed by confession), while an intensely insular local identity formed the bulk of a person's daily character. Peasants and townspeople alike (but peasants more so) had much to fear from strangers and outsiders and stayed in close-knit communities built on ties of kinship and long familiarity. Well beyond the nineteenth century, people tended to identify themselves by local parishes or villages and tended to see even relatively near neighbours as foreign, untrustworthy and outsiders.

In the mid- to late eighteenth century new religious identities provided some of the first breaks from these long-held, insular and closed concepts of identity. The Moravian brethren swept through parts of modern-day Latvia and Estonia and its adherents began to see themselves as of a different identity. Later, in the twentieth century, nationalist historians erroneously and somewhat disingenuously tried to recast these Pietists as early proto-nationalists. This was unfair. The Moravian brethren had little interest in secular reform, but their religious beliefs and fervour moved them away from traditional religious hierarchies and their proselytizing zeal overcame traditional parish boundaries. In this sense their changing sense of religious identity and of a community defined by this identity was an early example of new senses of identity in the lands of modern-day Estonia and Latvia. The nineteenth-century phenomenon of mass conversion to Russian orthodoxy was a similar profound change of identity as well as a calculated move for material improvement.

By the end of the eighteenth century and the beginning of the nineteenth, European intellectual trends re-examined the peasantry and discovered a potentially potent social order. Those transfixed by the French Revolution saw within the peasantry (and from the Pugachev rebellion more close to home) a potential for violent upheaval, something along the lines of a traditional European jacquerie, or peasant uprising. Others, including Johann Herder (who lived in Riga for several years), saw within the peasants a more pure social force less tarnished by Enlightenment thinking and rationalism. To these Romantic intellectuals, the peasant nations were fonts of rebirth. The long-considered oddities and anachronisms of peasant life – their songs, beliefs, customs and dress – were celebrated. Both these views of peasants were common in intellectual circles among the Baltic German aristocracy but, as they percolated down to handfuls of upwardly mobile, educated sons of peasants and then to peasants themselves, they suggested that a grand future waited for Estonian and Latvian peasants (but not always simultaneously), and that their difference and strength grew from folk conditions. Through the nineteenth century ethnic identity as a mobilizing tool took root in modern-day Estonia and Latvia.

In the mid-nineteenth century the first generation of Estonian and Latvian national figures laboured to deliver the Estonian and Latvian nations respectability. Although often working side by side, two separate and at times contradictory strains of national identity emerged. One narrative anchored identity in the folk, while the other aspired to mobilize ethnic achievements to raise its stature to that of other nations in the family of European nations. This dichotomy has continued to develop to the present day.

Champions of the folk concept of nation celebrated the peasant by trying to record peasant culture, and thereby reclaim a peasant past as the foundation of the modern nation. In the middle and late nineteenth century these adherents scoured the countryside recording folk proverbs, tales, fables and most importantly songs by the hundreds of thousands. Traditional peasant costume and dance joined an emerging pantheon that attempted to demonstrate the inherent value of a culture and identity based on a peasant past and present. To the modernizers among the ethnic national elites, peasant identity was, if noble, still lacking. To the champions of this national concept, the Estonian, Latvian or later Lithuanian nation needed the full complement of accomplishments and achievements of other European nations in order to be recognized and respected as such. These activists introduced a modern vocabulary to peasant tongues so that the world of high culture and science could be appropriately expressed. These activists further highlighted the international achievements of any member of their ethnic group in any field, from botany and other hard sciences to architecture and engineering, practical sciences and the humanities, as a marker of the rise of the entire ethnic group.

More often than not, these two visions of ethnic identity coexisted, although each continued to stress its own interpretation of events. For example, in the last quarter of the nineteenth century great ethnic song festivals were organized in modern-day Estonia and Latvia. These two strands of identity contested the meaning of these festivals. On the one hand, they were festivals devoted to folk songs, the very core of the folk concept of nation. But they also often included educational self-help seminars, and above all else were demonstrations of organizational ability. The ethnic organizations that organized and managed the festivals were flexing their organizational and logistical muscles and implying their ability to shepherd and speak for an emerging nation.

At other times the two visions of ethnic identity clashed (if politely) over the future direction of ethnic development and mobilization. The modernizers, most neatly summarized in the career of the early Latvian nationalist Krišjānis Valdemārs, encouraged the development of wealth and prosperity in order to capture more respect and power. Valdemārs and modernizers like him realized that peasant agriculture in modern-day Estonia, Latvia and Lithuania was a poor vehicle for rapid economic growth. Among other schemes, Valdemārs encouraged Latvians into the merchant marine and into agricultural schemes in more fertile areas of the Russian Empire far from Baltic German political control. Valdemārs, who worked in the Tsarist bureaucracy, evolved into a political realist eager to make compromises with other ethnic and socio-economic groups to advance the material conditions of Latvians. All of this activity was anathema to those nationalists that saw strength in the peasant roots and identity of the nation. To them urbanization and modernization entailed more risks than rewards. By the end of the nineteenth century these two separate visions were clearly formed: one embraced modernity and hoped to place an expansive Estonian, Latvian or Lithuanian nation within this brave new world, while the other celebrated the authentic, rural and almost transcendental insular world of Estonian, Latvian and Lithuanian peasants.[1] These conflicting ideals of ethnic identity appear consistently across the pages of nineteenth-century literature and in the fine arts of the time.

By the turn of the twentieth century increasing cases of radicalism among young intellectuals and some industrial workers might suggest that a new theme emerged in ethnic identity. By and large it did not, since radicals (ultimately gravitating towards some degree of Marxist thought) were more generally a subset of modernists eager to raise the material condition of the population. The radicals' driving force for change was neither the past nor peasant culture. If anything, they followed the earlier path of creating accomplishments that mirrored developments in other parts of Europe; literature, for example, took on a realist veneer similar to a Victor Hugo. Within political struggles the competition between ethnic and class mobilization was more an obsession of the elites than of the masses. In modern-day Estonia and Latvia, and slowly in modern-day Lithuania as well, the struggle between exploiters and exploited seemed to overlap with ethnic animosities and grievances and incendiary language was borrowed from both. After the unsuccessful Revolution of 1905 some revolutionaries did turn forcefully away from ethnic identity as a politically mobilizing force, seeing it as a false consciousness meant to dilute the unity of workers, but the earlier questions about the permanence of general ethnic identity seemed fixed.[2] In other words, 50 years earlier an educated Estonian or Latvian could choose, more or less, to become German or to embrace a new emerging ethnic identity. Twenty-five years earlier, an educated Estonian or Latvian could choose to throw himself into a more Russian identity within a Russian Imperial system pushing the benefits of Russification. Tens of thousands took this option to a geographic extreme by resettling to other parts of the Russian Empire (occasionally forming ethnic enclaves, but mostly losing ethnic distinctiveness within a few generations). By 1905 and its aftermath Estonians and Latvians could choose a host of political agendas and trajectories that covered a spectrum of how central ethnic identity would be to political action, but their ethnicity was most likely firmly set as Estonian or Latvian.

If ethnic identity had cemented in the minds and hearts of intellectuals, it had yet to ossify in the countryside. Through the late nineteenth and early twentieth century the borders of ethnic identity were still debated. Initially in the nineteenth century Latvians in the province of Livland wondered about the inclusion of Latvians from the province of Courland into their nation and vice versa. They regularly commented on the inclusion of singing choirs from Courland at song festivals as a positive unifying step, but were still unsure of its ultimate success. Through much of the twentieth century (and to some, even today) ethnic unification with Latvians from the southeast, from Latgale, remained an ongoing project. Latgalians had experienced a different socio-economic development; they were mostly Catholic, and their language was similar to Latvian, but not the same. Latvians and Latgalians alike struggled (and continue to struggle) with the proper relationship: were they related separate nations, or separated parts of a single ethnic whole? In either case, should Latgalians and Latvians continue to develop side by side or should they attempt to merge into one (and, of course, how would such a merger be negotiated)? With the ethnic Estonian nation, a similar parallel development existed with the Seto people, and in Lithuania, conversely, where the move towards ethnic consolidation happened slightly later, the difference of regions became less pronounced. Many of these issues and concerns affected a relatively small number of people for as long as Estonians, Latvians and Lithuanians navigated the waters of a multi-national Russian empire. With the achievement of independent statehood, the importance of identity took central stage and re-emerged even more hotly contested. Would identity continue to develop on an ethnic basis? Would the power of the state be used to forge identity? How would alternate, competing and/or contradictory identities co-exist in independent states?

Initially, following independence, the identity debate was somewhat muted. The new republics' constitutions defined the nation geographically, not ethnically, and most government leaders and politicians were generally in the modernist mould on the identity scale. If anything, government leaders were keen to show that Estonians, Latvians and Lithuanians fitted well on the European diplomatic stage. Diplomats in top hats and formal dress attire became the international faces of the new states. These politicians seemed particularly to recoil at Western stereotypes of Baltic backwardness or novice abilities at statecraft. For every glib comment that the old Baltic German aristocracy could scarcely believe that their former carriage drivers had taken the reins of power, the new ministers and diplomats took greater pains to show European accomplishments. The resurgence of the insular, peasant narrative did not take firm root in government-sponsored productions until the late 1920s, and most particularly after authoritarian coups came to power (in 1934 in the case of Estonia and Latvia), although in Lithuania the singular obsession remained the irredentist desire to reclaim Vilnius for Lithuania over all other potential narratives. With time, however, the identity battles sharpened into focus across Estonia, Latvia and Lithuania. The debate about identity slowly manifested itself in the guises of developments in architecture, the fine arts, music, *belles-lettres*, public spectacles and rituals, popular sports and slowly in the mass media. This debate, and the abovementioned venues, continues to this day. Instead of tracking the larger identity issue chronologically, we will look at the developments of each venue in terms of contested identity through the twentieth century and beyond.

The aforementioned song festivals, even the first ones in the second half of the nineteenth century, included substantial arguments about song selection, the use of flags and banners, and the proper methods of celebration. Even the way in which songs were sung hinted at the dichotomy between a revivalism of peasant culture and aspirations to high European culture. The song programmes almost always included new compositions that drew inspiration from folk songs as well as folk songs themselves. Even the folk songs were stripped of their more authentic and original singing style (often with droning, and call and response) and forced into a nineteenth-century, European choral mould. At the end of the nineteenth century all three nations, Estonians, Latvians and Lithuanians, could claim to be singing nations, but this was not unique. In many respects their folk singing culture was simply still extant by the time ethnographers took note. Across Europe singing traditions had been strong and dominant, but began to subside with the modern era.[3] By the time intellectuals took note of them, songs and singing traditions were disappearing. In Estonia, Latvia and Lithuania the importance of folk songs was imported into the region before folk singing fell into crisis. Still, the recorders of folk songs brought nineteenth-century, bourgeois values with them to the countryside and an inclination to expurgate bawdy texts (or relegate them to appendix-like volumes of songs). They also tended to value lyrics more than the style of singing. As a result folk songs became choral songs. Similarly folk dances became staged attempts at folk dance dominated by the popular polka step, which traced its own origins to a European dance craze of the mid-nineteenth century.

Nevertheless folk songs, folk dances and song festivals became staples of ethnic identity through the late nineteenth century. Even the location of a song festival would be imbued with meaning. Latvia's song festival of 1873 (often referred to as the first even though several smaller regional festivals occurred earlier) was seen as particularly important in Latvian ethnic mobilization because it brought the peasant nation and its culture to the metropolis of Riga, even immortalizing the step in a popular song written for the festival, 'Riga dimd'. This was a direct challenge to the idea that the cities were Germanic. A later song festival in Jelgava was likewise a challenge to the hegemony of Riga over Latvian affairs, but this experiment would end quickly, as this was the only all-encompassing song festival to be held outside of Riga. Through these song festivals and a vibrant choir movement personified in countless singing societies, a litany of ethnic national hymns and anthems coalesced. In the twentieth century the song festivals lost ground to other forms of popular music, hastened by records and radio. Popular musical taste turned to schlager music and even jazz. By the late 1930s popular music was overwhelmingly represented by melodramatic ballads, early dance-hall music or gross reproductions of popular hits elsewhere in Europe.

After the Soviet occupation song festivals took on a new significance in terms of content, even if their form remained remarkably similar, if not enhanced. Soviet song festivals in Estonia, Latvia and Lithuania were the most lavishly produced, well-funded productions in the history of song festivals. This seems to be a perfect example of the Soviet Union as an 'affirmative action' state that funded national differences, and indeed it is a strike against academics that see in Soviet rule an attempted genocide of the Estonian, Latvian, and Lithuanian nations. Soviet-era song festivals, however, brought fundamental changes. Initially, in the Stalinist years, praises to Stalin in musical harmony were included, and throughout the Soviet era the most stridently nationalist songs were absent from the song programme. More insidiously the Soviet song festivals included songs in Russian as well as performances from or for other members of the brotherly nations of the USSR. Songs and dances from visiting choirs and dance groups from as far afield as Uzbekistan or even beyond Soviet borders were often crowd favourites, but diluted the original intent of a homogenizing message within an ethnic song festival. The Soviet song festival posited Estonians, Latvians and Lithuanians within a range of socialist nationalities all eagerly building socialism in one country. This was the polar opposite of the original intent of song festivals: to highlight the uniqueness and intrinsic value of Estonian, Latvian or Lithuanian peasant culture. Soviet song festivals, however, could also act as places of quiet resistance as folk songs with little overt political message or symbolism took on a quasi-protest aura. This confusion about the message of song festivals has not retreated with the re-establishment of independence. They remain popular events that claim a special right for state support, but in hard financial times are also targets for budget reductions.

Popular song and music also developed in at times contradictory directions during the Soviet era. The Soviet regime recognized the legitimizing power that popular cultural figures, singers among them, could wield and tried unsuccessfully to coax a few émigré singers to return to Soviet Estonia, Latvia and Lithuania. Through the 1950s recorded and performed music was very tightly controlled. In the 1960s popular music became a much larger industry and created singers and songwriters with mass appeal. The most successful, in terms of popularity and acclaim, were those that had considerable support from the regime, but were still able to portray, at the least, the image of an independent artist. The best example of this phenomenon might be Raimonds Pauls in Latvia. Pauls, born in 1936, studied at the Latvian Academy of Music and began his career as an accomplished pianist in the 1950s. During the course of the 1960s Pauls led the Riga Light Music Orchestra and began to compose musical scores for theatre and film. By the late 1960s and through the '70s Pauls's musical style moved closer to pop and his popularity grew throughout the Soviet Union. Pauls's musical career was a curious mix of state support and acknowledgement and popular adulation. Few of his songs can be seen as aggressively propagandist for the Soviet state; instead, he mined sentiments of love and nostalgia. He was consistently feted by Soviet authorities (and seen as an influential and accomplished performer and songwriter in the Soviet Russian sphere) while also being the author of life's soundtrack for much of the Latvian generation that came of age through the 1960s, '70s and early '80s. His musical legacy includes composing the soundtracks for many iconic films of Latvian film history, writing and/or singing many of the most popular lyrical songs of the 1960s and '70s, and acting as a kind of incubator for musical talent throughout this time period. Pauls and his song catalogue managed to encapsulate Soviet Latvian music for almost three decades, but he also had an appeal that far outlasted Soviet rule.

While Raimonds Pauls and other singers and songwriters with official Soviet support charted their way through the last decades of Soviet rule, fringe elements survived and with time flourished across Soviet Estonia, Latvia and Lithuania. Musicians (Pauls included) had long experimented with jazz despite the regime's periodic official displeasure with the musical style. By the 1960s and '70s the slightly more porous borders of the Soviet Union witnessed the first arrivals of Western pop and rock music. The regime frowned upon the new music even more than jazz and tried to limit its spread while also offering sanitized alternatives. But music and musicians offered one of the few venues for, if not open opposition, than open non-conformity. Small hippie groups emerged in Estonia, Latvia and

Lithuania and pushed the limits of non-conformity, but had little chance for mass appeal. Rock music was far more popular. Small unofficial bands began in all three republics in the 1960s, playing covers of mostly British rock. These bands performed at the youth periphery of official Soviet leisure and recreation, at social clubs and dances, and often quickly garnered underground followings. In the 1970s some of these bands became more official musical groups that recorded and toured across the USSR. Yet the authorities worried about the potential of resistance and rebellion within this musical style and about the behaviour of its devotees. Soviet authorities increasingly tried to keep close surveillance on these bands and on their musical shows.[4] But even when the Soviet authorities became so alarmed as to act, they did so relatively tamely, by limiting group performances or recording options. On the one hand, musicians were reminded of Soviet authority, but on the other their continued presence in Estonian, Latvian and Lithuanian society kept them as symbols of non-conformity. By the 1980s the emergence of punk rock and heavy metal in Estonia, Latvia and Lithuania offered a far more strident, anti-society message. These bands and their followers were more closely monitored and more intensely demonized by the Soviet state, but they also continued to exist on the periphery of late Soviet society.

A revival in folk music ensembles mirrored the alternative music on the periphery that was not sanctioned, but somewhat tolerated, in the late Soviet era. Together with ethnographers (professional and amateur), folk singing groups across Estonia, Latvia and Lithuania began to resurrect folk singing styles from before their standardization into choral harmonies. Peasant musical instruments, arcane droning and call and response song styles slowly resurfaced. This new folk movement did not begin as a political statement, but it did challenge the modernist paradise of an industrial Soviet society. The same critique continues to hold for the modernist, free-market society of the EU, and the vibrant folk movement in all three countries continues to suggest a return to ethnic traditions, albeit with modern packaging and flair. Some groups, such as Latvia's neo-pagan heavy metal band Skyforger, have succeeded in finding similar audiences and musical currents across Scandinavia and into Europe. Along with electric guitars, bass and drums, Skyforger include traditional musical instuments and sing folk songs in heavy metal arrangements. These diverse musical styles share a celebration of ethnic pride, and have managed the difficult trick of garnering some wider international fame and accomplishment while performing in a style passionately devoted to ethnic uniqueness.

Since independence the popular music scene in Estonia, Latvia and Lithuania has had more difficulty in creating a uniquely Estonian, Latvian or Lithuanian sound while simultaneously crossing over into wider European markets. Musical bands follow Western and global musical patterns closely and to differing degrees mimic or incorporate them into original songs. Music as an industry struggles with the small markets of Estonia, Latvia and Lithuania. A hit album in a large market can be the beginning of a massive financial windfall. In Estonia, Latvia and Lithuania, however, musical groups must produce consistent hit records and also plumb the depths of soundtrack scores, commercial soundtracks and even political jingoes. These bands have great name recognition and fame, but the riches are more modest. The golden bullet is always the song or album that crosses over to a larger market, either in Europe with an English-language hit or in Russia with a Russian hit. The results have been inconsistent at best, and usually the music most exposed to European consumers becomes indistinct from the many other such bands and songs from across Eastern Europe that clog the Eurovision Song Contest on an annual basis.

This is a shame, because as with the dichotomy in musical identity from years past, the current musical scene in Estonia, Latvia and Lithuania often includes a vibrant and creative non-commercial current.[5] Bands experiment and create with myriad styles and introduce Estonian, Latvian and Lithuanian components, but the music is not driven by commercial sales. As a result bands either slip out of existence and into other professional endeavours, or out of Estonia, Latvia and Lithuania to greater markets and greener pastures in the large, multi-ethnic, cosmopolitan musical centres of Europe and the world. There they may rise to become central figures in their respective genres, but are lost to Estonia, Latvia and Lithuania. Only in the most successful cases are these musicians re-embraced by Estonian, Latvian and Lithuanian society, and only on the merits of their international achievements, a pattern repeated in opera.

With independence after the First World War, song festivals and folk music battled with popular music for mass attention, but all three states poured money into national operas (as well as national theatres). Embracing the opera seemed an odd step, since the musical form had primarily been the preserve of Baltic Germans before the war, but the opera was a step toward European respectability, and opera houses proliferated across Eastern Europe. The quality of the opera was helped by the influx of Russian artists fleeing upheaval in the Soviet Union, and quickly became a point of pride in recollections and nostalgia of the interwar period. The pride, however, may have been somewhat misplaced: diplomats privately belittled the opera even if they raved about it to the press. The opera also struggled to find common, mass acceptance. Ticket prices were affordable and workers filled the worst seats of the opera fairly faithfully, but the cost, extravagance and luxury involved singled out the opera as one of the first targets of common anger in periods of government austerity. Peasants frequently wrote petitions bemoaning government support of the opera when material conditions in the countryside were so poor. The same phenomenon recurred in the 1990s and 2000s when difficult government cuts were considered. The opera exemplifies the curious relationship with European high culture in Estonia, Lithuania, or Latvia. In good times it is a point of pride, with considerable press attention paid to innovative stage design and costuming and the calibre of new productions. The choice of a season's schedule is parsed for greater meaning: whether the inclusion of a Tchaikovsky opera is a signal of warming relations with Russia, for example. In times of want, however, the opera is as quickly jettisoned as a superfluous luxury and one that is not essentially Estonian, Lithuanian or Latvian. Still, the desire to be seen on Europe's stage leads international acclaim and success to trump other concerns. When Elīna Garanča, for example, received rave reviews for her perform-ances at the Metropolitan Opera in New York (in *The Barber of Seville* and *Carmen*), she and the opera were feted in Latvia as proof that Latvians had made a mark on the international stage.

The case of the celebrated Estonian composer Arvo Pärt is a curious amalgam of both of these phenomena. Pärt was born in 1935, but most of his musical educa-tion was in Soviet Estonian schools, most importantly at the Tallinn Conservatory. Initially Pärt composed neo-classical scores, but through the 1960s he began to compose music at odds with the Soviet musical establishment. Some of his works were censored and he responded by withdrawing from active work. During this time he became increasingly interested in choral music from the early Renaissance. He increasingly wrote sacred music, further alienating himself from official Soviet musical circles. Ultimately he emigrated in 1980, moving first to Austria and later to Germany. From the 1980s Pärt became one of the world's most well-known and celebrated composers of sacred music. Ultimately he returned to independent Estonia. His work is warmly received and celebrated in his native land, where an International Arvo Pärt Centre is under construction. His accomplishments and Western recognition are feted in Estonia, even if his music does not specifically draw from Estonian folk motifs. His inspirations are primarily old, sacred music, and his references are frequently religious, often with text in Latin or Church Slavonic. Pärt has often drawn attention to dissidents in Russia, including Anna Politkovskaya and Mikhail Khodorkovsky, rather than engaging in the Estonian political milieu. However, he did write a composition to Estonia's President

Lennart Meri, which was played at the president's funeral. All in all, Pärt, like many other musicians across Estonia, Latvia and Lithuania, has been celebrated at home when recognized abroad, even if his work is not essentially, in this case, Estonian.

Similar trajectories can be traced across many of the disciplines that play a role in defining identity. The fine arts are another example. Until the mid-nineteenth century there were almost no Estonian, Latvian or Lithuanian painters. A few painters can likely be traced to Estonian, Latvian or Lithuanian ancestry, but they did not identify themselves as such, nor did their artwork present some specific characteristic of Estonian-ness, Latvian-ness or Lithuanian-ness. By the second half of the nineteenth century a handful of painters, trained in the St Petersburg academy tradition or at various German schools, can be identified as the fathers of Estonian, Latvian, and Lithuanian painting.[6] As a result, by the end of the nineteenth century and into the twentieth, there was a bevy of talented Estonian, Latvian and Lithuanian painters, such as Johann Köler, Karl Ludvig Maibach, Kristjan Raud, Jānis Rozentāls, Jānis Valters and Vilhelms Purvītis, who all produced accomplished and celebrated artwork that fitted broadly into European art patterns. Their style, subject-matter and composition were all more generally European rather than being narrowly focused on Estonian, Latvian or Lithuanian identity. Some painters produced seminal works showcasing local subjects, such as Rozentāls' *After the Service (Leaving the Church)*, or Köler's *Portrait of Dr F. R. Kreutzwald*, but stylistically they remained essentially European.

The difficult balancing act for Estonian, Latvian and Lithuanian artists was to remain a part of European currents in the art world, particularly with the rapid spread of different art movements at the dawn of modern art, without drifting apart from the lived experience of Estonians, Latvians and Lithuanians. Often they failed, and their artwork was either a pale imitation of a movement or a particular canvas or was completely foreign to their fellow countrymen. On rare occasions they succeeded in accommodating the distinctive message of Estonian, Latvian and Lithuanian life in a modern oeuvre. The Estonian painter Kristjan Raud may be the earliest example of this skill. Jāzeps Grosvalds's highly emotional, somewhat abstract paintings of Latvian soldiers and refugees during the First World War are equally compelling.

Through the 1920s a new generation of artists in Estonia, Latvia and Lithuania dutifully replicated Cubist and Constructivist principles on their canvases. Their works of art were often accomplished, but struggled to define something particularly local and were hence often misunderstood or unappreciated by the mass of Estonians, Latvians and Lithuanians. A few artists tried to return to the attempt to meld a distinctive local message with a modern style. Romans Suta, for example, tried to accomplish this through using traditional designs and motifs in new forms. He followed the local arts and craft movement, which placed high value on ceramics, woven fabrics and other handicrafts. Suta began to create avant-garde representations of Latvian folk motifs on porcelain plates. This was a strikingly innovative and successful attempt and one that reinvigorated an entire approach to art and raised the status of the arts and craft movement simultaneously. To this day artists from this region who work in decorative and applied arts are perhaps more skilled and accomplished than many of their Western counterparts, in part due to Suta's marriage of high and applied art. This same trend can be seen in the central importance placed upon stage and set designs for opera and theatre.

Other artists understood the imperative of accommodating a distinct Estonian, Latvian or Lithuanian message with a modern oeuvre differently. Kārlis Padegs in Latvia saw a profound change in local identity from the artists before him. Rather than painting stylized peasants or drawing from folk motifs, he painted the gritty underbelly of urban life as central to modern Latvian identity. His sketches of thugs and prostitutes corresponded closely with similar literary approaches from writers such as Aleksandrs Čaks, who wrote of an unapologetically urban world. An unabashedly urban Estonian, Latvian or Lithuanian artistic and cultural identity was first seriously presented only in the twentieth century.

Through most of the 1930s, and particularly after authoritarian regimes had come to power in Estonia, Latvia and Lithuania, art and artist served the state in a manner similar to how they did in other authoritarian regimes across Europe at the time. Some art and its relentless glorification of the regime bears a striking familial resemblance to the art most favoured by Europe's most infamous twentieth-century tyrants. The dictators' aesthetic is apparently often similar. Often local identity was exaggerated to such a degree that the simple artistic quality of works produced suffered considerably. Artists that refrained from producing regime-friendly work, although not specifically persecuted, found it difficult to survive financially in a new society where most outlays on culture came from the state and not individuals.

Through the first decades of Soviet occupation, artistic production was rigidly controlled and defined by the state. Dissident artists were imprisoned and banned from exhibiting works and the drab commandments of official Socialist Realism determined creative expression.[7] Even in these years, however, the differences in artistic quality and skill between one painter and another was clear. Recently Estonia, Latvia and Lithuania have tentatively looked back at the decades of Socialist Realism to winnow out the artistic talent from the rest. In Riga a major exhibition, 'The Mythology of Sovietland', showed nearly 120 paintings and 50 sculptures through most of 2008. Still, the more celebrated Soviet Estonian, Latvian and Lithuanian artists are those, like the musicians, that walked the fine line between degrees of financial support (and ability to show art) from the regime and veiled or implied references to a distinct local message or a critique of the Soviet system. Artists such as Auseklis Baušķenieks or Maija Tabaka are good examples of this trend. They benefited from regime support for some of their creative work, but also touched a popular chord.

With independence restored in the 1990s, artists, like musicians, have had to conform their creative abilities and production to the vagaries of a free-market society. Although state support of the arts remains, it pales in comparison to the degree or generosity of Soviet state support to regime-friendly artists. Art schools and museums have had to rapidly readjust to a system of operations that is determined in part by financial viability. How art and identity will continue to develop is still an open question. Artists may increasingly focus on market-friendly art, they may supplement wages by using their creative talents elsewhere (in marketing campaigns or in merchandising and display, for example), or they may take their talents and seek their fortunes abroad. Still, the remnant of the idea that art should combine a distinct local message with a modern oeuvre has not entirely vanished. In 1995 the author had the pleasure of listening to the public defence of Masters degrees by a graduating class of painters at Latvia's Academy of Art. As with the artists of the 1920s, many of the young artists were dutifully replicating the artistic trends of the rest of the world (often with considerable skill and accomplishment) with relatively little direct local content. One painting stood out for being almost diametrically opposed to local content; the painting seemed to reference Central American modern religious murals. The academy faculty pointedly criticized the artist for producing a painting that was not 'Latvian art'. A faculty member cited the production of 'Latvian art' as the purpose of the Latvian Academy of Art. The relationship between art and artist and state and people continues to be debated in contemporary Estonia, Latvia and Lithuania.

Other artists in all three states, or from all three states, produced groundbreaking works that did not pay homage to a distinct local message. These artists were outsiders either politically or ethnically. Chaïm Soutine, a celebrated Jewish artist, for example, was born in modern-day Belarus, studied at the Vilna Academy of Fine Arts and emigrated to Paris in 1913. In France he developed a unique style that approached Abstract Expressionism. He is perhaps best known internationally for a series of paintings of a rotting beef carcass. Soutine died during the Second World War while hiding from the Gestapo. Philippe Halsman, one of the founders of Surrealist photography, a much sought-after portrait photographer and an important early high fashion photographer, was a Jew from Riga who lived for most of his professional life in the USA. Mark Rothko, a Jew from Daugavpils, moved to the USA while still a child. He became a leading figure in Abstract Expressionism and his simple yet powerful paintings are immediately recognizable. Even though one of his paintings seems inspired by the Latvian flag, he did not reference a Latvian element in his artistic career.

Gustavs Klucis, who joined the Communist Party soon after the Revolution and became a central figure in the avant-garde movement in Soviet Russia in the 1920s, was also a Latvian. His pioneering work in photography and the use of photomontage for political propaganda is still appreciated internationally. There was in his art, however, little or nothing that drew upon or referenced a Latvian message or identity. The artistic legacy of Klucis, Soutine and Halsman, or of similarly internationally accomplished film figures such as Sergei Eisenstein or Ladislas Starevich, has been a difficult one to digest for the art worlds of Estonia, Latvia and Lithuania. In the 1920s and '30s they were not recognized by these art worlds. During Soviet rule those artists that were accepted by Soviet authorities received some attention and inclusion, but most fell beyond this. From the 1990s and more aggressively in the twenty-first century, the famous artists, filmmakers, thinkers (Isaiah Berlin) and writers with any tenuous connection to Estonia, Latvia and Lithuania have been publically embraced by the intellectual worlds of each of these states, although more for show than in any meaningful way. In crude terms, these famous artists are surrogates and proxies that stand in for Estonian, Latvian and Lithuanian accomplishment on a world stage.

There is a wide constellation of additional activities that shape and define identity in Estonia, Latvia and Lithuania. These activities include literature, film, public celebrations and spectacles, and even sport. Across all of these, a common, all-encompassing theme is the struggle between expressing a unique, local identity for Estonians, Latvians and Lithuanians and claiming for these peoples a place on the world stage. Even the physical landscapes of all three states are contested sites in these battles around identity. Our well-worn themes and debates about identity can be seen in how nature is defined and imagined, how architecture is transforming cities and how public projects – from national libraries, to roads and bridges, to the creations of monuments for an equally contested historical memory – invest meaning in city spaces. In literature and film the outsider usually cannot easily access this ongoing debate. The Estonian, Latvian and Lithuanian languages act as enclosed spaces for Estonians, Latvians and Lithuanians. Within these spaces the theme of contested identities is commonplace. The first novel in Latvian, *The Time of the Surveyors* by the Kaudzītis brothers, included a character that was a parody of a Latvian attempting to be a German. The figure, Švauksts, has become a cultural archetype and is still referenced often. In this case Švauksts was comical precisely because he had failed on both accounts: he was not accepted in a German world and had turned away from an authentic Latvian identity. If the character of Švauksts failed, other authors succeeded. The development and success of authors mirrored the trajectory of musicians and painters quite closely. The most successful Estonian, Latvian and Lithuanian authors of the late nineteenth and early twentieth centuries borrowed from and referenced European currents, but also captured something local. Likewise, the most successful and popularly respected authors of the Soviet period balanced between regime approval (needed to publish) and an independent streak. The Latvian poet Imants Ziedonis managed to be chairman of the Soviet Latvian Writers' Union, but also developed into a veiled opponent of Soviet rule. His mashing together of folk concepts with biting descriptive commentary on societal ills in the seemingly innocuous form of children's tales are triumphs of Latvian literature. He managed in literature to create the distinctive Latvian message within a Soviet oeuvre that spoke to a larger world as well. In 2011 Ziedonis was nominated for the Astrid Lindgren Memorial Award, which is the world's largest prize for children's literature. Māra Cielēna, the contemporary Latvian children's author, has assumed this mantle. Cielēna consistently produces charming, unique stories for children that feel intrinsically Latvian, but could be readily accessible to an international audience.

The list of subject-matter to examine for further insights into these contested identities is almost limitless. Estonian, Latvian and Lithuanian filmmakers, for example, follow similar trajectories and face many of the same challenges today as artists and musicians. Early films were produced during the period of inter-war independence (even during tsarist rule), but most of the beginnings of a canon of Estonian, Latvian and Lithuanian film are from the Soviet era. As with other media, the most successful Soviet films had to tread difficult waters between official regime permission and a presentation to a viewing public that suggested uniqueness and autonomy. Filmmakers were some of the most vocal members of the cultural elite that pushed for reform and radical change in the late 1980s. With independence restored, Estonian, Latvian and Lithuanian filmmakers were faced with two great new challenges. Suddenly they were free to create films free of

Soviet censorship, ones that spoke of the difficult pasts of Estonia, Latvia and Lithuania. Simultaneously, however, the funding of films became dependent on market forces: films had to make money or hold out the prospect of making money. Some films have tried to do both; in each state relatively lavish productions of films either set during the wars for independence, during the loss of independence or during resistance to Soviet rule have struggled with a new balancing act. They have attempted to match the glitz, glamour and pacing of the Hollywood blockbusters with which they must compete at the box office. They have also tried to choose stories that are patriotic and triumphant, yet still remain roughly accurate to historical events while not alienating potential film viewers. The results are mixed. Other filmmakers have crafted films that fit in larger international film styles. Some, such as the Latvian film *Vogelfrei* (2007), an omnibus film of four connected stories told by four directors, succeed in presenting a film that is not overtly Latvian, but skilfully depicts Latvian society. Other successful films, as with literature, are on children's topics. The Latvian film *The Little Thieves* (*Mazie laupītāji*, 2009) touches on current economic crises, corruption and traditional rural values and strengths, all within a children's tale. The Estonian and Latvian animated film series *Lotte*, about an inquisitive and adventurous girl dog in a world of animals, captures a little of the spirit and sensibilities of Estonians and Latvians while still being immensely approachable and enjoyable for an international audience.

One public spectacle that may be largely devoid of the battle for identity is in mass spectator sport. If in many of these other areas there is a constant push and pull between creating and nurturing a unique, local, insular identity and a contradictory impulse to prove Estonian, Latvian, and Lithuanian merits on a European or world stage, in sports it is almost entirely the latter. Whenever an Estonian, Latvian or Lithuanian athlete receives international accolades, he or she almost instantly becomes a symbolic proxy for their homeland's international standing. Even if the sport is little followed or pursued in Estonia, Latvia or Lithuania, international success breeds recognition and celebration at home. In Lithuania these achieve almost rapturous levels for achievements in basketball (and there have been many achievements, including three bronze medals running at the Olympic Games, and a bronze medal at the FIBA World Championships in 2010). Latvians react similarly to achievements in ice hockey, where travelling Latvian fans have become as feted at international events as the teams. Latvia's qualification for the 2004 UEFA European Football Championship held in Portugal was a similar accomplishment. Much of this passion for basketball, ice hockey and football comes from its long roots in Lithuania and Latvia (through the interwar years and during the Soviet era). Equally important, however, is the national sense of pride in competing on the world stage in such internationally popular events. Each victory against a historic enemy is particularly savoured. In Riga, for example, hockey fans march to the embassy of defeated foes and leave flowers in a mock funerary procession. The most relished of such events are victories against Russian teams, although the embassy of the USA and others have received the same treatment. There is, however, more to this fanatic following than a proxy for geopolitical antagonisms. The most central aspect of the cultish place of basketball, ice hockey and to a lesser degree football for identity is that international achievement reinforces Latvian and Lithuanian beliefs in themselves on a larger stage. In this light some of these achievements are impressive. For Lithuania, for example, when the national team of a country of a little more than three million people defeats a national team from the USA composed entirely of NBA superstars, the victory becomes a national celebration for Lithuania. Perhaps even more astonishingly, there are less than 4,500 registered hockey players in all of Latvia. This includes all men, women and junior players. Nevertheless, from those four thousand players, Latvia is able to field a national team that competes on the international stage against countries such as Canada, which draws from almost 600,000 registered players! This is why boisterous throngs of Latvian fans follow their team to international events across the globe and remain generally ecstatic even in the face of the occasional crushing defeat.

Identity is always in flux, and no less so in Estonia, Latvia and Lithuania. This very cursory introduction to common themes in how identity is defined and contested across the Baltic states is woefully incomplete. There are always more artists, musicians, authors and events that could be added to the discussion. Hopefully the thematic framework outlined will accommodate these additions.

CHAPTER 6

Prospects

At the dawn of the twentieth century, the imprint of Estonians, Latvians and Lithuanians on the wider European world was almost negligible. There had been famous individuals who had made names for themselves in specific fields, professions or disciplines, and a handful of travellers and specialists that were knowledgeable about the region. But most Europeans knew almost nothing about conditions along the eastern coast of the Baltic Sea or about the aspirations of the area's inhabitants. Estonian and Latvian participation in the Revolutions of 1905 brought the region some international attention and notoriety, but that soon ebbed into stereotypes about Russia as a prison of nations. Through the First World War the region was known mostly as a battlefield and as the site of great and ominous German victories in the east. By the war's conclusion the region had received international attention for almost the first time. Estonian, Latvian and Lithuanian delegates arrived at the Versailles Peace Conference as the embodiment of Woodrow Wilson's much quoted claim that if he had known how many nations would declare their right to self-determination he would not have raised the issue in the first place. The idea of statehood for Estonia, Latvia or Lithuania was not readily embraced by any of the great powers, but since the alterative seemed to be Bolshevik power, and as local armies and governments demonstrated their viability, statehood was achieved. Many diplomats and government figures across Europe, however, doubted the long-term feasibility of the three states, either betraying their bias against small states or expecting a resurgent German or Russian power to reassert itself across Eastern Europe. When that moment arrived, when Nazi Germany and Soviet Russia divided Eastern Europe between themselves, neither Estonia, Latvia nor Lithuania received more than faint moral support in the face of upcoming aggression. When Soviet occupation descended across all three states in June 1940 Europe showed relatively little interest, since Paris had been occupied by German troops a few days before. After the Nazi invasion of the Soviet Union the tragic plight of Estonia, Latvia and Lithuania became rather awkward. The Soviet Union, the aggressor and occupier in the case of all three, had become a crucial ally in the war against the Axis powers. After the war ended Estonia, Latvia and Lithuania were the only pre-war states to lose their formal sovereignty, but what could be done?

Through the long decades of the Cold War the plight of Estonia, Latvia and Lithuania became a common trope for discussing Soviet rule in general. Estonian, Latvian and Lithuanian émigré communities skilfully fed the narrative that free-dom-loving people were captives in the Soviet prison of nations. Mass deportations and terror, coupled with relentless planned heavy industrialization and Russian immigration, were defined as the hallmarks of Soviet rule. Early on, during the Stalin years until 1953, much of this was accurate, but there was more to it. Estonian, Latvian and Lithuanian Communists and fellow travellers had helped build this system. Soviet accounts described incorporation into the Soviet Union as the last act of popular revolutions by peoples that eagerly embraced the Soviet experiment. Much of this was baseless propaganda, but there were still developments that were popularly appreciated. After Stalin's death, politics and development in the Estonian, Latvian and Lithuanian Soviet Socialist Republics became an elaborate game of pushing reforms within a closed, restrictive and oppressive system. The All-Union Communist Party was the paramount authority and ultimate arbiter, but in small spaces and small ways the republic-level party and government asserted some power as well. Individuals' lives and careers had firm boundaries, particu-larly in terms of political participation, but people still learned to carve out more specific personal successes and failures. Estonians, Latvians and Lithuanians did the best that they could within the Soviet system and at times enjoyed its best benefits. There seemed to be no other option; there was no viable avenue for radical political change.

In the 1980s, with the approval and instigation of Mikhail Gorbachev and like-minded Communist Party leaders, gradual reforms began to appear across Eastern Europe and even inside the Soviet Union, often in the Estonian, Latvian and Lithuanian Soviet Socialist Republics. These early simple economic reforms and the opening of political discourse quickly accelerated into demands for radical change. Revolutions toppled Communist regime after Communist regime in Eastern Europe, and the Soviet Union did not interfere (in the case of East Germany, the USSR even pushed for revolution and against the status quo). Emboldened, Estonians, Latvians and Lithuanians called for similar reforms and began to question the fundamental legitimacy of Soviet rule. Through 1988 and 1989 Estonia, Latvia and Lithuania seemed to be the conscience of the new USSR that Gorbachev hoped to create. Gorbachev faced two intractable questions: could he contain popular demands in Estonia, Latvia and Lithuania without using force or without acquiescence, and would his hoped-for reformed Soviet Union survive the popular exit of three constituent republics? In the end he could manage neither; but, much to the surprise of most observers, Estonia, Latvia and Lithuania regained statehood with relatively little loss of life. The successful, popular movements became known as the singing revolutions, and the dramatic and ultimately joyous result brought Estonia, Latvia and Lithuania into central focus on the world stage, perhaps more so than at any time before.

The goodwill and joy of the singing revolutions, however, did not last. If, in the late 1980s and early '90s, Estonia, Latvia and Lithuania were known globally for principled, non-violent and brave stands for independence in the face of an overwhelming foe (the Soviet Union), the 1990s brought considerable disappointments. The legacy from decades of a failed economic programme was exceedingly difficult to overcome. Reconstruction and state-building was long, torturous work that also tended to breed corruption and massive disparities in wealth and power in a society that had previously had little of either. In all three states, but most specifically in Estonia and Latvia, state-building included defining the status of hundreds of thousands of Soviet-era migrants. The principled absolutes of songs in the face of tanks and human chains in the face of handcuffs descended into the more pedestrian, complicated and relativistic merits of citizenship and language laws. Uninterested in these specifics, the international view of the Baltic states (and the international community almost always lumps the three together as the Baltic states) became defined by the question of non-citizens, of people disenfranchised, of the justness of naturalization processes and language laws. The casual observer often concluded that these were people once oppressed that now used political power and independence to oppress others themselves. Citizenship laws have been mollified and the number of disenfranchised has dropped steadily, but ethnic conflict has become the hallmark of Latvian politics specifically.

The first years of the twenty-first century seemed to suggest a kind of terminal achievement for Estonia, Latvia and Lithuania. If European powers and peoples had known little of Estonia, Latvia or Lithuania just decades ago, now they were all formal and equal members of the European Union and the North Atlantic Treaty Organization. Estonia, Latvia and Lithuania were unabashedly on the European stage, a dream fulfilled after more than a century of struggle. West

European prosperity was the last elusive dream and through the rapid growth of the better part of the first decade of the twenty-first century, the Baltic Tigers seemed a step behind the Celtic Tiger in rapid transformative change. By 2009 this dream was dashed by the global economic recession. Estonia, Latvia and Lithuania were all early casualties in this recession and also early recipients of international financial assistance that included demands for rapid and severe governmental fiscal restraint. Still, being early recipients, Estonia, Latvia and Lithuania have also emerged from recession more quickly. But they have done so in a badly shaken EU where recovery is still uncertain. Where do Estonia, Latvia and Lithuania go from here?

In the autumn of 2010 and the spring of 2011 Latvia and Estonia were presented with the possibility of a radical break from the politics of the past two decades. In each state the head of government and his political party seemed to enter parliamentary elections from a decidedly weak position. The head of government had presided over severe austerity measures, in part dictated by international financial organizations. The economy seemed to still be retracting, wages and real estate values had dropped sharply, and official unemployment figures hovered near 20 per cent, with many more underemployed. Although, in each case, the head of government could shift blame (in Latvia to the preceding government and in Estonia to the international recession), electorates are notoriously angry at standing powers in times of economic crisis. In both states, however, the head of government and his political parties emerged victorious. The Western media cooed about the magical abilities of each politician, and imagined, as did most, that the coalition governments from before the election would return to run Estonia and Latvia. After brief negotiations Estonia and Latvia saw the return of pro-Western, right-of-centre coalition governments. Each coalition included a difficult political partner, and tension existed between politicians, but there seemed to be few other options. The parliamentary elections were a victory for the status quo of politics in post-Soviet Estonia and Latvia; a status quo that saw the rising and waning fortunes of political parties and politicians over the course of many elections, but produced a string of generally pro-Western, pro-market-reform coalitions of centre and right-of-centre parties that appealed primarily to ethnic Estonians and Latvians. Ethnic Russians and other Slavic-speakers, after years of naturalization, voted in ever greater numbers and supported a large political party that continued to remain outside of power.

In both states, but particularly in Latvia, there was a brief moment of political calculus wherein political scientists and media analysts understood that the party of the head of government (in Latvia's case, Valdis Dombrovskis and the unfortunately titled political union Unity, or Vienotība) could form a grand coalition with the 'Russian party' (again in Latvia, the equally unfortunately titled political union Harmony Centre, or Saskaņas centrs) and usher in a new political era. With the exception of the muddled returns of the 1995 parliamentary elections, governance on the national level had been the preserve of centre and right-of-centre ethnic Latvian parties. Russian political parties had consistently manned the official opposition. As a result, political development atrophied on both sides. On the ethnic Latvian side, the reality of removing at least a fifth of parliamentary seats from potential coalition-building increased the value of the remaining seats. Not surprisingly this bred and accelerated corruption. Even when political parties campaigned against corruption and did well at the polls (as in 2010) without including a 'Russian party' in government, they were forced to turn to the parties that they had lambasted as corrupt in electioneering. At the most, a strong showing by an anti-corruption, anti-oligarch party could minimize the role oligarchs would play in government, but they remained in coalitions nonetheless and poisoned the political environment around every key decision: would bold decisions on policy and legislation be hijacked yet again to keep a coalition in power? The status quo has been no kinder to the development of 'Russian parties'. Denied a role in governing, they have enjoyed the freedom that not governing gives to a parliamentary opposition. The 'Russian parties' have been able to criticize mistakes and offer alternatives (often removed from reality), but never have to live with the consequences and compromises of forming consensus about national policies in a coalition government. There has been little incentive to be involved in political give and take, to sacrifice some policy goals for the attainment of others. This is all the more serious since these parties represent an ethnic minority with considerable grievances against the states in which they live. Essentially, with Russian parties out of government, the Russian community is kept out of political decision-making on a national level, and as a result their political voice is consumed with airing grievances and making promises.

In Latvia in the late autumn of 2010, and in Estonia in the spring of 2011, Valdis Dombrovskis and Andrus Ansip could have broken this cycle. Dombrovskis' Unity Party could have crafted a two-party coalition government with Harmony Centre built on two foundations: the inclusion of the largest Russian party into Latvian national political governance, and a campaign to break the oligarchs' and corruption's grip on national politics. There would have been two immediate implications of such a bold move. First, a coalition of the two largest parliamentary parties, one primarily ethnically Latvian and one primarily ethnically Russian, would have shaken the foundations of status quo ethnopolitics. Even in the most self-serving calculations of ethnic Latvian politicians, the invitation and inclusion of a Russian party into government would set a far better long-term precedent than the alternative of a future parliament where a Russian party is able to force its way into government on its own terms. Russian parties as part of the national government of Latvia or Estonia would equally reverberate in international relations. Second, the decision to form a government with a Russian party would have instantly devalued the political parties that used their relatively few seats for coalition-making. This in and of itself would have been a blow against corruption and the resulting coalition government would have been more unencumbered when it came to prosecuting past and current abusers of political power.

Such a grand coalition government may have been short-lived. The demands of each other's electorates may have been too uncompromising. Rifts and differences between the two parties could have scuttled such a government even before creation or forced its fall soon after.

In Latvia the year 2011 saw a degree of déjà vu. Valdis Zatlers, the state president, moved to dissolve parliament in the late spring of 2011. He reacted when parliament refused to sanction police searches of sitting deputies in an ongoing corruption investigation. Soon after, Zatlers lost in his bid for a second term (chosen by parliament). The national referendum on dissolving parliament in July 2011 produced a landslide: almost 95 per cent of the electorate voted to dissolve parliament. Extraordinary elections for a new Saeima took place in September 2011. The 'Russian party' did exceptionally well, winning 31 seats, but the party of the sitting minister president (Dombrovksis) and of the dismissed state president (Zatlers) did well enough to form the next coalition government with the support of an occasionally extremist nationalist union of parties. Again, a potentially gilded moment to create a grand, multi-ethnic governing coalition has gone by the wayside. Nevertheless a bold political move to break the status quo seems increasingly essential. Even as Estonia, Latvia and Lithuania emerge from the economic crisis of 2008–10 and again enjoy economic growth and political stability, far larger issues loom on the horizon.

In late 2011, after yet another failed attempt to break the ethnic ceiling of coalition governments in Latvia, Russian language activists began collecting signatures to force a referendum on whether the Russian language should become a second official language. The petition process succeeded and a referendum was held on 18 February 2012. The national referendum process is a curious and flawed provision within Latvia's constitution. The number of citizens' signatures required to force a referendum is relatively low (10 per cent of the electorate), while the chance of such a referendum succeeding is equally low (it must be approved by 50 per cent of the electorate). In the history of Latvia's referendums, opponents have encouraged their supporters to simply abstain from voting to ensure the threshold is not met. In this particular referendum, considering the demographic collapse of the ethnic Russian community, victory for the Russian language was almost impossible. Even with a unanimous vote from all ethnic Russian voters, the law could not pass. Nevertheless, the campaign to hold the referendum was almost a desperate plea for attention and change from a disaffected minority within the state. Ethnic Latvians, however, understood the referendum as an assault on the Latvian language and even national survival. Often, rather than debating the specifics of why the Russian language should not receive official status, ethnic Latvian campaigners descended to accusing their opposition as traitors. The ethnic Latvian nation mobilized and delivered a crushing electoral defeat to ethnic Russian political hopes. Voter turnout was heavy, with well more than a million ballots cast (more than 70 per cent), and of those almost 75 per cent were against Russian as a second official language. At first glance, this result suggests that politics will continue to exclude 'Russian parties' and the Russian electorate. There can be little incentive for ethnic Latvian politicians to suggest ethnic inclusion or rapprochements in the light of this electoral statement. The results, however, also suggest a deepening and more troublesome political future: a Latvia split into two: one part primarily ethnically Latvian and politically involved, the other a Russian minority (either with or without citizenship) outside of government and beyond the realm of the state. The geographic distribution of votes is indicative of this split. In Latvia's west, in areas where there are few ethnic Russians, the referendum suffered a cataclysmic defeat. In the district of Aizpute, for example, one electoral station returned 393 votes against Russian as the official language, with only one vote for. In Russian districts of Riga, however, three times as many votes were for the Russian language initiative. In the eastern province of Latgale, this support for the Russian language was even more pronounced. In the city of Daugavpils, for example, 34,459 people voted for Russian as the official language to 5,816 against. At many polling stations, support for the initiative outpaced the no vote by ten times. As a result, Latvia's politics are stymied: on the national, parliamentary level there is even less interest in a conciliatory approach to the Russian minority, while in a handful of Russian cities and neighbourhoods this status quo is almost unbearable, but there is little political hope for redress.

Ultimately the people living in a state define its prospects. In Estonia, Latvia and Lithuania there are fewer and fewer people. All three states face daunting demographic crises and severe public health and welfare obstacles to prosperity. In the simplest and starkest terms, people – citizens and non-citizens – are leaving all three states in droves, and far fewer children are born than people are dying. The populations of all three states are in a state of collapse. As a matter of perspective, more people have emigrated from Estonia, Latvia and Lithuania since independence was restored than were deported by the Soviet regime during the Stalinist era. From April 2009 to April 2010 the population of Latvia declined by 14,000 people. In the following year this drop accelerated to almost 20,000. Since Latvia is, by age distribution, old (with many more people over 50 than under 20), this trend will probably continue to accelerate. It is likely that there will be fewer than two million people living in Latvia in fewer than five years. This would be a loss of nearly 700,000 people in the span of a little more than 25 years. Although the reasons for this demographic collapse are varied, the simple reality is that economic development and the future of the state will be heavily influenced by new demographic realities.

Beyond the alarming decline in population, the health and welfare of people in Estonia, Latvia and Lithuania is worrying. In all three countries alcoholism and alcohol-related disease and illness is an endemic problem. The sexual imbalance in alcohol abuse (far greater among males) contributes significantly to the far shorter life expectancy of men than women. Alcohol's social costs are equally disruptive. Recreational drug use has also increased significantly in the post-Soviet era. Beyond substance abuse, Estonia, Latvia and Lithuania suffer from several other severe health crises. Tuberculosis is widespread, particularly virulent multi-drug-resistant strains of tuberculosis. Sexually transmitted diseases are also on the rise, although none of the three countries experienced an AIDS epidemic of the degree that was anticipated in the early 1990s. One glimmer of hope has been a drop in infant mortality rates over the last decade. Still, Estonia, Latvia and Lithuania are unhealthy places. Even their roads add to the miserable state of health; all three countries have alarmingly high rates of vehicle-related fatalities.

There is also, however, a story of success hidden within the demographic data of Estonia, Latvia and Lithuania. The most recent elections to the European Parliament in 2009 and the parliamentary elections in Estonia and Latvia (in Latvia in the elections of 2010 and of 2011) witnessed the first time that citizens born and raised only during a period of independence were able to vote in their own, independent state. Lithuania will reach this milestone for its parliamentary elections in 2012. In the interwar period the electorate consisted only of people born before independence. By the time children of the new state were legally entitled to vote, democratic rule had ended. Similarly, in all of the elections from 1990 until 2009, the fact that voters must be at least eighteen years of age meant that only citizens born during Soviet occupation could vote. Throughout this book one of the repetitive themes is the lack of stability and continuity; rulers and economic systems change frequently. After more than twenty years of independence Estonia, Latvia and Lithuania are producing, for all of its fits and starts, democratic, political continuity and stability. Ilves described Baltic identity as being defined by shared unhappy experiences; the coming of age of a new political generation will further weaken the already weak allegiances to a Baltic identity. For the most recent generation of voters, and for all to come, the hallmarks of this type of Baltic identity, be they repression or resistance, will not be personal memories. The high point of Baltic identity, when hundreds of thousands of Estonians, Latvians and Lithuanians linked hands to form a Baltic Chain from Tallinn to Vilnius, is the lived experience of parents; and its nadir, when hundreds of thousands experienced the loss of statehood and mass deportations and forced population displacement, is that of grandparents.

The sad state of the demographic condition and social health of Estonia, Latvia and Lithuania is a classic case of the glass half-full or half-empty. Undoubtedly conditions would be as grave if not more so if the three states had remained in some political union loosely based on the model of the Soviet Union. The demographic and social health situation of the bulk of the former Soviet republics is decidedly worse. Direct investment from the EU and the increase in wealth and prosperity from 1991 (even factoring in the recent economic crisis) arguably ameliorated matters in Estonia, Latvia and Lithuania. Still, two fundamental nagging questions remain after nearly two decades of renewed independence. If the goal was greater wealth and prosperity, it was attained, but the loftier goal of convergence with West European (or European Union) norms remains distant. If, however, the goal was to create an intrinsically Estonian, Latvian or Lithuanian model within a modern Europe, the goal seems equally distant. The three states and societies struggle with many divisions. Economic transformation has created massive gaps between economic classes, which in turn has fostered a political system that is open and democratic in theory and practice, but also substantially favours the wealthy and powerful. The scourge of a crossover between real political decision-making and economic wealth, the oligarch phenomenon, is as real in Latvia and Lithuania, and to a lesser extent Estonia, as it is across most of the former Soviet

Union and Eastern Europe. The existing political elite, in turn, exploit the ethno-political divisions in society for future electoral gain; or, in other words, the spectre of a Russian party in power is used to keep the same basic political economic powers in a constant reshuffling of coalitions that slightly favour one oligarch or another. A portion of the electorate and society, increasingly angry at the political status quo but unwilling to give up the ethnopolitical paradigm, lash out in ever more radical and intolerant ways. The occasional spasm of intolerance toward minorities (racial, ethnic, sexual orientation or other) is a sign of a political environment that belittles consensus-building and compromise. This is still a minority in each country, but increasingly a larger share of the active political society. More and more people are turning away from politics as a hopelessly corrupt and pointless exercise. Not surprisingly, more and more people, by questioning their place in Estonian, Latvian or Lithuanian society (most obviously by enter-taining the idea of emigration), are questioning the very value of Estonia, Latvia and Lithuania.

The values – or rather the accomplishments and ongoing challenges – of each state are as unique as they are similar. Without a doubt Estonia has covered the most ground in economic and societal transformation. If, during the heady days of Popular Front opposition to Soviet rule in the late 1980s, the Estonian, Latvian, and Lithuanian Popular Fronts jockeyed with each other to take the lead in acti-vism, Estonia has lapped Latvia and Lithuania in the last two decades. Estonia most aggressively embraced market reforms in the early 1990s and has religiously followed a policy of low taxation together with minimal government deficits and debts. This unwavering dedication to market reform relative to Latvia and Lithuania has worked very much like the principle of compounded interest in a savings account. In any given year, the growth and development of Estonia relative to its southern neighbours has not seemed astronomical, but year after year the gap between them grows. After a decade or two Estonia looks considerably more pros-perous and dynamic. Furthermore Estonia has transformed fundamental aspects of its society in a more revolutionary way than most Western European states. Government and business have embraced technological innovation, particularly the Internet and mobile technologies. Often dubbed 'E-stonia', much of the nexus between government and citizen is virtual. Even Estonia's experience as the victim in one of the world's first cyberwars has not slowed this transformation. In the spring of 2007 Estonian government and business servers were overwhelmed with millions of requests for data in an attempt to crash multiple systems. The source of the attack seemed to be from within Russia, although the Russian state officially denies any involvement. Nevertheless, despite the limited cyberwar, Estonia has continued to base its continued economic growth and development on a robust incorporation of technological innovation.

Though Estonia has enjoyed considerable successes, disparities remain. Economic development is most centred in and around Tallinn, with rural areas considerably less fortunate. Despite growing prosperity and increasing GDP rates, the ongoing economic recession has affected Estonia severely. Unemployment remains near 10 per cent and is markedly higher in certain regions. Many of the poorest regions are those areas of Estonia that have the greatest concentrations of Russians, many of whom do not have citizenship. This is one of Estonia's greatest challenges. Formal citizenship laws and naturalization processes are not enough. Estonia is faced with a disenfranchised community within its borders which has little attachment to the state. The demonstrations and riots surrounding the removal of a Soviet-era war monument (the Bronze Soldier) demonstrated how volatile this situation could become.

In Latvia economic progress, although formidable, has suffered from the pervasive influence of corruption. Even more troubling, as with Estonia, is the development of two ethnic solitudes within the state. If in social settings and workplaces this trend may not be as pronounced, the continued political ethnic divide is dangerous and counterproductive. A gross oversimplification of nearly twenty years of parliamentary history is that all manner of coalitions have been formed to keep any Russian party from coming to power. Importantly this is not to keep a Russian party from sole power, but to keep such a party from any power in any coalition government. After a brief flurry of activity in the early twenty first century to facilitate social integration, the Latvian state seems inclined to allow natural attrition to solve the problem of non-citizens within its borders. The most recent parliamentary election results, widely seen as a victory against oligarchs, has a potentially more tragic subtext. The 'Russian party' polled better than ever before and has a plurality in parliament, yet they are unlikely to be a part of government. The lesson Russian politicians and activists may learn is that even with the best polling possible, ethnic Latvian parties will work together to keep Russians from government. Ultimately there will be consequences to the creation of a political system that effectively denies governing participation to more than a third of the populace. Either that third will become more confrontational, as they understand the political system as one designed against them, or they will become laconic and disinterested in their state. In either case this becomes a civil rights issue in moral terms, and in economic terms a colossal waste of human capital.

In Lithuania the power of the state president has overshadowed parliaments and placed Lithuanian political developments on a slightly different track than that of Estonia and Latvia. The relatively small ethnic Russian population has removed much of the ethnic dimension from politics, although there is considerable acrimony between Lithuanians and the small community of Poles in Lithuania. Still, Lithuania shares an ongoing discourse with Latvia and Estonia about the proper relationship with Russia, struggles with corruption, and the debilitating demographic crises mentioned above.

Despite all of the developments of the past twenty years, all three states continue to lack a grand, unifying and inclusive idea (either jointly or separately), one that explains their past and girds them towards an uncertain future. In this there is something Baltic, something shared between Estonia, Latvia and Lithuania, even if there is little shared Baltic identity. More than just Baltic, however, this malaise is European – if not global. The challenges that face Estonia, Latvia and Lithuania, and there are many – from demographic and social health crises to creating growth and development, shaping identity that credits the past but does not handicap the future, and building a more inclusive, just and responsive political environment – are challenges faced by many states and societies. The most compelling reason why the Baltic states demand closer international attention is that they are the canaries in a twenty-first-century coalmine. Estonia, Latvia and Lithuania are examples of much of what will define the twenty-first century globally. Their successes and failures, and the consequences of each, should inform a much larger debate. If this were to be the case, the Baltic's chronic struggle to be noticed and respected on an international stage would be finally realized.

If this book began with Toomas Hendrik Ilves disparaging the idea of the Baltic, it rightly ends with a re-examination of this infamous quote. Ilves had distanced himself from the Baltic controversy, particularly when the concept regained further appeal in 2007 and 2008. When Estonia suffered from a cyberattack in 2007 and when Russia invaded Georgia in 2008, political leaders in Estonia, Latvia and Lithuania vocally pledged their continuing support for each other. Toomas Hendrik Ilves, as state president of Estonia, was at the forefront of the reaffirmation of Baltic unity and solidarity. Ironically this renewed interest in the Baltic concept reaffirmed his earlier dismissal of the term. The Baltic idea returned when the threat of future 'shared unhappy experiences' re-emerged. If Estonia, Latvia and Lithuania fail – if they collectively slump or are victims to some renewed territorial aggression or intimidation – they will do so as Baltic states, and will probably resist as Baltic states as well. If, on the other hand, Estonia and/or Latvia and/or

Lithuania succeed as states and societies, the bonds of past unhappy experiences will become ever weaker. If Estonia succeeds in reinventing itself as a Nordic state, its shared Baltic identity will cease to exist. If Lithuania develops closer ties with Central European states, its shared Baltic identity will fade. If Latvia loses interest in the concept, it will fade even more quickly. The final word is that if the traditional Baltic states, Estonia, Latvia and Lithuania, succeed in becoming integrated, prosperous members of the EU, their common Baltic identity based on a collection of 'shared unhappy experiences' will be relegated to history books. If the Baltic states succeed, they will stop being the Baltic states. If such long term developments transpire, organizations such as the Council of the Baltic Sea States (CBSS) will become more than a 'political forum for regional inter-governmental cooperation'. The CBSS could become the contextual framework for identity in the future, a framework that incorporates local uniqueness, regional similarities and European commonalities.

References

Introduction

1 *Wall Street Journal* interview as quoted in the interview of Ilves' opponent by Anna-Maria Galojan in *The Baltic Times*, 3 February 2011, at www.baltictimes.com, accessed 31 January 2012.
2 Ilves softened this earlier combative assertion, particularly after being elected president of Estonia in 2006.
3 Ilves, 'Estonia as a Nordic Nation', speech to the Swedish Institute for International Affairs, 14 December 1999.
4 Daunis Auers in Z. Ozoliņa, ed., *Latvia's Foreign Policy and 'Border Spanning'* (Riga, 2006), p. 49; see Dzintra Bungs, *The Baltic States: Problems and Prospects of Membership in the European Union* (Baden-Baden, 1998).
5 David Kirby, *The Baltic World, 1773–1993: Europe's Northern Periphery in the Age of Change* (London, 1995).
6 Alan Palmer, *The Baltic* (New York, 2007).
7 Romuald Misiunas and Rein Taagepera, *The Baltic States: Years of Dependence, 1940–1990*, expanded and updated edn (London, 1993).
8 Georg von Rauch, *The Baltic States: Years of Independence, 1917–1940* (Berkeley, CA, 1974).
9 Of John Hiden's many books, including John Hiden and Thomas Lane, *The Baltic Nations and Europe: Estonia, Latvia and Lithuania in the Twentieth Century* (New York, 1991), his most successful, unique contribution may be John Hiden, *Defender of Minorities: Paul Schiemann, 1876–1944* (London, 2004).
10 David Smith, Artis Pabriks, Aldis Purs and Thomas Lane, *The Baltic States: Estonia, Latvia and Lithuania* (London, 2002).
11 Andrejs Plakans, *The Latvians: A Short History* (Stanford, CA, 1996); Toivo Raun, *Estonia and the Estonians* (Stanford, CA, 2002).
12 Andres Kasekamp, *A History of the Baltic States* (Palgrave Essential Histories) (London, 2010); Andrejs Plakans, *Concise History of the Baltic States* (Cambridge, 2011).

13 Jörg Hackmann and Marko Lehti, eds, *Contested and Shared Places of Memory: History and Politics in North Eastern Europe* (London, 2009).

14 Dovile Budryte, *Taming Nationalism?: Political Community Building in the Post-Soviet Baltic states* (Aldershot, 2005)

15 Juris Dreifelds, *Latvia in Transition* (Cambridge, 1996); Marja Nissinen, *Latvia's Transition to a Market Economy: Political Determinants of Economic Reform Policy* (London, 1999).

1 Historical Background

1 See Prudence Jones and Nigel Pennick, *A History of Pagan Europe* (London, 1995).

2 For a more balanced perspective, see Eric Christiansen, *The Northern Crusades: The Baltic and Catholic Frontier, 1100–1525* (Minneapolis, MN, 1980).

3 See S. C. Rowell, *Lithuania Ascending: A Pagan Empire Within East-Central Europe, 1295–1345* (Cambridge, 1994).

4 See Alfred Erich Senn, *The Emergence of Modern Lithuania* (New York, 1959).

5 See Eric R. Wolf, *Europe and the People Without History* (Los Angeles, CA, 1982).

6 See Robert I. Frost, *The Northern Wars: War, State and Society in Northeastern Europe, 1558–1721* (London, 2000).

7 See David G. Kirby, *Northern Europe in the Early Modern Period: The Baltic World, 1492–1772* (London, 1990).

8 See Frost, *The Northern Wars*.

9 See Andrejs Plakans, *The Latvians: A Short History* (Stanford, CA, 1995).

10 See Tomas Balkelis, *The Making of Modern Lithuania* (London, 2009).

11 See Abraham Ascher, *The Revolution of 1905: A Short History* (Stanford, CA, 2004).

12 See Toivo Raun, 'The Revolution of 1905 in the Baltic Provinces and Finland', *Slavic Review*, 43 (1984), pp. 453–67.

13 Katrina Z. S. Schwartz, *Nature and National Identity after Communism* (Pittsburgh, PA, 2006), pp. 7–12.

14 See Anders Henriksson, 'Riga: Growth, Conflict and the Limitations of Good Government, 1850–1914' in *The City in Late Imperial Russia*, ed. Michael Hamm (Bloomington, IN, 1986); see Laimonis Briedis, *Vilnius: City of Strangers* (Central European Press, 2009).

15 See Peter Gatrell, *A Whole Empire Walking: Refugees in Russia During World War One* (Bloomington, IN, 1999).

16 See Vejas Liulevicius, *War Lands on the Eastern Front: Culture, National Identity, and German Occupation in World War I* (Cambridge, 2005).

17 See Aija Priedīte, 'Latvian Refugees and the Latvian Nation State during and after World War One' in *Homelands: War, Population and Statehood in the Former Russian Empire, 1918–1924*, ed. Nick Baron and Peter Gatrell (London, 2004).

18 See Baron and Gatrell, eds, *Homelands*.

19 See Stanley Page, *The Formation of the Baltic States* (New York, 1970).

2 Potemkin Republics

1 See Hugh I. Rodgers, *Search for Security: A Study in Baltic Diplomacy, 1920–1934* (Hamden, CT, 1975).
2 See John Hiden and Thomas Lane, *The Baltic States and the Outbreak of the Second World War* (Cambridge, 2003).
3 See Tomas Balkelis, 'War, State, Ethnic Conflict and the Refugee Crisis in Lithuania, 1939–1940', in *Contemporary European History*, XVI/4 (2007), pp. 461–77.
4 See Andrejs Plakans, ed., *Experiencing Totalitarianism: The Invasion and Occupation of Latvia by the USSR and Nazi Germany 1939–1991: A Document History* (Bloomington, IN, 2007).
5 See Aldis Purs, 'Soviet in Form, Local in Content: Elite Repression and Mass Terror in the Baltic States, 1940–1953', in *Stalinist Terror in Eastern Europe: Elite Purges and Mass Repression*, ed. Kevin McDermott and Matthew Stibbe (Manchester, 2010).
6 See Horst Boog et al., eds, *Germany and the Second World War*, vol. IV: *The Attack on the Soviet Union*, trans. Dean S. McMurray et al. (Oxford, 1998).
7 See Toivo Raun, *Estonia and the Estonians* (Stanford, CA, 2002).
8 See Andrievs Ezergailis, *The Holocaust in Latvia, 1941–1944: The Missing Center* (United States Holocaust Memorial Museum, Riga, 1996).
9 See Anton Weiss-Wendt, *Murder Without Hatred: Estonians and the Holocaust* (Syracuse, NY, 2009).
10 See the official website of Yad Vashem at www1.yadvashem.org.
11 See Valdis O. Lumans, *Latvia in World War II* (New York, 2006).
12 See Aldis Purs, 'Working towards "An Unforseen Miracle" Redux: Latvian Refugees in Vladivostok, 1918–1920, and in Latvia, 1943–1944', in *Contemporary European History*, XVI/4 (2007), pp. 479–94.
13 See Geoffrey Swain, *Between Stalin and Hitler: Class War and Race War on the Dvina, 1940–1946* (London, 2009).
14 See Modris Eksteins, *Walking Since Daybreak: A Story of Eastern Europe, World War II, and the Heart of our Century* (Toronto, 2000).
15 See Plakans, ed., *Experiencing Totalitarianism*.
16 See Arvydas Anausauskas, ed., *The Anti-Soviet Resistance in the Baltic States* (Vilnius, 1999).
17 See G. Reklaitis, *Cold War Lithuania: National Armed Resistance and Soviet Counterinsurgency*, The Carl Beck Papers in Russian and East European Studies, no. 1806 (Pittsburgh, PA, 2007).
18 See Yuri Slezkine, 'The USSR as a Communal Apartment, or How a Socialist State Promoted Ethnic Particularism', *Slavic Review*, LIII/2 (1994), pp. 415–52.
19 Gregory Meiksins, *The Baltic Riddle; Finland, Estonia, Latvia, Lithuania – Key Points of European Peace* (New York, 1943).

20 See Amir Weiner, 'Nature and Nurture in a Socialist Utopia: Delineating the
   Soviet Socio-Ethnic Body in the Age of Socialism' in *Stalinism*, ed. D. L. Hoffmann
   (Oxford, 2003), p. 272.

21 See Amy Knight, *Beria* (Princeton, NJ, 1995).

22 See William Prigge, 'The Latvian Purges of 1959: A Revision Study', in *Journal of
   Baltic Studies*, xxxv/3 (2004), pp. 211–30.

23 As quoted ibid, p. 223.

24 Prigge's article, ibid., admirably outlines the close relationship and rise of Pelše
   and Suslov.

3 Soviet Union to European Union

1 To see the text of the letter, go to www.letton, accessed 31 January 2012.

2 The made for television movie was *The Defection of Simas Kudirka* (1978). The
  film was shown on the American network channel CBS and won two Emmy
  awards.

3 See Romuald J. Misiunas and Rein Taagepera, *The Baltic States: Years of
  Dependence, 1940–1990*, expanded and updated edn (Berkeley, CA, 1993).

4 Andris Grīnbergs is the filmmaker and the film *Pašportrēts* (Self Portrait) (1972).

5 See Misiunas and Taagepera, *The Baltic States*.

6 See Mikhail Gorbachev's own *Perestroika: New Thinking for our Country and the
  World* (New York, 1987).

7 See Artis Pabriks and Aldis Purs, *Latvia: The Challenges of Change* (London,
  2001).

8 Almost all books published in the last twenty years that look at developments in
  Estonia, Latvia and Lithuania include a discussion of the popular movements
  against Soviet rule and the campaign to re-establish independence. One of the
  earliest sources, which continues to stand up to the test of time, is Anatol
  Lieven, *The Baltic Revolution: Estonia, Latvia, Lithuania and the Path to
  Independence* (New Haven, CT, 1993).

9 See the film documentary *The Singing Revolution* (2006), which showcases the
  Estonian singing revolution.

10 See David Smith, 'Estonia: Independence and European Integration', in *The
   Baltic States: Estonia, Latvia and Lithuania*, ed. David Smith et al. (New York,
   2002), p. 88.

4 Economic Developments

1 See David Kirby, *The Baltic World, 1772–1993: Europe's Northern Periphery in an Age
  of Change* (London, 1995).

2 See Andrejs Plakans, 'A Century of Reforms', in his *The Latvians: A Short History*
  (Stanford, CA, 1995), pp. 80–111.

3 See Theodore H. von Laue, *Sergei Witte and the Industrialization of Russia* (New York, 1969).

4 See Peter Gatrell, *A Whole Empire Walking: Refugees in Russia During World War I* (Bloomington, IN, 1999).

5 See Edgar Anderson, 'The USSR Trades with Latvia: The Treaty of 1927', *Slavic Review*, XXI/2 (1962).

6 See John Hiden, *The Baltic States and Weimar Ostpolitik* (Cambridge, 2002).

7 See Nicholas Balabkins and Arnolds Aizsilnieks, *Entrepreneur in a Small Country: A Case Study Against the Background of the Latvian Economy, 1919–1940* (Hicksville, NY, 1975).

8 See James C. Scott, *Seeing Like a State: How Certain Schemes to Improve the Human Condition Have Failed* (New Haven, CT, 1998).

9 See William G. Rosenberg and Lewis H. Siegelbaum, eds, *Social Dimensions of Soviet Industrialization* (Bloomington, IN, 1993).

10 Nikita Khrushchev used this example in his push for de-Stalinization.

11 See Jari Ojala, *Road to Prosperity: An Economic History of Finland* (Helsinki, 2006).

12 See Marja Nissinen, *Latvia's Transition to a Market Economy: Political Determinants of Economic Reform Policy* (London, 1999).

13 The phrase was used by Professor Daunis Auers of the University of Latvia during a BBC interview.

5 Identity

1 See Katrina Z. S. Schwartz, *Nature and National Identity after Communism: Globalizing the Ethnoscape* (Pittsburgh, PA, 2006).

2 See Andrejs Plakans, 'The Latvians', in *Russification in the Baltic Provinces and Finland, 1855–1914*, ed. Edward C. Thaden (Princeton, NJ, 1981).

3 See for example Eugen Weber, *Peasants into Frenchmen: The Modernization of Rural France, 1870–1914* (Stanford, CA, 1976) for an example of peasant singing and culture that was largely lost before ethnographic interest peaked.

4 See Timothy Ryback, *Rock Around the Bloc: A History of Rock Music in Eastern Europe and the Soviet Union, 1954–1988* (Oxford, 1990).

5 See the web-site www.tornis.lv for a veritable treasure trove of non-commercial music in contemporary Latvia.

6 See S. A. Mansbach, *Modern Art in Eastern Europe: From the Baltic to the Balkans, ca. 1890–1939* (Cambridge, 1999).

7 An excellent example is a document outlining acceptable themes for art in Andrejs Plakans, ed., *Experiencing Totalitarianism: The Invasion and Occupation of Latvia by the USSR and Nazi Germany 1939–1991: A Documentary History* (Bloomington, IN, 2007), pp. 322–5.

Further Reading

Balkelis, Tomas, *The Making of Modern Lithuania* (London, 2009)

Baron, Nick, and Peter Gatrell, eds, *Homelands: War, Population and Statehood in Eastern Europe and Russia, 1918–1924* (London, 2004)

Briedis, Laimonas, *Vilnius: City of Strangers* (Budapest, 2009)

Budryte, Dovile, *Taming Nationalism? Politial Community Building in the Post-Soviet Baltic States* (Burlington, VT, 2005)

Christiansen, Eric, *The Northern Crusades: The Baltic and Catholic Frontier, 1100–1525* (Minneapolis, MN, 1980)

Clemens, Walter C., *Baltic Independence and Russian Empire* (London, 1991)

Eksteins, Modris, *Walking Since Daybreak: A Story of Eastern Europe, World War II, and the Heart of our Century* (Toronto, 2000)

Ezergailis, Andrievs, *The Holocaust in Latvia, 1941–1944: The Missing Center* (Washington, DC, 1996)

Gatrell, Peter, *A Whole Empire Walking: Refugees in Russia During World War I* (Bloomington, IN, 1999)

Gorsuch, Anne E., and Diane P. Koenker, eds, *Turizm: The Russian and East European Tourist Under Capitalism and Socialism* (Ithaca, NY, 2006)

Grover, Alexander, *The New Estonian Golden Age: How Estonia Will Rise To Be One of Europe's Five Richest Nations* (Armstead, Estonia, 2009)

Hackmann, Jorg, and Marko Lehti, eds, *Contested and Shared Places of Memory: History and Politics in North Eastern Europe* (London, 2009)

Henrikkson, Anders, *The Tsar's Loyal Germans: The Riga German Community: Social Change and the Nationality Question, 1855–1905* (Boulder, CO, 1983)

Hiden, John, *The Baltic States and Weimar Ostpolitik* (Cambridge, 1987)

—, *Defender of Minorities: Paul Schiemann, 1876–1944* (London, 2004)

—, and Patrick Salmon, *The Baltic Nations and Europe: Estonia, Latvia and Lithuania in the Twentieth Century* (London, 1991)

Jones, Prudence, and Nigel Pennick, *A History of Pagan Europe* (New York, 1995)

Kasekamp, Andres, *A History of the Baltic States* (Palgrave Essential Histories) (London, 2010)

Kirby, David T., *The Baltic World, 1772–1993: Europe's Northern Periphery in an Age of Change* (London, 1995)

Lehti, Marko, and David Smith, eds, *Post-Cold War Identity Politics: Northern and Baltic Experiences* (London, 2003)

Lieven, Anatol, *The Baltic Revolution: Estonia, Latvia, Lithuania and the Path to Independence* (New Haven, CT, 1994)

Liulevicius, Vejas, *War Land on the Eastern Front: Culture, National Identity and German Occupation in World War I* (Cambridge, 2000)

Lumans, Valdis, *Latvia in World War II* (World War II: The Global, Human and Ethical Dimension) (New York, 2006)

Mansbach, S. A., *Modern Art in Eastern Europe: From the Baltic to the Balkans, ca. 1890–1939* (Cambridge, 1999)

McDermott, Kevin, and Matthew Stibbe, eds, *Stalinist Terror in Eastern Europe: Elite Purges and Mass Repression* (Manchester, 2010)

Misiunas, Romuald, and Rein Taagepera. *The Baltic States: Years of Dependence 1940-1990*, expanded and updated edn (London, 1993)

Nissinen, Marja, *Latvia's Transition to a Market Economy: Political Determinants of Economic Reform Policy* (Basingstoke, 1999)

Page, Stanley, *The Formation of the Baltic States: A Study of the Effects of Great Power Policies on the Emergence of Lithuania, Latvia, and Estonia* (Cambridge, MA, 1959)

Plakans, Andrejs, *The Latvians: A Short History* (Stanford, CA, 1995)

—, *A Concise History of the Baltic States* (Cambridge Concise Histories) (Cambridge, 2011)

Rauch, Georg von, *The Baltic States. Estonia, Latvia, Lithuania: The Years of Independence, 1918–1940* (Berkeley, CA, 1975)

Raun, Toivo, *Estonia and the Estonians: Updated Second Edition* (Stanford, CA, 2002)

Rislakki, Jukka, *The Case for Latvia: Disinformation Campaigns against a Small Nation: Fourteen Hard Questions and Straight Answers about a Baltic Country* (Rodopi, 2008)

Rowell, S. C., *Lithuania Ascending: A Pagan Empire Within East-Central Europe, 1295–1345* (Cambridge, 1994)

Schwartz, Katrina Z. S., *Nature and National Identity After Communism: Globalizing the Ethnoscape* (Pittsburgh, PA, 2006)

Senn, Alfred Erich, *Lithuania Awakening* (Berkeley, CT, 1990)

Smith, David, Artis Pabriks, Aldis Purs and Thomas Lane, *The Baltic States: Estonia, Latvia and Lithuania* (New York, 2002)

Snyder, Timothy, *The Reconstruction of Nations: Poland, Lithuania, Belarus, 1569–1999* (New Haven, CT, 2004)

—, *Bloodlands: Europe Between Hitler and Stalin* (New York, 2010)

Stukuls-Eglitis, Daina, *Imagining the Nation: History, Modernity and Revolution in*

Latvia (University Park, PA, 2005)

Swain, Geoff, *Between Hitler and Stalin: Class War and Race War on the Dvina, 1940–1946* (New York, 2004)

Thaden, Edward, ed., *Russification in the Baltic Provinces and Finland, 1855–1914* (Princeton, NJ, 1981)

Vardys, V. Stanley, and Judith Sedaitis, *Lithuania: The Rebel Nation* (Boulder, CO, 1997)

Weiss-Wendt, Anton, *Murder Without Hatred: Estonians and the Holocaust* (Syracuse, NY, 2009)

Whelan, Heidi, *Adapting to Modernity: Family, Caste and Capitalism among the Baltic German Nobility* (Bohlau, 1999)

Acknowledgements

If I have foregone the traditional footnote, referencing and thorough construction of an academic argument, I should also forego the equally traditional list of acknowledgements. There are too many people to list. If my References suggest where to turn for sources on any given topic, the acknowledgements in my past and future work will have to suffice. I would be remiss, however, to not acknowledge the tireless work and devotion of this book's publisher, Michael Leaman. Without him this book would not exist, although I am entirely responsible for all errors in fact or judgement within these covers. I am also indebted to András Bereznay for the excellent maps.

Finally, acknowledgements almost always include an apology and thanks to a partner and children. This book is no different, although much about the book will be a surprise (hopefully a happy one) to them. To my two wonderful daughters, Lilja and Teika, now they know why on some mornings (after long nights of work) I was even more irritable, grumpy and curt. My apologies and thank you always for your patience and understanding. To my amazing wife Ann-Marie, a sentence or two in a book cannot relay more than what I try to relay by my actions, words and thoughts on a daily basis, although here too I could do more. I should have used you more as an advisor throughout this process; you know the Baltic as well as I do.

Index

'National Salvation Committees' 91, 92
naturalization 110
Nazi Germany 50, 51, 59, 125, 172
Nazi-Soviet Non-Aggression Pact
    (Molotov-Ribbentrop Pact) 49, 55,
    82, 88
'near abroad' former republics 103
Netherlands 151
Nevsky, Alexander 26
New Era Party 100
Nicholas II 39
Nissinen, Marja 19
NKVD 67, 70
Nordosteuropa 11
North Atlantic Treaty Organization
    (NATO) 105, 106, 107, 108, 146, 174
    NATO's Prague Summit 105
Nuremberg Trials 50

October Manifesto 39, 41
oligarchs 143, 176, 180, 182
opera 163–4
OstEuropa 125
Ottoman empire 43

Pabriks, Artis 18
Padegs, Kārlis 166
Paksas, Rolandas 98, 101, 102
Paldiski 103, 139
Palmer, Alan 11, 17
Parex Banka 149
Pärt, Arvo 164–5
partisans 61, 62, 77, 127, 131
patronage 122, 135, 136, 140
Päts, Konstantin 47, 52
Pauls, Raimonds 161
Pelše, Arvīds 69, 70, 71
People's Party 99–100
perestroika 82, 136
Peter I 33
Pit-Comb Ware Culture 23
Plakans, Andrejs 18

Poland 44, 48, 49, 50, 51, 56, 57, 62,
    103, 106, 122, 154
Poles 73, 109, 153, 183
Polish rebellions 39
Politburo 70
Popular Fronts 84, 85, 86, 87, 88, 89,
    90, 91, 92, 94, 95, 96, 181
Portugal 105, 148, 151
Primorsk 130
Prussia 38
Pugo, Boriss 71, 92
purges 134
Purvītis, Vilhelms 165

quotas 134, 135

radicalism 35
Radio Free Europe 9
Rauch, Georg von 17
Raud, Kristjan 165
Raun, Toivo 18
real estate 147, 148
Red Partisans 59
Reformation 32
refugees 60
Reichsmark 58
repatriation 51, 96
Repše, Einars 100
restitution 142, 143
Revolution of 1905 39, 40, 43, 119, 157,
    172
Rice, Condoleezza 107
Riga 26, 39, 42, 44, 46, 55, 57, 60, 73,
    74, 79, 82, 91, 92, 118, 123, 130, 144,
    147, 150, 160, 167, 178
Riga Automobile Factory 73
Riigikogu 9, 94, 112
rock music 162–3
Roma (Gypsies) 58, 73, 153
Romania 43
Romans 24
Rothko, Mark 168